PRAISE FOR COLLEEN CARROLL'S
The New Faithful

"Colleen Carroll has done a masterful job of bringing together the profiles of a diverse generation of fervent young Christians who are shaking up the American religious scene. She marshals the anecdotes and studies in such a way that she offers the best sociological indication and explanation of what those who work with young people see that they want—authentic, personal, and convinced Christianity. If you are making plans for your church in the next decade, you can't afford to leave this book unread."

> —FR. BENEDICT J. GROESCHEL, C.F.R., author of
> *Behold, He Comes*

"*The New Faithful* reveals the first lights of an unexpected dawn: the growing youth movement toward Christian orthodoxy. If Carroll's discernment and clarity are typical of young believers, the future of the faith is bright indeed."

> —FREDERICA MATHEWES-GREEN, author of *The Illumined Heart,*
> columnist, and NPR commentator

"Colleen Carroll shows how a new generation of Americans has found truth, beauty, and fulfillment not in the trendy hot tubs of New Age spirituality but in the bracing truths and disciplines of an ancient faith—traditional and orthodox Christianity. The stories she tells are deeply moving. The sense of hope they offer to the spiritual future of this nation is warmly encouraging. This is a marvelous book."

> —DAVID AIKMAN, senior fellow at the Trinity Forum, author of
> *Great Souls*

"Colleen Carroll writes boldly and beautifully about today's young adults embracing Christian orthodoxy. Her research, worthy of a competent journalist and scholar, is impressive. Her findings create credibility that faith will be an increasingly important part of building a better world."

> —RICHARD LEONARD, former editor of the *Milwaukee Journal,*
> Nieman Chair Emeritus at Marquette University

"Colleen Carroll deserves serious congratulations. This narrative of her quest for the religion of some of the most thoughtful young Americans is as readable as its implications are profound. For anyone seeking a proper understanding of the immensely complex forces at work in our culture, *The New Faithful* charts a course to the truth."

—NIGEL M. DE S. CAMERON, principal of Strategic Futures Group, LLC, dean of the Wilberforce Forum

"This is an important book. Colleen Carroll has captured the deep yearnings of the generation just emerging from college into the work world. In their own words, these new faithful deliver a powerful message: Life is about more than amassing toys, the spirit matters, and they intend to be heard."

—HOWARD MEANS, author of *Money and Power: The History of Business*

"In contrast to many of the previous generation, great numbers of those born between 1965 and 1983 are finding the church to be a faithful mother giving birth to a renewed spiritual life. Carroll explores the uniqueness of this resurgence of belief, which is evangelical in spirit, seeks to engage rather than to ignore the culture, and seeks to transform the world. This engaging book, which is not hesitant to present the criticisms that have been directed to the younger generation, is an important tool for understanding the growing number of young, active Christian believers. It would be invaluable for anyone engaged in ministry to this generation, with its great spiritual hunger."

—FR. JAMES F. GARNEAU, PH.D., academic dean of the Pontifical College Josephinum, Columbus, OH

"Carroll shines a light into the lives of young spiritual seekers that dispels gloomy assumptions about the decline of orthodox Christianity. She sensitively explores how Christian faith informs and fortifies attitudes about sexuality, vocation, and education for large numbers of young adults. With its smart cultural critique and journalistic flair, *The New Faithful* is a groundbreaking study of religion in America."

—JOSEPH LOCONTE, William E. Simon Fellow in Religion and a Free Society at the Heritage Foundation, NPR commentator

"This is an important story, well told by one of our finest young religion writers. *The New Faithful* should be on the reading list of every church leader and anybody interested in the future of the faith in this country."

—DAVID SCOTT, author and former editor of *Our Sunday Visitor*

"In *The New Faithful,* Colleen Carroll combines her religious sensibilities and consummate reporting skills to take readers on an insightful tour through the world of Generation-X orthodox believers. She sketches the lives of young men and women who draw strength and fulfillment from traditional religious beliefs and practices—and who act on these beliefs in their schools, jobs, and homes. Those immersed in lives of faith will find this book a great affirmation, while those not so immersed may find it a great revelation."

—COLE C. CAMPBELL, fellow at the Charles F. Kettering Foundation, former editor of the *St. Louis Post-Dispatch*

"As if to prove that the worst of times are also the best of times, Colleen Carroll heartens us with a detailed and documented tale of how the young are turning to Christian orthodoxy. She engaged in vast and exhaustive research to bring the good news that there is indeed a groundswell of orthodoxy among the young. In her book, you hear their voices, and they will warm your heart."

—RALPH MCINERNY, professor of philosophy at the University of Notre Dame, author of the Father Dowling Mysteries

THE NEW FAITHFUL

THE NEW FAITHFUL

WHY YOUNG ADULTS ARE EMBRACING CHRISTIAN ORTHODOXY

Colleen Carroll

LOYOLAPRESS.

CHICAGO

LOYOLAPRESS.

3441 N. ASHLAND AVENUE
CHICAGO, ILLINOIS 60657

Interviews for this book were conducted between May 2000 and February 2002.

Interior design by Nick Panos

Library of Congress Cataloging-in-Publication Data

Carroll, Colleen.
  The new faithful : why young adults are embracing Christian orthodoxy / Colleen Carroll.
      p. cm.
Includes bibliographical references.
  ISBN 0-8294-1645-5
  1. Generation X—Religious life. I. Title.
  BV4529.2 .C37 2002
  277.3'083'0842—dc21

2002002225

Printed in the United States
02 03 04 05 06 07 08 09 M-V 9 8 7 6 5 4 3 2 1

To my parents, Tom and Mary Carroll,
in gratitude for their gifts of faith, hope, and love.

CONTENTS

ACKNOWLEDGMENTS

The year that I spent researching and writing this book was perhaps the best of my life. Showered with grace and laden with challenges, it was a year spent relying on the kindness of strangers.

First, though, I must thank my loved ones. My parents, Tom and Mary Carroll, have given me so much support through the years that I find it difficult to convey my gratitude. I will be eternally grateful to my mother and father for the faith that they have passed on to me, and for their example of selfless, committed love.

I am also grateful to my brother, Tom Carroll Jr., for long, edifying conversations that fueled my desire to surrender myself to a project like this one.

And I am honored to know John Campbell, who in a short time has become such a source of joy, love, and strength for me that I can scarcely remember life without him.

This book would not exist if not for the generosity of Thomas Phillips and the trustees of the Phillips Foundation, who awarded me a $50,000 journalism fellowship that allowed me to devote myself full-time to this project. John Farley, secretary of the foundation, also deserves thanks for his encouragement and administrative support. Without the Phillips Foundation, I would never have had the chance to pursue this dream. I will always be grateful for that chance.

I would also like to thank the many people at Loyola Press who worked on the publication and promotion of this book, particularly Jim Manney, whose enthusiasm for the project fueled my own, and Heidi Hill, whose careful, insightful editing made this a better book.

Joe Loconte, who served as my mentor on this project, was a wonderful support to me, and the generous gift of his time and many contacts was invaluable.

I am grateful to Christine Bertelson and the *St. Louis Post-Dispatch* for giving me a hearty recommendation for the fellowship and a leave of absence with benefits that made this project's success possible.

I am thankful for the host of teachers, editors, mentors, and friends who have encouraged me over the years by reading and remarking on my work and by pushing me to pursue my writing vocation. I would particularly like to thank my unofficial career advisor and former editor at *Washingtonian* magazine, Howard Means; my mentor and former professor at Marquette University, Dick Leonard; and a former editor of *Our Sunday Visitor* who generously served as one of my references for the fellowship, David Scott. I am also grateful to Krista Ratcliffe, one of several professors at Marquette who stoked my passion for writing at a crucial time.

The spiritual support I have received—in my writing career and in all of life—is a gift for which I am indebted to many. Most of all, I thank my parents for a faith formation that I have come to recognize as a priceless gift. I am also grateful to my grandmother Beatrice "Queen Bea" Linzmeyer, whose love of life has captivated me from childhood; to a dear family friend, the late Sr. Mary Veronica "Reets" Sudholdt, C.S.J., who prayed ceaselessly for my soul and my success; and for my late aunt Verna Linzmeyer, who patiently clipped my articles for years and chronicled my life in her meticulous scrapbooks. Fr. Dick Tomasek, S.J., Sr. Carol Ann Smith, S.H.C.J., and Fr. Andy Thon, S.J., blessed my life at Marquette and beyond; Sr. Maristelle Schmitz, O.S.B., and Fredel Wiant encouraged me in Colorado Springs; Sr. Maria Joseph Walsh, C.S.J., and Carole Brown edified me during visits to Steubenville, Ohio; and Stephanie Moergen supported me in St. Louis.

While researching this book, I was astounded time and again by the willingness of so many bright, articulate, fervent young adults to share their stories with me. Many of the people who most generously gave of themselves never made it into the pages of this book because I found myself with far more stories, sources, and support than I ever imagined, and far more than this book or its acknowledgements could contain. Their kindness and honesty humbled me, their words of encouragement and prayers heartened me, and their practical help—from compiling contact lists of like-minded friends to offering me books, emergency rides, and help finding accommodations—sustained me.

Finally, I am grateful to the God who answered the call of my restless heart. Without him, nothing else would be possible or meaningful.

1

THE FAITHFUL

Don't let anyone look down on you because you are young, but set an example for the believers in speech, in life, in love, in faith and in purity.

1 TIMOTHY 4:12

Thirty minutes after students had belted out the last hymn at the praise-and-worship service in Catholic University of America's Caldwell Chapel, more than half of them—about five dozen college students—had not yet left. They lingered under the chapel's softly lit arches on this unseasonably warm October night, kneeling in silent prayer before the tabernacle set on an altar now crowded with makeshift confessionals. So many students had been clamoring for the chance to confess their sins to a priest that the college chaplain had to double the ranks of his confessors to accommodate them. But half a dozen priests still could not handle the demand generated after an evening of prayer, song, and eucharistic adoration. The students seeking reconciliation kept coming, and the priests—seated on chairs at the edges of the altar, at the sides of the church, anywhere they could find a semiprivate spot—planned to stay until midnight hearing confessions.

Sitting on the right side of the altar, not far from the piano where a student sang a muted version of the evangelical Protestant favorite "Lord, I Lift Your Name on High," was a young blond-haired woman wearing a faded T-shirt. She huddled with a priest in a black collar who looked only a few years older than she was. Their chairs faced each other and their bent bodies formed a human arch that mirrored the concrete one above them. With eyes closed and foreheads nearly touching, they sat in silence. She had already confessed her sins to him. He had already extended his hand over her, resting it on her shoulder in the formal act of absolution that usually takes only an instant.

But she did not leave. Crumpled under the weight of that hand of forgiveness, she seemed unable—or perhaps unwilling—to go. Instead, she simply wept. Her entire body shook with the force of her silent sobs in the safe darkness of the chapel. The priest, looking somewhat unsure of what to do in the face of such raw emotion, kept his hand on her shoulder as she absorbed the meaning of his gesture.

Finally, she stood. She hugged the priest, hanging on for several minutes. When she let go and wiped away her tears, a radiant smile washed across her face. As she headed toward a nearby pew to pray, she passed another student who was eagerly ascending the altar steps to take her place.

An Irresistible Attraction

Many Americans—and many American Catholics of the generation that reared these students—regard the confession of sins to a priest as superfluous, the neurotic act of guilt-ridden traditionalists. The necessity of regular confession is laughable, and the notion of college students packing a chapel to pray on their knees before a consecrated communion host is absurd.

But not here. Here, in a chapel littered with backpacks, past a staircase where dozens kneel or stand because they cannot fit inside the chapel itself, students do not ridicule eucharistic adoration or the rite of reconciliation. They gush about it. The peace, the freedom, the supernatural sense of forgiveness—this, they say, is almost inexplicable. The benefits far surpass those of psychotherapy, chats with friends, even private prayer. For them, the sacraments and devotions of the institutional church allow them to be cleansed, healed, and strengthened. For young adults like the one who kept clinging to that promise of pardon, these rites offer something so powerful that they weep in the face of it, so irresistible that they cannot walk away from it.

"It's kind of hard to describe," said Lori Agnew, a tall, attractive Catholic University junior who stood in flip-flops outside the chapel while the confessions were taking place.

Agnew turned twenty-one years old that night—a prime time for a pub crawl—but she spent the first few hours of her landmark birthday in church instead.

"There's something there," she said. "In our hearts, we know the truth. And this holds the truth. It's not fluff. It's real."

Why are young adults who have grown up in a society saturated with relativism—which declares that ethical and religious truths vary according to the people who hold them—touting the truth claims of Christianity with such confidence? Why, in a society brimming with competing belief systems and novel spiritual trends, are young adults attracted to the trappings of tradition that so many of their parents and professors have rejected? Is this simply the reaction of a few throwbacks to a bygone era, a few scattered inheritors of a faith they never critically examined? Is it the erratic behavior of young idealists moving through an inevitably finite religious phase? Or are they the heralds of something new? Could these young adults be proof that the demise of America's Judeo-Christian tradition has been greatly exaggerated?

"It's a massive turning of the tide," said Boston College philosopher Peter Kreeft after addressing an auditorium full of students during Jesus Week at Harvard University in April 2001.

Citing enrollment spikes at orthodox Catholic seminaries and the general demeanor of the students he has met in the last decade, Kreeft said today's young adults are rejecting "the old, tired, liberal, modern" mind-set in favor of a more orthodox one.

"Even though they know less history or literature or logic" than students ten or twenty years ago, Kreeft said, "they're more aware that they've been cheated and they need more. They don't know that what they're craving is the Holy Spirit."

Across the nation, from the runways of beauty pageants to the halls of Ivy League universities, a small but committed core of young Christians is intentionally embracing organized religion and traditional morality. Their numbers—and their disproportionately powerful influence on their peers, parents, and popular culture—are growing. The grassroots movement they have started bears watching because it has thrived in the most unlikely places, captured the hearts of the most unlikely people, and aims to effect the most unlikely of outcomes: a revitalization of American Christianity and culture.

In Search of Structure

Recent media reports and statistical surveys—though hardly consistent or conclusive—suggest the stirrings of renewed interest in organized religion and conventional morality among young adults. According to a 1997 Gallup poll, nearly 80 percent of teens thirteen to seventeen considered religion a significant influence in their lives.[1] A 1999 study by George Barna found that 42 percent of "baby busters"—those born between 1965 and 1983—were likely to attend church weekly, as compared to 34 percent of their baby boomer parents. The busters also were more likely to read the Bible (36 percent to 30 percent) and to pray (80 percent to 70 percent).[2]

Gallup polls of teenagers in the 1990s found that 70 percent rejected the notion that religion is "not an important part of the modern world," and they identified as "religious" by an almost identical margin. Nearly nine in ten polled by Gallup said they believed in the divinity of Jesus.[3] And the federally financed National Longitudinal Study of Adolescent Health has recently found that two-thirds of teenagers describe themselves as "religious" or "very religious."[4]

Much of the renewed vigor of organized religion is concentrated in its most traditional forms, and young adults often are the ones clamoring for convention. *Time* magazine reported in 1999 that the number of U.S. Catholic dioceses hosting the traditional Latin Mass had risen from 6 in 1990 to 131 in 1999, and more than 150,000 people attended them weekly. The article attributed the increase largely to "Gen-X interest" and quoted several young Latin Mass–goers who were "part of a retro-revolt among U.S. Catholics."[5] A survey of young Catholics, conducted by sociologists Dean R. Hoge, Mary Johnson, and Juan L. Gonzales Jr., and William Dinges, a professor of religious studies, suggested that the three core elements of the faith of today's young Catholics are belief in God's presence in the sacraments (including the presence of Jesus Christ in the Eucharist), concern for helping the poor, and devotion to Mary as the mother of God—all key tenets of an orthodox Catholic faith.[6] And another Hoge survey found that the priesthood has grown "increasingly conservative on theological questions" since the 1980s. Young priests, it seems, have more in common with conservative elderly priests than with the more liberal middle-aged baby boomers who directly preceded them.[7]

The popularity of traditional services in mainline Protestant churches—like the Sunday night compline service at St. Mark's Episcopal Cathedral in Seattle that has drawn crowds of more than six hundred, most of whom are young adults—has garnered attention in secular publications, including the *New York Times*.[8] Old-time Protestant theology and morality, even when not delivered in a High-Church setting, is also booming among young adults. Evangelical Christian groups are particularly popular on college campuses and in the Ivy League, as noted by such publications as *Fifteen Minutes,* the weekend magazine of the *Harvard Crimson,* which published a cover story in 2000 about the rise of evangelicalism among Harvard students.[9] Promise Keepers, a grassroots evangelical-style movement for Christian men that emphasizes conventional morality, has reached more than 3.5 million men through ninety-eight stadium and arena conferences since 1991[10] and has sparked an equally vast amount of media scrutiny. And evangelical megachurches—where Christian rock bands and video shows are mixed with morally conservative sermons—attract hearty crowds of young Christians who want a conventional message delivered in an unconventional style.

A parallel movement is seen in the attraction of young secular Jews to orthodoxy, a shift that has generated substantial media attention in recent years. In a *Boston Globe* article that profiled some of the young adults known as *ba'alai tshuvah,* or "returning," in 2000, Sylvia Barack Fishman, a professor of contemporary Jewish life at Brandeis University, estimated that a "core group" of 25 to 30 percent of young Jews "is actively seeking to connect with their heritage."[11] An *Atlantic Monthly* piece in 1999 noted rising enrollments at Jewish schools—the sort of schools that observant young Jewish parents choose and the sort that tend to produce observant young Jews. According to the article, the number attending such schools has more than tripled since the early 1960s, to about two hundred thousand, out of about a million Jewish school-age children.[12]

Signs of more conventional sexual behavior and morality among young adults also have surfaced sporadically in secular media reports and surveys. Talk of a sexual "counterrevolution" was spurred in the late 1990s by the popularity of such books as *The Rules: Time-tested Secrets for Capturing the Heart of Mr. Right* by Ellen Fein and Sherrie Schneider and *A Return to Modesty: Discovering the Lost Virtue* by Wendy Shalit. The True Love Waits campaign has made headlines for persuading more than half a million young adults to pledge sexual abstinence until marriage.[13] In 1997, the government's National Survey of Family Growth announced that between 1990 and 1995, the percentage of sexually active teenagers had declined for the first time since 1970.[14] The Centers for Disease Control and Prevention found that teen pregnancy rates had dropped 20 percent from 1991 to 1999.[15] Recent studies from the University of Chicago, the University of California at Los Angeles, and the Urban Institute have documented less approval of casual sex and legalized abortion among young adults.[16]

The latest surveys and media reports also show parallel trends toward other manifestations of conventional morality and altruism among young adults, including an inclination toward community service. A 1999 Gallup survey estimated that 109 million Americans volunteered in some form in 1998, a 36 percent increase from the estimate of 80 million volunteers in 1987.[17] If a 1998 study by the American Youth Policy Forum is any indication, that trend can be explained at least partly by a rising tide of youth voluntarism. The study found that more than 15 million young people volunteered through groups like Habitat for Humanity.[18] The 1999 American freshman survey from UCLA found that a record percentage of incoming college students—nearly three-fourths—said they had volunteered during their senior year of high school, while only about one-fifth of them said they were required to do so for graduation. More than 80 percent of the freshmen queried listed attending a religious service as one of their activities during their senior year of high school.[19]

An embrace of traditional religion and morality often begins with a rejection of relativism. In a culture where young adults are frequently told that no universal moral standards or religious truths exist, many have begun to question that dictum and search for the truth that they believe is knowable.

Jean Bethke Elshtain, an ethics professor at the University of Chicago Divinity School, said the rebellion against relativism among her students is "quite noticeable."

"I certainly have detected among my students a sort of quest for some kind of purpose or meaning," said Elshtain, who sees that quest among "my students who are the most thoughtful and the most demanding. Some have been out in the world and they could not take the way it was being presented to them."

Even more surprising, she said, is how many students arrive at her secular university with a religious faith and experience a deepening of that faith during their years on campus. The students often surprise professors by starting Bible studies and prayer groups on their own, then asking faculty to lead them.

Elshtain said she believes the trend has staying power: "I think something is really afoot."

Andy Crouch, editor in chief of *re:generation quarterly,* a magazine for young Christians, first saw the stirrings of this interest in traditional religion at Harvard, where he worked with the Inter-Varsity Christian Fellowship for nine years, beginning in 1991.

In the last fifteen years, participation in campus religious groups has been rising "across the board," Crouch said. "Everybody is talking about it."

He noted that the rise has most benefited conservative campus groups, explaining, "Orthodoxy thrives in pluralism."

Campus Crusade for Christ, a conservative evangelical group that stresses strict moral standards and salvation by Jesus Christ, has seen its ranks swell in recent years. Mike Tilley, who oversees campus expansion in America, said participation in the group nearly doubled between 1995 and 2000, rising from twenty-one thousand to forty thousand students. Some chapters have several hundred active students, and a few have nearly a thousand. At seven hundred of the campuses where the group operates, the chapters are organized by students, not Campus Crusade staffers.

Countertrends clearly exist, especially in the realm of sexual behavior and morality. Divorce is rampant among evangelicals. Many Catholics disregard Vatican bans on contraception, premarital sex, and remarriage without annulment. And New Age spirituality—which often accompanies a movement away from moral absolutes—is gaining steam in many circles of American culture and in many American churches. Many polls of young adults reveal a high tide of moral relativism among the next generation and a deep suspicion of objective standards of truth and beauty. Indicators such as these do not portend a universal embrace of Christian orthodoxy and conventional morality.

But those countertrends may ultimately strengthen the appeal of orthodoxy to young adults who want an alternative to the secular status quo.

"[They] have witnessed the breakup of their own families or friends' families," said Brad Wilcox, a postdoctoral fellow in sociology at the Center for Research on Child Wellbeing at

Princeton who has authored studies on Christian marriage and family issues. "They have experienced the dark side of the sexual revolution and are seeking some kind of meaning and structure."

Purpose and Methodology

Clearly, something new is happening. These snapshot surveys and reports hint at an emergent interest in religious tradition and the conventional morality that often accompanies it. But they tell only half the story—and sometimes less—of the romance of Christian orthodoxy and young adults.

The full story of this budding bond is both less and more complex than it appears in most statistical analyses and secular media reports, which necessarily focus on only specific slices of this trend and often do so through a purely sociological lens. It is less complex in that the various images of young adults embracing tradition—in religion, morality, even clothing and pop-culture fads—are diverse yet interrelated expressions of the same trend. It is more complex in that the reasons why young adults are attracted to tradition, and the ways in which they express and act on that attraction, are copious and sometimes conflicting. And when it comes to deeply held religious and moral convictions, this trend stems from something more than a pendulum swing, though a reaction against today's moral relativism and religious pluralism surely accounts for much of the inverse appeal of orthodoxy. Many young adults who count themselves among the renewed devotees of orthodoxy in America recognize the cultural influences that have swayed them. But they also speak eloquently about a desire too deep to be explained by sociology, too timeless to be peculiar to Generation X and its famous "spiritual hunger."

This book is an attempt to explore and explain that desire, using not only statistics and expert analyses but also the stories of the young adults who have experienced it most intensely and acted on it most boldly. As a twenty-seven-year-old Catholic and a journalist in the secular media, I have spent years listening to my twenty- and thirtysomething peers and to young orthodox believers with whom I strongly identify. I have heard them speak of their weariness with secularism, their thirst for meaning, and their conviction that they will not repeat the mistakes of the generation that preceded them. I have seen flashes of insight in the mainstream media about my generation's "spiritual emptiness." I have witnessed the well-intentioned attempts of religious leaders to assuage that emptiness. And I have heard snippets of young believers' voices in the public square, describing their beliefs and commitments with honesty and passion.

What I have not heard is the story of these young orthodox believers presented in a way that scrutinizes seemingly disparate trends in the Christian tradition to unearth their unifying themes. What I have not seen is a coherent explanation of this draw toward organized religion and traditional morality that gives credence to sociological explanations but refuses to stop there. What I have not read is an extensive account of this phenomenon that allows young adults themselves to explain what experiences led them to a place many never intended to go and to envision where they want to go from here.

So I decided to write it myself. Thanks to a generous journalism fellowship from the nonprofit Phillips Foundation of Potomac, Maryland, I had the opportunity to spend a year researching, reporting, and writing on this trend. In that year, I interviewed dozens of sociologists, religious leaders, college professors, theologians, and youth ministers for their insights on this trend. I sorted through statistics to quantify, where possible, its scope. Most important, I visited cities across the nation and talked with hundreds of young believers who fit the profile of a young orthodox Christian. I heard—in their own words, through their own stories—how and why they have chosen this life. And I witnessed how their daily lives have been shaped, and shaken up, by their countercultural choice to embrace moral and religious absolutes in a postmodern age.

Defining the Faithful

Though I intend to examine the trends and countertrends related to this attraction to Christian orthodoxy among young adults, my subjects are not the ones so often celebrated by a culture that revels in the "spiritual search." These young adults have had many yearnings and formative experiences that are common to all spiritually inclined Americans. Yet they are qualitatively different from many of their peers and parents who seek spiritual growth while rejecting either organized religion or its more conventional, demanding, or morally strict manifestations.

These young adults are not perpetual seekers. They are committed to a religious worldview that grounds their lives and shapes their morality. They are not lukewarm believers or passionate dissenters. When they are embracing a faith tradition or deepening their commitment to it, they want to do so wholeheartedly or not at all. When they are attracted to tradition in worship or in spirituality, they want to understand the underlying reality of that tradition and use it to transform their lives. That sense of commitment and total acceptance of orthodoxy sets them apart from many of their peers and fellow believers who share their affection for the trappings of religious tradition but reject its theological and moral roots.

The young adults profiled in this book also differ substantially from their grandparents, though their moral attitudes and devotional practices often look surprisingly similar. Most of their grandparents inherited a religious tradition that either insulated them from a culture hostile to their beliefs or ushered them into a society that endorsed their Christian worldview. Today's young Americans, regardless of their religious formation, have never had the luxury of accepting orthodoxy without critical reflection. The pluralistic culture they live in will not permit it. Nor do most of them want to be religious isolationists confined to spiritual, religious, and cultural ghettos of their own construction. They intuitively accept the religious tolerance that marks a postmodern culture, yet they refuse to compartmentalize their faith or keep their views to themselves. Though they express their values in different ways, most of these young adults are intent on bringing them to bear on the culture they live in and on using their talents and considerable influence to transform that culture.

These are not your father's believers—or your grandfather's. So who are these young adults? What drives them? How do their beliefs shape their own lives and the lives of those around them?

The young adults profiled in this book constitute, in many ways, an eclectic mix. They are college students, monks, beauty queens, rocket scientists, and landscape architects. They come from fallen-away and devout Catholic families; fundamentalist, evangelical, and mainline Protestant families; and families with no religious affiliation at all. They tend to be cultural leaders, young adults blessed with talent, intelligence, good looks, wealth, successful careers, impressive educational pedigrees, or charisma—or some dynamic combination thereof. They are the sort of people who, according to conventional wisdom, do not *need* religion; though they have had their share of rough times, most did not arrive at their convictions out of utter desperation or a lack of alternatives. Rather, they made conscious commitments that are having an impact far greater than their numbers would warrant. The believers who form this small but growing core are the sort of people whom religious leaders say they want in their congregations—dedicated, committed, capable of leadership—though their presence sometimes seems to alarm as many fellow believers as it inspires. They are the sort of people other young adults look to when considering what to do, how to live, and what to believe. So what they do, how they live, and what they believe matters to America—a lot.

"When they speak, even the skeptics are listening," said Dr. Leon Kass, a bioethicist and humanities professor at the University of Chicago who sees signs of increased interest in traditional religion among today's students. Whether attending now-packed High Holy Day services with other Jews at the campus Hillel or discussing the biblical creation story with students in his class on the philosophical theory of Genesis, Kass has found that the students who defend organized religion are some of his best and brightest.

"The kids that I see are more intellectually serious," Kass said. "That generally means they're more attracted by the weighty religious traditions. And there's a new recognition that religion is not just superstition or the refuge of the ignorant."

The young adults profiled in this book were born between the years of 1965 and 1983, with a few exceptions on either end of the age spectrum. Most belong to the cohort known as Generation X, though the younger ones fall into Generation Y. Their religious affiliations span the Christian spectrum, but my focus—on orthodox young adults who are in positions of cultural influence and on churches where this trend is most vibrant—tended to lead me to Roman Catholics and evangelicals, as well as some mainline Protestants and Orthodox Christians.

This movement is broader than the boundaries carved by the time and space restraints of this book project. Its ripple effects reach across the church and culture, and its adherents are represented across the spectrums of race, class, and denomination. But in this book, I chose to focus on those young believers whose faith commitments will most directly and disproportionately impact American culture writ large. There are many other stories to tell, but the stories in this book paint the broad strokes of a phenomenon that has gone largely unnoticed in the secular media and even within the church.

A note about orthodoxy: The dictionary often equates orthodoxy with conventionality or traditional values. G. K. Chesterton aptly summarized the meaning of *orthodoxy* in a Christian context in his 1908 religious autobiography, *Orthodoxy*. He wrote: "When the word 'orthodoxy' is used here it means the Apostles' Creed, as understood by everybody calling himself Christian until a very short time ago and the general historic conduct of those who heed such a creed."[20] The Apostles' Creed confesses belief in a triune God who created heaven and earth; in the full divinity and humanity of his son, Jesus Christ; and in the Holy Spirit, who proceeds from the Father and the Son. The creed also affirms the existence of a universal church, one baptism, the forgiveness of sins, and eternal life, among other doctrines. Its embrace over the centuries has generally implied adherence to the Ten Commandments—which forbid such things as murder, theft, and adultery—as well as the embrace of faith, hope, and love, and acceptance of the Beatitudes delivered by Jesus at the Sermon on the Mount. For the Christians introduced in this book, the acceptance of a transcendent moral authority as revealed in the Scriptures translates into a commitment to regular worship and prayer, a belief in absolute truth, and a recognition of objective standards of personal and public morality.

On the subject of values and beliefs, a few other definitions may be helpful. *Relativism*, as noted above, is the theory that all values or judgments are equal and none are absolute or universal, since they all vary according to circumstances and to the people or cultures that hold them. In the moral and religious realm—the context for my use of the term—relativists argue that no belief system or ethical code is superior to another, because there is no objective standard of truth or morality against which the systems can be measured.

Pluralism has several meanings, including its definition as a theory that two or more kinds of ultimate reality exist—so contradictory religious truth claims are not necessarily mutually exclusive. In this context, *pluralism* most often refers to the cultural condition of having manifold religions, cultures, and belief systems represented in one society. America has a pluralistic culture, and that condition allows today's spiritual seekers to sort through an overwhelming array of options.

Postmodern, in this context, describes today's epoch in American culture, which is characterized by a rejection of the Enlightenment-era emphasis on reason, science, and progress and by a new blending of old patterns, beliefs, and styles. Postmodernism, the reigning ideology in today's culture, is closely linked in this book to the theories of relativism and pluralism. All reject or undermine universal standards and absolute-truth claims, and all celebrate the leveling of hierarchies and the equalizing or blending of diverse ideologies.

Amid the swirl of spiritual, religious, and moral choices that exist in American culture today, many young adults are opting for the tried-and-true worldview of Christian orthodoxy. They are not a uniform group, but most of these young believers share key characteristics that often make them more similar to one another than to the less orthodox members of their own religious traditions. A few examples:

- Their identity is centered on their religious beliefs, and their morality derives from those beliefs.
- They are attracted to a worldview that challenges many core values of the dominant secular culture while addressing their deepest questions and concerns. Time-tested teachings and meaningful traditions appeal to them.
- They embrace challenging faith commitments that offer them firm guidelines on how to live their lives.
- Their adherence to traditional morality and religious devotion often comes at considerable personal cost, and the sacrificial nature of these commitments is often precisely what makes them attractive.
- They yearn for mystery and tend to trust their intuitive sense that what they have found is true, real, and worth living to the extreme.
- They seek guidance and formation from legitimate sources of authority and trust these authorities to help them find lasting happiness and avoid repeating their own painful mistakes or those of their parents and peers.
- They strive for personal holiness, authenticity, and integration in their spiritual lives and are attracted to people and congregations that do the same. Conversely, they are repelled by complacency, hypocrisy, and pandering.

- Their beliefs and practices—though usually completely compatible with the core tenets of their faith traditions—often defy conventional wisdom about their generation, the expectations of religious leaders, and existing classifications of believers within individual denominations (for example, charismatic or conventional, liberal or conservative).
- They are, for the most part, concerned with impacting and engaging the larger culture. Yet they are equally committed to living out their beliefs in the context of authentic communities that support them and hold them accountable.

That, in a nutshell, is what sets these young Christians apart from the many seekers, dissenters, and tepid believers in their midst. It even sets them apart from the passionate believers in their own faith traditions who embrace parts of the tradition but want to reshape doctrine or moral teachings to fit the circumstances of a modern—and now postmodern—world.

These young adults understand the challenges that traditional morality and orthodoxy pose. They sometimes empathize with members of their religious traditions who want to "update" teachings to make them more relevant, and many of these young believers happily embrace worship styles that make Christianity more accessible to seekers. But they resist any compromise of the essential tenets of orthodoxy as capitulation to secular culture. These young orthodox believers defend Christianity's timeless moral teachings and its scriptural and ecclesiastical authority with vigor because they believe that any other approach would endanger the integrity of the faith they hold so dear.

An Overview

How did today's young Christians come to be defenders of orthodoxy in an age that denigrates dogma? How did they come to embrace views that so many in their schools, congregations, culture—even, in some cases, their own families—consider reactionary, intolerant, or dangerous?

Each story, like each person who tells it, is unique. But just as they share key characteristics, the young adults profiled in this book also have shared some variation of two key experiences that led them to a fuller embrace of orthodoxy and the morality it demands. Those experiences—a spiritual search and the resulting commitment to organized religion and traditional morality—are explored in more depth in chapter 2.

First, a brief sketch of the path to orthodoxy taken by today's young Christians. The search begins with the realization of spiritual hunger or of the desire for a deeper, more authentic expression of spirituality. Sometimes subtle, sometimes acute, this crisis of meaning often arrives on the heels of significant success in the secular world at an early age, which leaves these young adults feeling surprisingly unsatisfied. For a stockbroker in San Francisco, the crisis came when he had more money than he could spend, a beautiful girlfriend, and a life that felt utterly empty. For a NASA engineer in Houston, the call to orthodoxy came when she decided that service to the cause of Christ should supersede her passion to put more people on the moon.

The young faithful who trek toward orthodoxy then begin an intentional spiritual search or make a critical reflection on their current beliefs and practices. Like many seekers, they may question childhood beliefs—or the lack thereof—or they may ask themselves if they are truly living up to the demands of the faith they already profess.

"People have a deepened sense of the need for meaning and belonging," said Os Guinness, a Christian author and founder of the Trinity Forum, a faith-based leadership academy in McLean, Virginia. "The reigning philosophy—postmodernism—has no powerful answers at all. And this has created a powerful search for meaning."

It is at this point that the young adults profiled in this book part company with many of their peers, parents, and pop-culture personalities who conduct endless, and sometimes aimless, spiritual quests. These young adults are not content to search forever. They want answers. For them, the search is not an end in itself; it is a means to an end. From the outset, many of them crave tradition, historical continuity, and time-tested approaches to metaphysical questions they know they did not invent, so their spiritual journeys head in the direction of organized religion. Others may not seek answers in organized religion until they encounter a person or a community living orthodoxy in an authentic, compelling way—a way that makes them want to join or at least give it a chance.

There are almost as many twists, turns, and false starts in these journeys as there are people who take them. None of the young adults in this book have wholeheartedly embraced orthodoxy without reflection, without challenge, without confronting a larger, secular culture that questions and even mocks their choice daily. And few who count themselves among these young orthodox believers would pronounce their conversions complete, the integration of their faith and daily lives accomplished, or God's will for their lives fully revealed. They see themselves as always either moving ahead or falling behind, always striving for holiness and never arriving at a place where they can rest on their spiritual laurels.

These believers have had powerful spiritual experiences that have engendered their faith in a transcendent God who knows them personally, has a plan for their lives, and wills their cooperation. At crucial times in their lives—often in crucial moments— each of these young believers has made a conscious, intentional decision to embrace this way of life despite external obstacles or internal doubts. That commitment sets them apart from other spiritual seekers.

Once committed to orthodoxy, these young adults do not quarantine their faith. It infuses every aspect of their lives, guides every major decision they make, and affects nearly every interaction they have at home, work, school, church, and in the culture at large. They frequently make their private faith known publicly, and its impact touches every aspect of American religion and culture that they do. Chapters 3 through 9 examine the ways that their religious worldview has been shaped by and has shaped their worship styles, faith communities, romantic relationships, voting patterns, campus environments, and career decisions.

The Cultural Challenge

Woven through the fabric of this book are several key questions, which are addressed in each topical chapter and tackled with particular intensity in the concluding chapter. Among them: Are the young adults who embrace organized religion and traditional morality inherently different from their less committed or irreligious peers, or have they simply had different experiences? Is this phenomenon purely a return to tradition, or is it something new? What are its historical roots and parallels? How widespread is it? What is its potential for growth? Will it last? What are its implications for American religion and religious leaders? What are its implications for politics, education, the arts, and the broader secular culture? What are its inherent dangers, tensions, and obstacles? What could derail it? What could fortify it?

History has been known to foil even the most promising predictions. But several features of this trend toward orthodoxy among today's young adults indicate that its cultural significance could be considerable. One feature is the circle of conversion that hooks so many young adults who eventually embrace organized religion and traditional morality. Here's how it works: they see the radical personal witness of a believer living his or her faith explicitly and authentically. They investigate that believer's convictions out of respect or curiosity. They adopt those convictions and embrace that faith. Then they, in turn, bear witness to other young adults. That dynamic—witness to conversion to more witness—allows for the possibility of an exponential increase in these orthodox young Christians in the years to come.

When thirty-year-old Dominican Brother John Paul Walker
was an undergraduate at the University of Illinois at Urbana-
Champaign, he was a lukewarm Catholic. Then he met a group
of committed Catholic students on a weekend retreat. They were
fun and friendly, the type, Walker said, who could joke around,
drink beer, watch football, "and still say, 'Jesus Christ is the most
important person in my life and I'm Catholic through and
through.'"

The way those Catholics lived their lives—and their willingness to proclaim their faith publicly—impressed Walker and led
him to "become one of them."

Walker's faith blossomed after that retreat and flourished while
he was in graduate school at Johns Hopkins University, pursuing
a doctoral degree in chemistry and environmental engineering.

"I was darn good at what I did," said Walker. "I could have
written my own ticket."

Instead, he chose to join the Dominican order and study for
the priesthood. He hopes to influence others through a radical
witness to his faith, the way those undergraduate students had
influenced him.

Another promising feature of this trend is that the young adults
who embrace organized religion tend to be cultural gatekeepers who
have a disproportionately large impact in academic, artistic, political,
and professional circles. Their talents, education, and positions of
influence make them natural trendsetters in the church and the culture. Successful young adults are not the only ones embracing orthodoxy, and orthodoxy is not the only path chosen by successful young
adults. But those who "have it all" and make serious Christian commitments are more likely to influence others to join them.

Religious leaders like Fr. C. John McCloskey believe that this
generation's best and brightest young proponents of orthodoxy,
who wield a disproportionately powerful influence in the culture,
hold the key to the future of the faith.

"If you want to change the world, what you usually do is go for
the best people," he said.

A former Wall Street financier, McCloskey is now a priest with Opus Dei, an ecclesiastical association that attracts many traditional lay Catholics who seek to glorify God in their secular pursuits. Opus Dei, which is Latin for "work of God," often sets up shop near prestigious universities to evangelize influential young adults who are poised to influence many others. McCloskey has spent much of the last fifteen years in campus ministry at Princeton, Yale, and Columbia, where he detected increasing hostility toward religious and moral absolutes among many faculty members and administrators. But he saw a corresponding openness to orthodoxy on the part of some students. McCloskey noted that when students are presented with ideas and teachings that sharply contrast with campus culture—church teachings against abortion and contraception, for instance, and orthodoxy's insistence on absolute standards of right and wrong—they often respond with surprise and interest. And the student leaders who embrace orthodoxy in these Ivy League settings often lead others by their example, McCloskey said, since they naturally attract imitators.

In the wake of terrorist attacks on the World Trade Center and the Pentagon in September 2001, the attraction to organized religion crystallized for many young adults—and the nation took notice. Many journalists expressed surprise at the outpouring of religious devotion seen in the public at large and among the young in particular. Campus ministers reported overflowing Catholic Masses, massive evangelical prayer huddles, and newly invigorated fellowship groups. Church leaders marveled at the young people who attended all-night prayer vigils and packed faith-sharing sessions.

At the First Evangelical Free Church in a suburb of St. Louis, thirty-three-year-old pastor Kevin Bauer watched the ranks of his young singles group multiply in the weeks following the attacks. A weekly meeting in October 2001—like so many evangelical events that have attracted young adults in recent years—centered largely on worshiping Jesus with a blend of contemporary worship and orthodox theology. A crowd of about five dozen packed a church hall where lights were dimmed and song lyrics were projected onto a movie screen. Led by a twenty-five-year-old software engineer strumming an emerald electric guitar, the crowd belted out "Amazing Grace" and plenty of contemporary praise songs.

"I want to know you," they sang in one ballad, their eyes closed and feet tapping. "I want to hear your voice / I want to know you more."

Bauer sang along from the corner, swinging his legs from the table where he was perched. When given a chance to address the group, the peer pastor ambled up to the front of the room and told his listeners that this was only the beginning of a religious revival.

"I really believe that God is going to bring more people into this," said Bauer as he addressed an audience of denim-clad computer programmers, engineers, and other young professionals. "I get a true sense that God is really moving in our church, and especially moving in our generation. You guys are leaders."

Many young believers have reached levels of secular success for which others their age—or older—are still striving. Other believers have grown up in an atmosphere in which nothing was forbidden and, having experienced so much freedom at such an early age, now find worldly pleasures unsatisfying, even banal. So they experience early "midlife crises" and embark on spiritual quests that lead them to commit to organized religion—often earlier and with more conviction than did their parents. Their world-weary outlook helps them relate to unbelievers and speak the language of their peers, even as they call them to make otherworldly commitments. Having "been there, done that," they know what it will take to make religion relevant to their generation, and they are eager to share their knowledge with religious leaders. They also have the authority—by virtue of the lives they have led, the conversions they have experienced, and the commitments they have made—to speak credibly to older members of their congregations, who cannot easily dismiss them as neophytes with no worldly wisdom or spiritual discipline.

Bill Haley, a thirty-two-year-old Episcopal minister and publisher of *re:generation quarterly,* a magazine for young orthodox Christians, traveled the world for more than a year on a fellowship designed to prepare him for the ministry. The insights he gleaned from his travels led him to establish Kairos, a community of young, professional, mostly evangelical Protestants who meet for weekly worship at The Falls Church (Episcopal) in Falls Church, Virginia.

At Kairos, Haley said, "we treat people like they have brains. I don't think a lot of churches do that. And I say that with sadness."

Haley hopes to offer young adults something they may not be getting elsewhere: authentic community, the challenge to live a moral life geared toward serving others, and a genuine connection to a transcendent God.

Before the 2000 presidential election, Haley preached about the sanctity of life in all forms, condemning abortion as well as voters who worry more about a good economy than the advance of a "culture of death." About 125 young adults heard his sermon, and Kairos members and their friends were still buzzing about it a week later.

"There aren't thousands hearing that message," Haley said, but unlike many who hear it in larger congregations, the young adults at Kairos "get it."

Even when they get it, life is not always easy for these young believers—or for those who live, learn, or work with them. Many of these believers have experienced radical conversions or swings toward religious observance that have driven wedges between them and the people, careers, and faith communities they love. They face tough choices and severe ridicule when embracing orthodoxy. They also face the danger of becoming defensive, judgmental, and isolated from a world that mocks their deepest values. Most of these young believers are committed to transforming the world rather than retreating from it. To do so, they must constantly walk a tightrope to avoid the two extremes they loathe—isolation from the world at one end and capitulation to its relativistic values at the other. That tension, and their sometimes deft, sometimes botched management of it, makes their stories especially compelling and relevant to the larger culture they seek to influence.

2

THE SEARCH

Our hearts were made for You, O Lord, and they are restless until they rest in you.

ST. AUGUSTINE, BISHOP OF HIPPO

When David Legge talks about the days before his religious conversion, he doesn't talk about hitting rock bottom. He talks about living the good life, the kind that makes young men ache with ambition and old men seethe with envy. It was the American dream—accelerated.

At twenty-four, Legge had two years of Yale Law School under his belt, a summer associate's job in New York that paid more money than he could spend, and dazzling prospects for a law career that promised more of the same. Legge, who looks like a slimmer version of Tom Cruise with lighter brown hair and the same intense eyes, also had a hopping social life. Four or five nights a week, he would hit the city's hottest restaurants and bars, splurging on lavish dinners and big bar tabs in a continuous quest to entertain himself. It was the summer of 1995, and the living was very, very good. It was also hollow.

"I wasn't very happy," Legge said, reflecting five years later on that summer. "I had a good time, I guess, but I didn't have that many real friends in New York. And I realized it was just kind of an empty life."

The party lifestyle that tempted and consumed him felt meaningless. And though Legge didn't make it to church more than once that summer, an intellectual interest in the Catholic faith of his childhood that had surfaced during his second year at Yale still lingered in his consciousness.

Earlier that school year, while sitting at his computer and reviewing a paper he was writing about Abraham Lincoln, Legge had realized that he had never applied as much intellectual rigor to the study of his faith as he had to his schoolwork.

"I thought, you know, I know so much more about Abraham Lincoln than I do about Jesus. And Jesus should be so much more important in my life. Maybe I should learn something about him."

Like many Generation-X Catholics who grew up in the 1970s and 1980s, Legge's religious formation had been spotty. Though he was raised in a churchgoing Catholic home and attended Catholic schools in the suburbs of Seattle, his religion classes consisted mostly of "psychobabble," he said, and he learned next to nothing about the sacraments or church history. It wasn't until after college that he realized what Catholics believe about the Eucharist—that after the consecration of the host at Mass, the body, blood, soul, and divinity of Christ are truly present in the communion wafer. Both Vatican II, the church council that had shaped Legge's experience of Catholicism, and Pope John Paul II, who has presided over the Catholic Church since Legge was nine years old, have hailed the Eucharist as the "the source and summit of the Christian life." But to Legge, the Eucharist was just another aspect of an inherited faith he did not understand. Yet it would be his attendance at Mass and his devotion to that particular Catholic reality—the Eucharist—that would lead him from emptiness to a sincere and radical Christian commitment.

The transformation took time. After Legge's realization in law school that he was ignorant of his professed—and largely unpracticed—faith, he headed to the bookstore to buy a Bible and the *Catechism of the Catholic Church*. He started reading Catholic classics by such authors as St. Augustine and Thomas Merton, who told stories of converting to Christ after realizing the dreariness of their decadent lives. He also began making time for Mass. In New York, the temptations of the fast track derailed his spiritual quest for several months. But Legge never forgot the acute emptiness he felt there, and it propelled him forward in his search.

Slowly, over the course of several years of receiving the Eucharist at Mass and struggling to surrender his secular impulses and freewheeling lifestyle, Legge's conversion to orthodoxy began to take hold. And his devotion to the Eucharist—which set the stage for a life-changing revelation he had while praying before the tabernacle—led him into a relationship that now consumes him more completely than the party lifestyle ever did.

The Evidence: A Mixed Bag

At first blush, studies and polls that track the spirituality and religious beliefs of young adults like Legge seem hopelessly contradictory. On the one hand, America's spirituality craze—and the spiritual hunger of younger Americans—is well documented. Opinion polls consistently show that more than 90 percent of Americans believe in God, and a Gallup poll found that the percentage of Americans who expressed a need for spiritual growth grew from 58 percent in 1994 to 82 percent in 1998.[1] Pollsters are also spotting enthusiasm for religion among the young. An August 2000 Gallup poll found that 85 percent of young adults said religion was important to them personally, and more than 60 percent said religion can solve all or most of today's problems.[2]

As for Christianity, a recent survey by evangelical pollster George Barna found that 86 percent of teenagers identify as Christian, and three of five say the Bible is completely accurate in all that it teaches.[3] A 1997 study of confirmed Catholics conducted by Mary Johnson, Dean R. Hoge, William Dinges, and Juan L. Gonzales Jr. found that 75 percent of non-Latino Catholics ages twenty to thirty-nine and 81 percent of young Catholic Latinos cannot imagine themselves as "being anything other than Catholic," and 90 percent of those confirmed as adolescents kept the faith.

The study also found that about 90 percent agree that in the Mass, the bread and wine actually become the body and blood of Christ.[4]

Yet ignorance like Legge's—about Scripture or core teachings of individual churches—abounds, as does indifference and relativism. The same Barna survey that found so many teenagers identifying as Christians also found that two out of three of them believe Satan is not a living being but only a symbol of evil, and just over half said that Jesus committed sins while he was on earth. Those beliefs run counter to orthodoxy, since historical Christianity holds that the devil is real and Jesus was sinless. A Gallup poll that found that 93 percent of Americans own a copy of the Bible or other Scriptures also found that only 42 percent of them could name five of the Ten Commandments.[5] And only 60 percent of the young adults in Gallup's August 2000 poll said they belong to a church or synagogue, as compared with 76 percent of people fifty and older.

On the Catholic front, the same study that found Catholic young adults identifying so strongly with the church also found about half of them agreeing that Catholics are "essentially no different than Protestants."[6] Only 31 percent reported attending Mass weekly, as practicing Catholics are obligated by church law to do.

The Seeds of a Search

Faced with the evidence, the question remains: Do young Christians lack essential knowledge about their faith and resist the teachings and standards that define their churches? Or do they harbor a deep spiritual hunger and curiosity about Christian tradition that makes them inclined to embrace orthodoxy in all of its rigor and particularity?

The answer may be both. While they lack religious knowledge and are conditioned to embrace a religious tolerance that bleeds into relativism, many young adults also show a genuine interest in orthodox Christianity. It starts with an interior, scarcely perceptible craving for something other than a life lived for pleasure, success, or self. It crystallizes into a desire for beliefs that mean something, demand something, change something.

That yearning—for meaning, for belonging, for something or Someone else—can take many forms, and the search it triggers can take many routes. But for the young adults who turn toward orthodoxy, the search often starts with a deep discontentment with the values thrust on them by their popular culture, schools, churches—sometimes even by their own families. That dissatisfaction manifests itself differently in each seeker, but four general patterns run through the stories of young adults attracted to orthodox Christianity:

- They have achieved secular success at a young age, and it leaves them hungry for meaning.
- They have been exposed to "watered-down" religion, moral relativism, or atheism, and they crave its opposite.
- They have practiced religion out of a sense of duty but now want a more personal relationship with God and a more intentional way to worship him.
- They have had personal religious devotion since childhood but long for a more integrated faith that is supported by community.

Not every young Christian committed to orthodoxy has conducted an intentional spiritual search. Many were born into devout Christian homes and grew steadily in the faith, never leaving the fold. Others stumbled upon belief in Christianity almost in spite of themselves, discovering God in a worship experience or through the witness of a Christian friend. Still others suffered a personal crisis that sparked a desperate desire for God. Nearly all of them tell stories of a faith journey characterized more by grace, hope, and joy than by a strident rejection of secularism or a conscious shift to orthodoxy. Still, at least one of the four themes cited above—and often several of them—generally surface in the stories of young Christians who have taken the countercultural trek toward orthodoxy.

The early midlife crisis:
Success and the call to serve

On Halloween night 2000 at the Dominican House of Studies in Washington, D.C., it was hard to tell who was in costume and who was not. Some Catholics in the twentysomething crowd were sporting religious robes to pay playful homage to their favorite medieval saints. Others were wearing the same robes they don every day, out of obedience to their religious vows.

But even in this eclectic crowd, the three Dominican brothers were hard to miss. Draped head to toe in white, they bore the easy smiles and confident air of natural-born leaders. They're tall—each easily clears six feet—and handsome. And like David Legge, they know what it means to rub shoulders with the best of the best, to glimpse the secular promised land of money, prestige, and power at an early age. They also know what it means to ache for more.

"It was this fundamental restlessness," said thirty-year-old Brother John Paul Walker as he stood in the midst of the pressing crowd, reflecting on what lured him away from a doctoral program in chemistry and environmental engineering at Johns Hopkins. "I've learned that's the key to discernment. If you're really doing what God wants you to do, you'll have peace and you'll have joy."

Walker said he now revels in that peace and joy, in his life as a Dominican studying for the priesthood. He no longer feels the nagging restlessness that consumed him while he was navigating—quite successfully—the secular career track.

Brothers Jonathan Kalisch and Nicholas Lombardo, Walker's friends and fellow Dominicans, also joined the order after achieving secular status and success. Kalisch, a Georgetown graduate, was working as a businessman in Poland when he took a trip to Israel and felt the tug of radical commitment.

"Being on the Sea of Galilee," Kalisch said, "I just felt called to give myself completely to Christ."

For Lombardo, committing wholeheartedly to Christ—and by extension, to a life of obedience with the Dominicans—meant a drastic departure from the ambition inculcated at Middlesex

School, his prestigious prep school on the outskirts of Boston. The Brown University graduate had intended to follow in the footsteps of his father, who had applied a doctoral degree in physics to the business world. But the seeds of a conversion that had been planted in Lombardo at a confirmation retreat in high school grew when he encountered Brown's Catholic campus ministry. He started to attend campus Masses and reconsider what mattered most to him. When he realized that God—not success or the pursuit of pleasure—was his top priority, Lombardo said, "it changed my life. I was just so much happier."

Most young Christians who commit to orthodoxy do not dump their secular careers and join a religious order, as Lombardo, Kalisch, and Walker did. But the restlessness that consumed those three men and caused them to reassess their priorities is a common factor in the spiritual search of today's young adults.

That restlessness is partly a reaction to American prosperity. Children born between 1960 and 1980 grew up in a culture saturated with consumerism and unprecedented wealth. The New Economy of the late 1990s only heightened prospects for material gain. Mendelsohn Media Research in New York reported that in 2000, nearly a third of millionaire American households were headed by someone between the ages of eighteen and thirty-nine.[7]

For those young adults blessed with a solid financial start in life, a top-notch education, or early professional success, a premature midlife crisis is a strong possibility. Many have reached positions of economic affluence and cultural status that their parents and grandparents only attained after middle age, if at all. They are already experiencing the best the material world has to offer. And like their baby boomer predecessors, many find it unsatisfying.

These young adults have the luxury of asking life's existential questions at an age when many of their parents were still working blue-collar jobs or climbing the corporate ladder. Of course, their peers who were born into poverty, deprived of a decent education, or raised in immigrant homes have fewer opportunities to ponder the pitfalls of money and power. But even many young adults who are struggling financially are asking why they should work so hard for the material comforts that left baby boomers chronically busy and dissatisfied. They know that the same New Economy that made their Silicon Valley peers rich in the last decade also left many young entrepreneurs penniless when the ride ended. And the same hard work that allowed their parents to succeed at work also failed to protect them from corporate layoffs or family problems resulting from their long hours on the job.

Whether reacting against the uncertainty of secular success or achieving that success at an early age and finding it empty, many of today's young adults see Christianity—and particularly, a commitment to Christian service—as a way out of the corporate trap. In the academic realm, that attraction to Christianity has led many students to spend their college years preparing to work for God, not just themselves.

Jeff Barneson, who heads the thriving evangelical InterVarsity Christian Fellowship graduate ministry at Harvard University, sees young Christians in Harvard's graduate law, business, government, and other programs seeking more than a prestigious degree. They have a sense that God has called them to Harvard for a reason, and that following his plan is more rewarding than chasing status and wealth.

"They are waking up earlier," said Barneson, of the students who refuse to wait until midlife to seek meaning in their careers and lives. "They're not like the social misfits, either. These are engaged, bright, articulate students. These are folks who've succeeded."

Sean Womack, an evangelical Protestant who was born in 1969, is one of the founding partners of the *Life@Work Journal,* a magazine that targets Christian baby boomers in the workplace. Womack and his partners are now working on a new magazine for Christian professionals under thirty-five, and he is writing a book about young professionals who are fed up with materialism and unwilling to wait until midcareer and middle age to ask life's biggest questions.

"They have decided that they do not need to wait until they are successful, i.e., have lots of money, before they do something significant—i.e., something they are called to or are passionate about," Womack said, of his twenty- and thirtysomething peers. "They don't want to play that game for their first forty years."

Indeed, some are opting out of the game altogether—at least for a while. At the University of Notre Dame, an estimated 8 percent of graduating students apply to the Alliance for Catholic Education (ACE), a faith-focused, university-run teaching program that sends its members to live in Catholic community houses and work in understaffed Catholic schools across the nation. The program, which started in 1994 and offers graduates a chance to do summer work toward a master's degree in education, attracts an average of 250 applicants each year to fill about eighty new teaching slots. Those looking to join ACE routinely pass up coveted job offers and graduate-school appointments, and about two-thirds of them stay involved in Catholic education after their two-year service stint ends.

John Eriksen, a 1999 ACE graduate, said the program's popularity defies conventional logic.

Eriksen arrived as a freshman at Notre Dame with "visions of law school and an M.B.A." But when spring 1997 rolled around and it was time to go to law school, the prospect left him cold. So he opted to take a break and try a new challenge, one that would force him to put his faith into action. He was accepted to the ACE program and moved to Baton Rouge to teach high school religion, earning an annual income of about eleven thousand dollars. At the end of his two years of teaching, his faith had crystallized, his law school ambitions had died, and he had fallen in love with Catholic education.

Fr. David Burrell, a Holy Cross priest and Notre Dame professor of philosophy and theology, thinks he knows what's going on. Students at a school like Notre Dame are among the best and brightest. They often feel pressure—both internal and external—to succeed. After a lifetime of academic success and four years of stiff competition, Burrell said, "they want to get off that whole merry-go-round. They really want something that can touch their souls. And a faith culture is the only thing that can respond to that."

The pendulum swing: In search of substance

On a Wednesday night in the fall of 2000, the upper room of Lulu's Club Mardi Gras in downtown Washington, D.C., was packed with hip young professionals sipping Corona and straining for a decent view of the small square stage in front. The bar, which looks like a cross between a comedy club and an airplane hangar, is hardly a predictable place for a religious revival.

But very little about this Theology on Tap speaker series is predictable. That's precisely the point. Theology on Tap, an event imported from cities like Chicago and Atlanta, exposes young Catholics to the teachings of the church in an unconventional setting. In Washington, D.C., speakers ranging from priests to graduate students address a standing-room-only crowd of twenty- and thirtysomething Catholics each week on topics spanning from sexual morality to religious devotions. The setup feels unconventional, but the theology is utterly orthodox. And the crowd eats it up.

On this October night, the audience was enjoying the antics of the burly, boisterous Fr. Bill Byrne, a campus chaplain at the University of Maryland at College Park who is in his midthirties. Byrne was wearing a Rodney Dangerfield grin, a Roman collar, and his black clericals.

"No, these pants are not leather," Byrne assured his amused audience, "just really old polyester."

Sweating under the spotlight, Byrne talked fast and loud, ridiculing himself as often as he dispensed doctrine. But his underlying message—all joking aside—was crystal clear. Go to Mass. Pray, preferably in a church where the Eucharist is reserved. And don't whine about Catholic guilt.

"First of all: Catholic guilt," Byrne said. "I hate that phrase, *Catholic guilt.* Because you know what? We're the only show in town offering forgiveness. Confession is not making you feel guilty. It's stripping off the layers of grime and varnish. I go every two weeks."

When he opened it up for questions, Byrne got them in rapid succession. A young woman asked how to prepare to confess her sins. Another asked how to pray. People in the back of the bar hollered for him to repeat his answers. When he told them that they all—including himself—needed structure and ritual in their lives to counteract laziness, a young woman in a pantsuit and platform heels leaned over to her friend and whispered excitedly, "That's totally true!"

After his stand-up routine, Byrne unfastened his collar, tied his jacket around his waist, and lit a cigarette. He waded into the crowd, sipping a drink and expressing no shock that his message went over so well. These young adults were reared on watered-down Catholicism and " '70s spirituality," Byrne said. So traditional Catholic teachings, when delivered in a language they can understand, are "radical"—and appealing.

"It's the truth," Byrne said, "and the truth hits."

The new generation's search for truth—and for a demanding, substantive religious message coupled, often, with a sense of tradition—might not surprise Byrne, but it has mystified many baby boomers. Catholics raised before Vatican II marvel that their children are embracing devotions like eucharistic adoration and the rosary, the very traditions that they happily shed in the 1960s and 1970s. Baby boomers in liberal mainline Protestant denominations watch their children defect in droves, opting instead for evangelical churches that preach the inerrancy of Scripture and the immorality of premarital and homosexual sex. And some evangelical pastors see young adults with a hunger for liturgy crossing over to Orthodox, Catholic, or conservative Episcopalian churches to satisfy it.

The most shocking aspect of this phenomenon, for many observers, is that many young adults drawn to orthodoxy had little or no religious formation as children. Their ignorance of the faith left many of them—particularly nominal Catholics—hungry for solid answers.

"There's a search for substance," said Vince Bernadin, who was born in 1978 and is now studying for the priesthood at Moreau Seminary at Notre Dame. "People are getting sick of trite little phrases. 'God is love' and 'God loves you'—what does that mean?"

Mark Holloway, a Holy Cross seminarian who was born in 1971, said he sees rising attendance at daily Mass on Notre Dame's campus as one sign of that search.

"They're rebelling against the rebellion," said Holloway. "They want tradition."

As the associate vocations director for Holy Cross, Fr. Bill Wack sometimes receives calls from young men who fire off such questions as "Do you wear your clericals?" "Do you defend and spread the faith?" "Are you faithful to the teaching authority of the church?"

"They want things to be more clear-cut, straightforward," said Wack, who graduated from Notre Dame in 1989. "They want to be sure that we're proud of who we are and that we're public about it."

Surveys of the priesthood by sociologist Dean Hoge have shown that the views of young seminarians are more similar to those of older conservative priests on issues like priestly celibacy and women's ordination. Those views stand in contrast to the opinions of baby boomer priests, who tend to be more progressive.[8] Religious orders that have attracted a substantial number of new recruits in recent years—like the Legionaries of Christ, Franciscan Friars of the Renewal, and Sisters of Life—also tend to be more traditional.

Psychologist and Catholic priest Fr. Benedict J. Groeschel credits the grace of God, as well as psychology and anthropology, for the shift. Groeschel, a founding member of the Franciscan Friars of the Renewal, said today's young adults are repelled by those who preach a "blah, middle-of-the-road" version of the gospel in mainline Protestant and liberal Catholic circles. Their attraction to orthodox Catholic and evangelical churches, he said, has a lot to do with the permissive culture around them.

"Where sin abounds, grace abounds all the more," Groeschel said, quoting St. Paul in Romans.

Young adults who have grown up in a culture that celebrates self-indulgence and sexual license and in churches that stress love of self more than service to God have seen the fallout of self-fulfillment fads. Families divided by no-fault divorce. Adults pursuing pleasure or careers with reckless abandon. Children left to raise themselves, making adult decisions—and adult mistakes—well before their time. The pendulum swings, and they find themselves captivated by Christianity's emphasis on self-restraint, sacrifice, and commitment.

Consider the case of Brother Luke Mary Fletcher. Like a lot of his twentysomething brothers in the Bronx-based Franciscan Friars of the Renewal, Fletcher did not hear God in the still, small whisper of his soul. He heard him in the thunderclap of a radical conversion, amid the excesses of a decadent lifestyle.

"People think we were always into God and prayerful," said Fletcher, who wears the characteristic long beard and floor-length gray robes of his austere and fast-growing religious order. "For almost all of us, that's not true."

Fletcher grew up "a pagan baby" in Tipton, Indiana, and was not baptized as a Catholic until age seven. His religious formation was spotty, and he was never confirmed. By his freshman year in public high school, Fletcher had fallen away from the church and was "just living a typical, secular life"—partying, dating, and indulging his interest in heavy-metal music. Tipton produced such famous bands as Blind Melon and Guns N' Roses, and Fletcher hoped to be the next hometown act to make it big. So he went to Ball State University in Muncie, Indiana, to study music engineering and classical guitar and submerge himself in the heavy-metal scene.

Halfway through his freshman year, while rocking a few feet from the stage at a heavy-metal concert, something jolted him. Singer Glenn Danzig was launching into a musical diatribe against God. As he urged his audience to "find hell with me," Fletcher felt something wrench inside him.

"The Holy Spirit came upon me," he said. "And the scales fell from my eyes: There is a God. There is a Satan. I just realized I was not with God. I saw everything in a new light."

Fletcher's life began to change. In the weeks after that concert, he started seeing the consequences of disobedience to God all around him, especially in the pain of his friends' lives. He felt the urge to confess his sins to a priest and begin praying regularly. After he did, he decided to attend a Catholic school that could strengthen his fledgling faith. So the next fall, he transferred to the Franciscan University of Steubenville, a charismatic Catholic school in Ohio that nurtured his eventual vocation to the Franciscans. Now Fletcher lives, prays, and works with a band of men who have been similarly attracted to a demanding, countercultural faith.

"Many of us come from a background—all of our peers and ourselves—of just kind of chasing after things the world tells you to chase after," Fletcher said. Embracing orthodoxy "is finding the truth, the light you're really attracted to."

Often, but by no means always, the swing toward orthodoxy begins with an intellectual quest. Children who are raised in secular homes or educated in secular schools may become dissatisfied with the worldview that is presented to them and start searching for answers.

Liz Sperry, a bright-eyed philosophy student in her early twenties, still recalls the answer her father gave her when she inquired about the afterlife as a child.

"When you die," he told her, "you're just compost."

Sperry, who is twenty-four and is pursuing her doctoral degree at St. Louis University, found that answer "really depressing. It really disturbed me that there was nothing after I die."

The Christian answer to Sperry's questions did not seem like a viable option during her childhood years in Norwich, New York. Her father had rejected his strict Baptist upbringing, and her mother had drifted away from her Episcopalian roots. Sperry had been baptized in a Methodist church that her mother attended for a few years, but its leaders seemed preoccupied with boosting self-esteem and adapting Christianity to fit their lifestyles—rather than the other way around. For the most part, church was something reserved for holiday visits with her grandmother. At her public school, Sperry's teachers openly espoused existential philosophy, self-help psychology, and the benefits of a selfishness that defends against the demands of others. Sperry tacitly accepted the values that saturated her school, but only because she could find no better answers.

Around the time that her parents divorced, Sperry, at age ten, met a boy who "became the center of my entire life." She dated him off and on for the next six years. At one point, she even ran away to live with him. So when he appeared at her door one day during the summer before her senior year of high school, fresh from Bible camp, his unruly long locks shorn, she paid attention. He told her about Jesus and gave her his Bible. Though she struggled to reconcile what she was reading with the behavior of the lukewarm Christians she knew, something about the answers she found in the New Testament made more sense than those she had encountered elsewhere.

In the Bible, life after death was no joke. Followers of Jesus were asked for total surrender, total trust, total sacrifice. As Sperry pored over the Gospel stories and Pauline epistles, she said, "I had a sense of their profundity and that what was in those letters was true."

One night, while reading the Bible in bed, Sperry came across the account of Christ's agony in the Garden of Gethsemane. In the story, Jesus prayed that God the Father would save him from suffering the crucifixion. But Jesus wanted to do the will of his Father regardless of the cost. The passage resonated deeply with Sperry.

"He was definitely afraid of what would happen if he gave himself over to the will of God," she said. "And I was afraid that if I gave my life to God, I would become a different person. I wouldn't be myself anymore."

Like Jesus, Sperry longed to trust God. She desperately wanted to believe the gospel promise of life after death. But she was afraid. What if she lost her independence, her identity? She had no church or Christian friends to guide or reassure her, and the thought of submission to God terrified her.

Then Sperry read Christ's prayer of surrender. His words in Mark 14:36—"Take this cup from me"—echoed her own fears and desires. Lying on her bed that night, she gave up her fears and repeated those words as her own.

"What I meant was, take my life from me and take it over," Sperry said.

After she said the prayer, Sperry said, she felt an instant physical change.

"I felt like there was something in me, running through me. I can only describe it as electricity, or water. I'd never felt anything like that before. I hadn't felt that from any human being. That really got my attention. I knew there was something to Christianity. And I had this conviction that I would keep pursuing it, even apart from my boyfriend."

The allure of Christianity—and dissatisfaction with a secular worldview—is apparent among many young adults who are steeped in secularism, as Sperry was. The spiritual search often begins on secular campuses, where students encounter an academic climate that scorns notions of objective truth and a unifying worldview. In that atmosphere, the truth claims of Christian orthodoxy can be a refreshing, even rebellious, alternative.

Doug Galbi, an economist in his late thirties, gravitated toward the Catholic faith while in graduate school at Oxford.

"Christianity was talking about things that no one else was talking about," said Galbi, who said he sometimes wonders, "If everyone was Catholic, would I still be Catholic?"

Virginia Harper-Ho leads the Harvard Law School Christian Fellowship, which regularly attracts between forty and sixty students to its campus meetings. Harper-Ho, herself a Harvard law student, said young adults are attracted to the time-tested teachings of Christianity because they contradict the "wishy-washy" mind-set of moral and religious relativism.

"There are hard truths in Christianity," she said. "It's not easy. Somehow the not easiness of it is attractive."

Evangelical faith: A Catholic craving

For many young Christians, the embrace of orthodoxy begins when they decide they want a more intentional way to worship God. Rather than abandoning organized religion because it seems spiritually lifeless, these young believers funnel their frustration into newfound zeal for Jesus and his church, thanks to the radical conversion experiences they have had. Like the charismatic movement that brought a wave of church renewal in the 1970s, today's trek toward orthodoxy is often marked by enthusiastic worship, vivid conversion stories, and the ardor of a younger generation set afire for God.

Natalie Barsoum brims with that fervor. A voice student with dimpled cheeks, beaming brown eyes, and reams of black curls, Barsoum always considered herself a Christian. She dutifully attended services at her Episcopalian church. She said she believed in God. But in retrospect, she said, "I didn't understand the concept."

Barsoum endured years of depression as a teenager. She drank and partied but always wound up unhappy, sure that there must be more to life than what she had found. On Pentecost weekend in 1998, while an eighteen-year-old freshman at Eastman School of Music in Rochester, New York, she took a trip to Rome.

Barsoum had been to Italy before, so she knew her way to St. Peter's Basilica. But once she stepped inside, she surprised herself by heading straight for the Chapel of the Blessed Sacrament, which is reserved for adoration of the Eucharist.

"I didn't know what I was doing," said Barsoum. "I was in there for, like, three hours, confessing my sins to the Lord. And I didn't know what else to do except give my life to him."

Barsoum became a born-again Christian—but not a Catholic— that day in St. Peter's. It was an odd place for the conversion of someone who did not even think Catholics were real Christians.

When she returned to Eastman, she started attending Inter-Varsity Christian Fellowship meetings and visiting a series of evangelical churches. Then she transferred to Catholic University in Washington, D.C., to study with a different voice teacher. Barsoum was worried about being surrounded by so many Catholics but figured she could use the opportunity to witness her evangelical faith to them. Instead, they converted her.

She attended praise-and-worship sessions that blended eucharistic adoration with evangelical songs. She met charismatic Catholics who were committed to Christ, the church—and the Bible. And she came to believe that Jesus Christ was truly present in the Eucharist.

"All of my views about Catholics started changing," Barsoum said.

Her views—that Catholics are guilt ridden and duty bound, that they do not intimately know Jesus, that they are not interested in the Bible or evangelism—are common among Protestants, and even other Catholics. But today's young orthodox Catholics are surprising their parents, professors, and Protestant peers with their boldness and fervor. They sing evangelical songs. They tell their conversion stories and facilitate the conversion of others. They stress the importance of a "personal relationship with Christ." They wear T-shirts with messages like "Eucharistic Adoration: Do It 24/7" and "Top 10 Reasons to Be Catholic." And they take Pope John Paul II's call to evangelize the world very, very seriously.

They are, as William Portier likes to say, "evangelical Catholics."

Portier, a professor at Mount St. Mary's College in Emmitsburg, Maryland, sees the in-your-face evangelical fervor of young Catholics as a natural response to religious pluralism. In a culture of competing messages, believers must proclaim their religious beliefs more boldly. And unlike their parents, most of today's young Catholics do not have the support or restrictions of a strong Catholic subculture. So the choice to be a committed Catholic is often conscious and dramatic.

Not all young Catholics have such spiritual awakenings in the Catholic Church. Many who feel drawn to an evangelical faith do not find it in Catholicism and seek it in other churches.

Pamela Toussaint, an author in her midthirties, drifted through a childhood of Sunday Masses and Catholic schools in Queens, New York, before intentionally committing her life to Christ. Her epiphany arrived while she was a twenty-year-old student at Fordham University, a Jesuit school in the Bronx. But it happened in Madison Square Garden, not a Catholic church.

Toussaint attended a revival there in 1985 with her West Indian mother and heard the evangelist give an altar call that pierced her heart.

"It was really clear that I was one of the people he was talking about," Toussaint said. "I went to that crusade and got saved."

When she returned to Fordham, she was eager to attend church. But she soon lost interest in Catholicism. The campus felt too homogeneous to her as an African American. The Masses did not appeal to her. And if the campus ministry program was actively reaching out to help young Catholics grow in their faith, Toussaint said, "it certainly wasn't reaching me."

Toussaint eventually found her way to a Protestant church that gave her the support she was seeking. American Catholicism has hemorrhaged scores like her over the years, who found Catholic worship lifeless and Catholics themselves unenthusiastic about the faith. Many gravitated to evangelical Christianity, which stresses the personal relationship with Christ that so many young Catholics seek.

While many Catholics leave the church in search of a personal relationship with Christ and wind up in evangelical churches, converts to Catholicism bring with them the features of evangelicalism they loved about their childhood churches. Many young Christians today are buzzing about this new trend of conversions *into* the Catholic Church. Young converts who embrace Catholicism are often attracted by its emphasis on exactly those elements that drove their baby boomer parents away: its structure, liturgy, strict moral teachings, and tradition. Often, the converts come from the very evangelical and mainline Protestant churches that attracted their parents away from Catholicism.

When they come, they bring an evangelical fervor that often proves contagious, even among formerly complacent cradle Catholics.

"They enrich the church because they're like leaven now in a lifeless pile of dough, causing it to rise," said Patrick Madrid, editor in chief of *Envoy* magazine and author of several books on Catholic converts. "They realize, 'This is the real thing. This is what I wanted all along.'"

Many young evangelical Catholics are "reverts": Catholics who flirted with other churches, then returned. Like converts, they tend to have a strong effect on the lifelong Catholics around them, who are inspired by the renewed enthusiasm of reverts for a faith that many cradle Catholics practice grudgingly, if at all.

Andrea Wray, one of the evangelical Catholics Natalie Barsoum encountered at Catholic University, had left the Catholic Church during her sophomore and junior years of high school. She liked the spirited worship she experienced in Young Life, an evangelical ministry to teenagers, and she did not see any Catholics around her in New Canaan, Connecticut, "who lived and acted like the Lord was Lord." Eventually, she found her way back to the Catholic Church after reading Catholic authors like Thomas Aquinas and uncovering the Catholic theology of redemptive suffering, which helped her deal with a cousin's suicide.

But Wray had learned from her experiences with evangelicalism, and she incorporated what she learned into a Holy Hour that she started at Catholic University in 1997. The event blends evangelical songs from her Young Life days with the traditional Catholic devotion of eucharistic adoration. Each week, the Holy Hour attracts more than a hundred students who, like Barsoum, find themselves captivated by a side of the Catholic Church they never knew.

Faith in action: Integration and community

If young Catholics are mimicking evangelicals in the realm of faith, evangelicals are copying Catholics in the world of works. Protestants reared in middle- and upper-class Bible churches in the 1970s and 1980s heard early and often about the authority of Scripture and the importance of a personal relationship with Christ. What they did not hear in some evangelical churches was how the gospel applies to such issues as poverty, racism, unbridled individualism, and materialism.

Many who grew up in evangelical churches have embraced Christianity with a zeal that continues to pulse through their adult lives. Many others, who heard only a message of personal salvation, hit a brick wall in adolescence or early adulthood. Sure, they're saved, and they'll spend eternity in heaven. But what do they do in the meantime? How should they engage secular culture? How can they stop compartmentalizing their Christian beliefs and start applying them to daily life?

The struggle to infuse faith into daily life is a perennial one for committed believers. In a secular, pluralistic culture where all religions are considered equal and none are entirely welcome in the public square, the challenge of integration looms even larger. Unlike their grandparents who embraced the same orthodox beliefs, today's young believers cannot count on American culture to encourage their pietism, because that culture is increasingly suspicious of moral absolutes, organized religion, and its own Christian heritage. The decision to be an orthodox Christian today entails a conscious choice, not a passive inheritance. And living that choice is a no easy task.

"A lot of people live fragmented lives," said Womack, of the *Life@Work Journal*. Womack, who was raised in a "very fundamentalist" church in Arkansas, sees some of his Protestant friends attracted to the Catholic Church because of its historic commitment to social justice. That attraction, Womack said, is a reaction against some Protestant churches that preach the "health and wealth gospel," which ties personal piety to prosperity and ignores the poor.

"Gen Xers got burned out on materialism in the evangelical church," he said.

Tara Haley is one of them. She grew up in a Christian home and accepted Christ as her personal savior at age twelve. She wanted to live a Christian life, but as she grew older, she became bothered by the tendency of some evangelicals to focus on how God relates to the individual and to ignore his role in the larger world. She admired the social-justice tradition of the Catholic Church, which translates biblical concepts of helping one's neighbor and caring for the less fortunate into concrete teachings on the role of Christians and Christianity in society. But the approach she saw taken in some evangelical churches—which emphasized the importance of saving souls but often neglected the corporeal needs of the poor—disturbed her.

"There's got to be something more to this," Haley told herself.

Her search for that "something more" culminated in 1994, when she took her first trip to India. Serving the poor there fed her soul and made her feel closer to Christ. Haley was hooked.

"My specific vocation came into focus," said Haley, a petite woman with blond hair and delicate features.

Haley now works for Christ House, a recovery facility for people who are homeless and ill in Washington, D.C. The facility is affiliated with Church of the Savior, an activist ecumenical church that stresses service to the poor. Above her desk, Haley keeps a picture of Mother Teresa and a photocopied image of Jesus stamped with this question: "How can you worship a homeless man on Sunday and ignore one on Monday?"

"God has been very gracious to me in giving me a vocation that makes my Christianity alive," said Haley, who attends an "evangelical" Episcopalian church where her husband is a pastor.

Rather than contenting themselves with simply securing their personal salvation or winning converts, many young Christians like Haley seek to serve and impact the larger culture and to make their childhood faith relevant to their adult lives.

For Deann Ayer, a slim, bubbly woman in her early thirties, the desire for integration came early. Ayer, who is white, grew up in suburban San Diego, attending a Baptist church and a mostly white private Christian high school with only a handful of black and Hispanic students. She committed to Christianity at age five, and she meant it.

But even then, she found herself drawn beyond her white, evangelical enclave, fascinated by stories of foreign missionaries and other cultures. After her freshman year at Westmont College, an evangelical school in Santa Barbara, Ayer decided she needed to move into "the real world," where she would encounter people unlike herself. So she transferred to the University of Arizona, a large secular school that offered her the chance to interact with non-Christians and test the strength of her convictions.

"I just feel that as Christians, we need to go out into the world," Ayer said, recalling how her Christian friends warned her that the move would endanger her faith. "We'll never be salt and light if we're all huddling together. We're supposed to be influencing the world."

Ayer loved Arizona. Teachers and students challenged her with questions about Christianity, forcing her to learn more about her faith. After graduation, she immersed herself in service, teaching and serving the poor from Tijuana to Brazil.

Ayer now lives near Capitol Hill at Esther House, a Christian community of young women who choose to live among the poor and foster racial reconciliation. She lives with roommates who are white, black, Catholic, Protestant. She worships in an evangelical church that is multiracial, multidenominational, and firmly Bible based. She works with teenagers and adults who live in her neighborhood. There are no clear divisions between the realms of Ayer's life. They bleed into each other, and her Christian faith pervades them all. That's the way she likes it.

"It's exciting to live what I believe," Ayer said. "I like that holistic thing where your life is not so compartmentalized, like 'Well, I go to work. And then I come home. And the people I go out with, they don't understand my work.' I guess it's because I'm very relational. It feels really good to have people get the different parts of my life."

Young Christians seeking integration in a fragmented culture often crave community. Many of them feel nostalgic for something they never experienced: the sort of place where you live, work, and worship with people who share your values and hold you accountable for living up to them. Shared values do not necessarily mean identical opinions or experiences, though. Many young adults, like Ayer and her roommates, are attracted to communities where they can share their lives with Christians of other denominations, races, or economic classes and learn to love one another in spite of their differences.

DeeShunna Ragland, an African American woman in her early twenties, graduated from Liberty University, a Christian school in Lynchburg, Virginia, with visions of tackling homelessness in inner-city Washington. But she did not want to do it from afar, by commuting to work and living apart from the people she served. And she did not want to do it alone.

"I wanted to live purposely in community, to get to know other Christians," said Ragland, who moved into Esther House after hearing about its mission from the pastor at Ayer's church. Sometimes, Ragland said, it's hard to be in a house where she is the only black woman. But the bond of faith she shares with her roommates is stronger than their differences.

"Even though we are different colors," Ragland said, "it's because of Christ that we can see past that."

The desire to integrate spirituality into daily life, and to find communities where others want to do the same, is not limited to evangelicals. Young Christians of every denominational stripe are working to establish community and coherence in every sphere of culture, driven by a desire to feed their hunger for a faith that matters now. And they are attracted to orthodox Christianity because they believe it does more than allow them to blend their private values and public lives. For them, Christianity demands that mix—and makes it possible.

Making It Stick: Keys to Commitment

A spiritual search does not always lead to a faith commitment. Confronted with the buffet of religious beliefs that is American pluralism, young adults often resist orthodoxy's demands: that they embrace only Christianity, that they follow stiff moral standards, that they commit to specific beliefs that cannot be compromised. Those demands scare away many young adults, who instead adopt a more liberal interpretation of Christianity or another belief system, or create their own spirituality and moral rules based on a blend of ideologies or their own proclivities.

Another obstacle to the spread of orthodoxy among young adults is the provisional nature of today's faith commitments. The strongest attribute of today's young believers is that they are choosing their religious beliefs with enthusiasm rather than simply inheriting them with indifference. But that's also their greatest stumbling block to full-fledged commitment. A commitment that is consciously chosen can also be consciously tossed aside when its appeal fades. Young adults who are forever searching for new spiritual highs and religious truths may find it hard to settle into the routine of daily devotion.

With so many religions and philosophies to choose from, in a culture that celebrates constant change, the path to orthodoxy can be torturously circuitous. Many young believers, seized with initial enthusiasm for Jesus, never make the long trek from embracing Christian beliefs to implementing them in their lives. They never become committed followers of Jesus who are ready to suffer and sacrifice for the cause of Christ. Their spiritual hunger predisposes them to hearing the Christian message, but their secular culture leaves them ill suited to put its moral and behavioral demands into practice.

"Today's culture makes it very easy to evangelize and very hard to make disciples," said Christian author Os Guinness.

Americans, Guinness said, "are conversion prone": they revere choice and change in their political leaders, fashions, and popular culture. Considering the postmodern consensus that all choices are equally valid, it's no wonder that Americans might be reluctant to embrace orthodoxy, which calls for self-denial and singular devotion.

In American culture today, Guinness said, "Truth—and conviction and commitment—is obscene."

The inevitable clash of orthodoxy and secular values forces young adults to make a choice for Christianity that may not have been as stark or countercultural for their parents and grandparents. So what does it take for young Christians to commit to orthodoxy?

Those who have embraced orthodoxy generally cite three factors that made their commitment possible: the grace of God, a supportive faith community, and personal resolve.

The grace of God

None of the young Christians whose stories run through these pages credit only themselves or their Christian communities for their conversions. Nor would they agree that their commitment to orthodoxy is simply a reaction against secularism or an autonomous decision based on their own designs and motives.

The glory belongs to God, they say, and to God alone. They see everything else—the sociological factors, the impulses toward tradition or away from relativism, even the personal crises that spark their searches—as a vehicle for his grace, as an addendum explanation that falls hopelessly short of capturing the true meaning of their conversions.

Natalie Barsoum, the born-again Christian who encountered evangelical Catholics in college, says that grace is the reason she committed to Catholicism.

After experiencing eucharistic adoration and meeting enthusiastic Catholics at Catholic University, Barsoum felt drawn to
embrace the faith. She went through the preparation classes that
lead to acceptance into the Catholic Church. But she worried
what her Protestant friends and family would think if she converted, and she still struggled with some concerns about becoming Catholic. So the weekend before she was scheduled to join
in December 1999, she dropped out of the classes and canceled
her entrance into the church. The abrupt change of plans was
necessary, she told herself, because "it was not God's time."

That weekend, Catholic University hosted a day and a half of
continual adoration of the Eucharist in honor of the start of the
Jubilee Year. Just as she had been drawn to the Blessed Sacrament chapel a few years earlier in Rome, Barsoum found herself praying in front of the Eucharist once again. The hours
slipped away as she prayed. By the end of the weekend, she had
spent six hours in adoration and had read Bible verses that reinforced her desire to join the church. She felt drawn by desire—
and something stronger—to make the commitment that she had
been postponing.

"I didn't think I could go through another whole year of not
receiving the Eucharist," Barsoum said. "It was almost like the
Lord was telling me that he wants me to be in the Catholic
Church and he doesn't care what obstacles are in the way."

Barsoum said God's grace overcame her fears and gave her the
strength to commit. So she called her parents, told her friends, and
took the plunge. When Barsoum reflects on what she experienced
in the stillness of those hours of prayer—first in Rome at age
eighteen and then in Washington a year later—she cannot believe
how much her life changed in such a short time.

"It's completely incomprehensible," said Barsoum, her brown
eyes glistening with tears. "The Lord lavishly pours out graces
and blessings on us in ways that are overwhelming. All you have
to do is take a little step toward him and he gives you a thousand miles."

Spiritual support

In a culture that often derides commitment, young adults need support to make faith commitments that last. In many Protestant churches, help often comes from accountability groups—small circles of peers who come together regularly to discuss choices made in daily life and to keep each other on track. Some Catholics have formed similar groups, and orthodox believers of all stripes say the choice of friends, as well as the support of formal faith communities, can make the difference between short-lived enthusiasm for Christianity and long-term commitment.

Phil Hurley experienced firsthand the difficulty of sticking to a faith commitment without the support of like-minded friends. Hurley, a slim man with piercing blue eyes, had attended Mass "in spurts" as a child, had belonged to a student-led Catholic youth group as a teenager, and had graduated from a Catholic high school before entering Loyola College in Maryland. His experiences gave him a passion for social justice, but little knowledge of his Catholic faith. By the time he was a freshman in college in 1993, he had other priorities.

Yet Hurley's connection to Catholicism continued, thanks in large part to his grandmother, a steadfast Catholic who had taught him his prayers as a child and served as his greatest spiritual mentor. In 1993, she asked him to attend World Youth Day, an international Catholic youth festival that is held every two years and hosted by Pope John Paul II. Though Hurley dismissed the idea, his grandmother persisted. She called him several times to tell him about the hordes of young Catholics from all over the globe who would soon descend on Denver to greet the pope.

Finally, he agreed to go. After all, he figured, it might give him a chance to practice his Spanish. And his grandmother was paying.

Hurley went with a group from the Franciscan University of Steubenville, who traveled in a fourteen-bus caravan. Surrounded by passionate Franciscans and prayerful young adults on the bus and at the gathering in Denver, he found himself drawn into a deeper prayer life and a new desire for God.

"It was the first time I'd really experienced, with that intensity, my peers just really on fire, really committed to their faith," said Hurley. "It was a real oasis in a spiritual desert."

Trouble was, it didn't last. World Youth Day ended, the crowd dispersed, and Hurley returned to Loyola and his old crowd of friends. Full of zeal but too timid to share it, Hurley struggled alone to keep the embers of his faith burning. After less than three months, his prayer life collapsed. He felt powerless to resist the undertow of partying and premarital sex on campus. He wanted to make a lasting faith commitment, but he could not do it alone.

A year later, Hurley found the support he had been craving. Some students from Loyola talked him into attending an evangelical Christian music festival in Pennsylvania. There, he met people he liked, down-to-earth students who were passionate about Christ. When Hurley returned to Loyola the next fall, he had an amplified prayer life and a new group of friends who shared his faith. Soon he was helping out with pro-life and social-justice groups on campus and spreading the message of chastity. The fellowship he found that summer grounded him in a Catholic faith that ultimately led him to study for the priesthood with the Jesuits.

Os Guinness, who has written several books for Christians seeking to solidify and deepen their faith, says all Christians need at least five or six close friends to encourage them and hold them accountable to their faith commitments.

"Community," said Guinness, "is essential."

Personal resolve

In the case of David Legge and so many other young orthodox believers, committing wholeheartedly to Christ required deliberation and determination. In February 1999, nearly five years after Legge rediscovered his faith at Yale Law School and began attending Mass again, he was working as a trial lawyer at the Department of Justice in Washington, D.C., and dating a woman who did not share his Catholic beliefs.

He thought that it might be best to end the relationship. But what if she was the one he was to marry? Confused, Legge went to a Benedictine monastery for the weekend to pray for guidance. Part of his retreat entailed meditation on an assigned Scripture passage: Luke 11, in which Jesus tells his disciples: "Ask, and it will be given you; seek, and you will find; knock, and it will be opened to you."

Legge meditated all day but found the passage irrelevant to his situation. After all, he thought, he was here to sort out his relationship with his girlfriend, not seek God. He had already found Jesus. That night, Legge sat outside and watched the monks process toward a statue of the Virgin Mary while singing the Litany of Loretto and asking her to send young men to join their order. Something about the procession struck Legge and moved him almost to the point of tears. He could feel something welling up within him, and he felt compelled to be alone in the presence of the Eucharist. So Legge ducked into the chapel, knelt before the tabernacle, and began to pray.

"It was like God hit me over the head with a bottle," he said.

> *I realized that the Scripture passage I had meditated on did apply to me. All this time I'd been thinking that it didn't. Then it hit me that I had never asked the Lord what he wanted me to do with my life. I was asking him to make this relationship work; I was asking him for what I wanted. But I wasn't asking him what he wanted. And I was just overwhelmed with fear because I thought,* I cannot possibly ask that question, because he might say, "I want you to be a priest." Or what if he says, "I want you to be a monk"? I don't want to be a monk! I want to be married, to this woman. I want to be a lawyer. I'm very happy with my job. How can I throw all those things away?

In fear and distress, Legge lingered on his knees for almost an hour. He wrestled with himself, trying to find the resolve to ask that question in the silence of his heart that would allow God to take complete control of his life.

"I was in anguish because I didn't know what to do," he said.

> *I just couldn't bring myself to ask that question. Finally I saw that if I didn't ask, I would be saying, "I don't want to do what you want me to do. I'm going to do what I want. And I'm going to hope that's what you want. But I'm not actually going to try to do what you want." And I knew that I would be rejecting him if I said that. So finally I said, "All right, Lord, you win. I give up. I can't resist you anymore. Lord, whatever you want, I'll do. You want me to be a priest, I'll be a priest. You want me to be a monk, I'll be a monk. Tell me what you want me to do." And that was the turning point for my life. At that moment, I received one of the most dramatic consolations that I've ever received. All of the fear that was weighing on me, it literally felt like something was lifted off of my shoulders. It disappeared. And I was just filled with joy and peace. And it was an intensity that's hard to describe. I had the clear sense that it was not coming from inside me, that it was being poured into me, just added into me. In that one instant, it just was apparent to me that all of the things that I thought were really important to me weren't important to me.*

Legge realized he could walk away from his career, his girlfriend, and any other part of his life that God might want to change.

"I still didn't know what he wanted me to do," he said. "But I wasn't afraid. I was actually kind of excited. I was very excited."

Legge's decision—to surrender his own will to God's—propelled him from a life of searching to a life of commitment. His problems did not instantly dissolve, Legge said, and he continued to have profound experiences of ever deepening conversion. But the resolution he made that night moved him from the company of "conversion-prone" seekers to the ranks of committed Christians. Legge has spent the months and years since that February night seeking to live his faith commitment more fully and to incorporate his faith into every aspect of his life. In the process, he discerned a call from God to become a priest, which he is now pursuing as a member of the Dominican order.

Young adults like Legge, who follow the path that leads from spiritual seeker to committed believer, have been shaped by many of the same experiences that influenced their less religious or irreligious peers. Their longings—for meaning, community, fulfillment—are typical of young Americans, as are their fears about repeating the mistakes of the generation before them. And like many young adults who encounter orthodoxy, they are intrigued by its moral rigor, spiritual depth, and eschatological promises.

But at crucial moments in their lives, these young adults have taken a step that other seekers did not. Relying on grace, peer support, and personal resolve, they stepped beyond seeker status into the realm of committed believers. They gave their lives to Jesus Christ and embraced the orthodox faith that they believe to be his gift. And they embarked on a journey toward integration that will take them the rest of their lives to complete.

3

THE CHURCH AND WORSHIP

Yet a time is coming and has now come when the true worshipers will worship the Father in spirit and truth, for they are the kind of worshipers the Father seeks.

JOHN 4:23

As the last rays of sunlight streamed through the church's stained-glass windows, crystal chandeliers and flickering candles compensated for the waning daylight. A crop of about forty young adults filed into the nave, each carrying one delicate white candle and a prayer book. Their faces illuminated by the tiny flames, the crowd faced the iconostasis, the tall glass screen decorated with doors and tiers of icons that separates the sanctuary from the main part of an Eastern Orthodox church.

That screen—and the purple-and-gold-clad priest who, at times, turned his back to the congregation—seemed almost incongruous with this congregation of twenty- and thirtysomething worshipers, many of whom wore jeans or khaki pants. The contrast between ancient and modern became even more pronounced when the priest began to sing a cappella. He sang for most of the two-hour service, accompanied at times by a cadre of men at the right of the iconostasis and at other times by the entire congregation. The music seemed to morph into a chant, a mournful, almost mystical melody that wafted through the church like the thick, sweet incense that saturated the April night air.

For all but a few moments during the service on this Monday night of Holy Week in 2001, the congregation stood. They repeatedly touched their fingers to their foreheads and chests, making the sign of the cross at each mention of Jesus, the Trinity, or Mary. Some rocked gently back and forth, their eyes closed, their lips mouthing the songs.

In a back pew, Andrea Whitson sat holding her candle to her chest. The flame bathed her delicate features in a soft golden glow that left her looking much younger than her thirty-one years. As the haunting music and incense enveloped her, she seemed lost in adoration, utterly at home in the mystery, rigor, and reverence that is Orthodox worship.

The Romance of Orthodoxy

It was not always that way. Like the white clapboard church where she worships in Cambridge, Massachusetts, Andrea Whitson used to be Protestant. Born in Texas and raised Southern Baptist, she joined an Episcopalian church eight years ago when she married her husband, John Whitson, who was also raised Southern Baptist.

Soon after they married, Andrea and John Whitson both wanted out of their Episcopalian church. They were alarmed by the national hierarchy's dissent from St. Paul's teachings on sexuality and by the ordination of sexually active homosexual clergy. Things seemed to be unraveling, and the Whitsons wanted a church that stuck to conventional moral teachings while offering sacramental grace.

But when John Whitson's inquiries convinced him that a conversion to Eastern Orthodoxy was the answer, his wife recoiled. The prospect of conversion to Orthodoxy attracted her husband, who had studied church history. But it left her feeling angry and miserable. She could not understand why she should stand through a two-hour service shrouded in unintelligible symbolism and conducted in a foreign language. Fresh into their marriage, the Whitsons—who were living in Texas at the time—faced one of their biggest fights.

"He convinced me logically, but I didn't want to make the change," said Andrea Whitson, a pretty, soft-spoken woman who attended MIT and now works as a research analyst in Boston. "It was very foreign."

Andrea Whitson missed the comfort of her childhood experiences in the Baptist church. And visiting a Greek Orthodox church with her husband made matters worse. Church members peppered her with questions about her and her husband's ancestry. When they realized that neither of the Whitsons was Greek, she recalled, "they literally said to us, 'Then why are you here?'"

Two days later, Andrea Whitson dreamed that she had returned to that Orthodox church. This time, she sensed that Christ was enthroned on the altar. But she couldn't see him clearly because angels were blocking her view. She recognized that the angels were serving as doors, much as the iconostasis separates the altar from the nave. A piercing question arose from that dream: "Do you want to worship God in the way he wants to be worshiped or in the way that makes you comfortable?"

That question changed Andrea Whitson's perspective. She began to see Orthodoxy in a new light and to believe that she had found a liturgy that mirrored the heavenly scene of Isaiah 6, which describes a house "filled with smoke" and angels stationed above the Lord's throne. She was impressed by the reverence and seriousness with which the sacraments were conducted in the Orthodox Church. Unlike the members at her Episcopalian church, these church members did not have vague or conflicting beliefs about the Eucharist—they believed that it contained the true presence of Jesus Christ. Confession was similarly serious business: the penitent stood in front of an icon and whispered his or her sins to the priest. Andrea Whitson said even her niece—a young girl who attended a Southern Baptist church—sensed the power of an Orthodox liturgy and the presence of God in the Eucharist. When she saw her aunt receive the Eucharist from the Orthodox priest, the little girl whispered, "That was really *it,* wasn't it?"

Once Andrea Whitson felt God's presence in the Orthodox liturgy and sacraments, she said, she could not return to the lecture-style service of a Baptist church without feeling that something was missing.

Now the Whitsons worship at St. Mary's Antiochian Orthodox Church of Cambridge, a formerly Protestant church brimming with formerly Protestant members, as well as Orthodox Christians who learned the faith in their Middle Eastern, Ethiopian, Slavic, and Greek homes. The services are held in English, and they attract a vibrant young crowd of Orthodox Christians who rave about the church's mystical liturgies, awe-inspiring traditions, and time-tested moral teachings.

St. Mary's pastor Fr. Antony Hughes knows the attractions of Orthodoxy. A fortysomething former Southern Baptist from Tennessee, Hughes converted while studying at Oral Roberts University. He sees young adults attracted by Orthodoxy's historical roots and mystical liturgy. The fact that Orthodoxy is relatively unknown in the United States, Hughes said, makes it more appealing than Catholicism to Protestants because "they don't have any prejudices against it, as they do about Rome."

"They're looking for something that's stable, but they don't really know what that stability is," Hughes said. In Orthodoxy, "they see something so beautiful and so solid. A lot of people discover that there is such incredible depth in Christianity. There's two thousand years of this."

A Hunger for Substance

Despite their generation's famous distrust of institutions and their parents' conspicuous quest for feel-good theology, many young adults are flocking to churches that preach conventional morality and employ traditional worship. Young adults who are disenchanted with the moral relativism and materialism that saturate popular culture—and many American churches—may find themselves viscerally attracted to the very aspects of Christianity that their parents' generation rejected. Churches that demand sacrifice and celebrate tradition often appeal to world-weary young adults.

"Generations X and Y have watched the parental seeking [of baby boomers] and don't have the same set of questions," said Phyllis Tickle, a contributing editor at *Publisher's Weekly* and national commentator on religion and spirituality. "They want to go to a spirituality that's rooted in tradition."

Tickle, who left Presbyterianism in college to become an Episcopalian, has edited and written dozens of books, including a trilogy of best-selling prayer manuals based on the sixth-century Benedictine Rule of fixed-hour prayer. Though she sees a split in the American consciousness between religion, spirituality, and morality—with many Americans now identifying themselves as "spiritual but not religious," for instance—she predicts that tide may turn with the next generation. For the past four or five years, Tickle said, she and her peers in the book business have been expecting to see a shift from generic and New Age spirituality to tradition. A 2000 Gallup youth survey confirmed that change, Tickle said, when it found that teenagers identified most strongly as "religious" (55 percent), instead of "spiritual but not religious" (39 percent) or "religious and spiritual" (2 percent).[1]

"That's a major shift," said Tickle, who expects to see morality eventually reunited with spirituality and religion. "It had to come."

Young orthodox believers often disagree on ecclesiastical and theological issues, such as the role of women and laity in the church and the authority of Scripture. Some also differ on hot-button moral issues, though most of the young adults interviewed for this book oppose the blessing of same-sex marriages, the ordination of noncelibate homosexuals, premarital and extramarital sexual relations, and abortion. For some, a good church is one with a solid preacher who derives his theologically and morally conservative message straight from the Bible. For others, a good church is one that can trace its lineage back to the apostles and offers the same traditional teachings and doctrines espoused by the early church fathers. For nearly all of these young orthodox believers, a good church gives them the fullness of the gospel and a worship experience that connects them to the mystery of God's presence.

The primary cravings of young orthodox Christians in America—for tough time-tested teachings and worship imbued with mystery and a sense of the transcendent—are often the result of deficiencies in their childhood spiritual diet. Those raised in mainline Protestant and Catholic churches typically complain that their faith formation consisted of vague platitudes about tolerance and love, not the "hard gospel" of sin and salvation. They recall church leaders so absorbed with chic social causes that they failed to lay the faith foundations for their service work. In evangelical circles, young adults often recall many sermons on personal salvation but few discussions of how Christians should treat the poor, engage the culture, or learn from Christian history and tradition. They complain of pastors focused more on winning converts than helping the converted live out their Christian faith and of worship leaders more interested in entertaining the congregation than encouraging reverence for God.

Today, many of these young orthodox Christians are embarking on spiritual searches that lead them to frontiers their parents never dreamed they would explore, both within and beyond their denominational borders. Many evangelicals—including many children of former Catholics and mainline Protestants—are drifting back toward those liturgical churches in a quest for historical Christianity. Others remain committed to evangelical Christianity but devoted to engaging—not ignoring or retreating from—popular culture and church tradition.

Many mainline Protestants and some Catholics continue to gravitate toward evangelical and Pentecostal churches that blend contemporary worship with Bible-based sermons. Others—like the burgeoning ranks of Catholic "reverts"—are bringing the evangelical emphasis on contemporary worship and overt evangelization back to their liturgical churches. Still others have never left their mainline churches but now show a particular affinity for the most traditional aspects of Christian devotion, including fixed-hour prayer and, for some post–Vatican II Catholics, the rosary, eucharistic adoration, and the Latin Mass.

"We are rapidly moving toward the third century," Tickle said, in reference to the popularity of traditional devotions and early church spirituality among the young. "It's a need to go back to mystery."

Not all young adults are attracted to Christian orthodoxy. Some relish the trappings of traditional worship without subscribing to the conventional morality and theology typically associated with it. They may like the sound of Gregorian chant, for instance, but overlook its connection to a transcendent moral authority. They may respect church tradition and orthodox Christian leaders like Pope John Paul II but not follow the church's teachings on matters of personal morality.

Other young adults flock to the same style of seeker services that have captivated baby boomers, services that blend contemporary worship with a message that some critics disparage as "Christianity lite." Still others gravitate toward faith traditions that are fundamentally distinct from orthodox Christianity. Scores of young adults have embraced Mormonism, thanks in part to its demanding moral code and emphasis on family life. Others have embraced non-Western belief systems, such as Buddhism or Hinduism, New Age or pagan spirituality, or some blend of each. Statistics show that some 70 percent of Americans say they can be religious without going to church,[2] and clearly many—perhaps most—Generation Xers fit the mold of the spiritual seeker who suspects organized religion and its moral absolutes.

Given those odds and popular culture's tendency to equate orthodoxy with intolerance, it is noteworthy that any young adults embrace conventional Christian theology and morality at all. Even more surprising is the fact that orthodoxy's appeal seems to be growing among young adults who have a disproportionate amount of cultural influence—those who set trends and lead others in academic, artistic, and political circles. Perhaps most astounding is that these young products of postmodern, relativistic America often incline toward Christianity's most morally rigorous teachings and most traditional devotions.

Consider the case of Catholicism and Eastern Orthodoxy. Conventional wisdom holds that these two historical, hierarchical Christian churches struggle for survival and attract few American converts. In terms of new church development, Catholic and Orthodox congregations clearly are not reproducing as evangelical congregations are. But many Catholics are buzzing about the influx of evangelical and mainline Protestants into the Catholic Church in recent years and about the popularity of books about such conversions, such as former Presbyterian pastor Scott Hahn's *Rome Sweet Rome*—cowritten with his wife, Kimberly—and Patrick Madrid's Surprised by Truth books. Lay ministries like Marcus Grodi's Coming Home Network have arisen to meet the needs of hundreds of Protestant pastors who have converted to Catholicism in the past decade. And the number of adult converts to Catholicism in America—which hit 171,000 in 2000[3]—has been steadily growing. According to a recent survey commissioned by the U.S. Bishops and conducted by sociologist Dean R. Hoge, 61 percent of the Catholic converts surveyed came from other Christian churches, and their average age was thirty-seven.[4]

Eastern Orthodoxy has enjoyed similar gains. About two decades ago, a group of about twenty evangelical Christian leaders with Campus Crusade for Christ converted to Orthodoxy, beginning a wave of conversions of Protestants disaffected by the liberalism of mainline churches and the ahistorical bent of evangelical churches. From 1967 to 1997, the number of American congregations affiliated with the Antiochian Archdiocese—the branch of Eastern Orthodoxy that has attracted the bulk of American Protestants—tripled, to some two hundred congregations.[5]

The trend toward tradition and mystery in worship transcends denominational lines. Magazines such as *Christianity Today* and

FaithWorks have run major features on the attraction of evangelical and Low-Church Protestants to traditional devotions and liturgical worship. Books such as Tickle's three-volume *Divine Hours* and Kathleen Norris's *The Cloister Walk* (which explores Christian monastic traditions) have become best-sellers. Consumers of all denominational stripes have gobbled up Gregorian chant from groups like Enigma, which has sold seventeen million albums since the early 1990s.[6] And crowds of young adults have fueled a revival of meditative compline services at Episcopalian cathedrals and Latin Masses at Catholic churches.

Traditional faith communities also have enjoyed attention from young Christians. Some one hundred thousand pilgrims from across the denominational spectrum travel each year to Taizé, France, to experience an ecumenical monastic community's life of shared work and ritualized worship. Taizé prayer groups—which have adopted the Christian monastery's prayer devotion of candles and icons, mantras and silence—have sprouted across the United States, from New York to San Francisco.

Matthew Pinto, author and cofounder of the Catholic *Envoy* magazine, believes young adults in postmodern America are drawn to the fresh, countercultural quality of orthodoxy and tradition.

"This stuff is so outrageous that it's attractive," he said.

Pinto has experienced that attraction firsthand. He founded a young-adult group at his San Diego parish that offers lectures on such weighty topics as the Eucharist, purgatory, and just war theory, all from a traditional Catholic viewpoint. Within six months of its start, the group was attracting a hundred regulars to its meetings—unusually healthy attendance figures in Catholic young-adult circles—and it is still going strong ten years later. Pinto credits Generation-X curiosity about Catholic doctrine and Christian tradition, a curiosity that was not satisfied by the spotty religious instruction so many Catholics received in the 1970s and 1980s.

"In many ways, our job is easier now than it was in the past, because people are starving," said Pinto, who compared the dissenting theology and catechesis of recent decades to fast food—easy and cheap but ultimately unsatisfying. "We've allowed ourselves to adopt a fast-food approach to everything in life, and we've actually come to convince ourselves that fast food is good food. It may take some time to take them from fast food to good food. But it's actually what they're yearning for."

The Hard Gospel

If you want to make a Generation-X Catholic laugh, ask him about his childhood religious education. Odds are he will share at least one wacky story about his post–Vatican II formation in the faith. Interviews of young Catholics conducted for this book yielded too many amusing anecdotes to recount, from stories of polyester-pantsuit-clad nuns spinning John Lennon records in high school religion classes to tales of agnostic confirmation instructors puffing on cigarettes while extolling existentialism to their teenage charges. One Catholic revert—who returned to the faith as an adult after an intense conversion experience—only recalls playing tag in his confirmation class. Another remembers spending his childhood CCD classes painting "Jesus loves you" on rocks. And many—like John Lovell—remember learning next to nothing about the details of the Catholic faith.

Lovell, a thirty-one-year-old New Jersey native, considers his Catholic upbringing stronger than most. His parents both practiced and understood the faith. But like many Catholics in his generation, Lovell learned precious little about Catholic teachings from the religious-instruction program in his parish. His eighth-grade confirmation classes made Christianity seem boring and irrelevant. He saw little fervor at the Masses he attended. So when Lovell encountered the enthusiasm of evangelical Christians in a high school Young Life group, he was "hooked."

Unlike his Catholic religion classes, the evangelical youth group stressed the importance of a personal relationship with Jesus.

Suddenly, the gospel excited Lovell, and the differences between Catholicism and Protestantism no longer mattered to him.

After high school, he attended Xavier University, a Jesuit school in Cincinnati. His theology professors there "were all over the map." One belonged to the Jesus Seminar, a union of scholars who debate the historicity of Jesus and who are known for deconstructing many tenets of orthodox Christianity. Others exposed him to interesting intellectual questions about Christianity, mostly from liberal viewpoints. The campus ministry leaders struck him as too liberal, wedded to "save the earth" causes but not core Christianity. None attracted him back to Catholicism.

Lovell spent his college years worshiping at a nondenominational "home church"—an informal seeker-oriented assembly of young evangelical Christians. At a typical meeting, the gang would gather around the campfire in someone's backyard, drink beer, and discuss the Bible or the writings of C. S. Lewis. When he moved back to New Jersey after college, Lovell bounced around various Protestant churches, shopping for a new home. He wound up in an evangelical Lutheran church, where he met and married his wife.

One day, Lovell opened up the neoconservative journal First Things and read that the Evangelical Lutheran Church of America (ELCA)—his denomination—was considering a change in its teachings to allow abortion and the ordination of noncelibate homosexuals. Though his local pastor said individual ELCA churches could go their own way, Lovell was disturbed by the fact that the leaders of his denomination were willing to take moral stands that seemed to fly in the face of Scripture. Lovell thought consideration of allowing abortion was "absurd." As for noncelibate homosexual clergy, Lovell said, "Gays and lesbians should be absolutely loved, but I don't think they should be in ministry."

Around the same time, Lovell began to notice that his favorite fiction writers—Flannery O'Connor, Walker Percy, Graham Greene—were Catholic. Something about the richness in their

writing and the way they saw holiness in obscure places had resonated with him despite his Protestant convictions. He started to
wonder if that richness stemmed from their Catholicism and if he
ought to give his old faith tradition a second look. When he considered the Catholic Church's staunch opposition to abortion and to
sexual relations between homosexuals, Lovell decided that he should
investigate further and learn more about the church teachings
that had not been clearly explained to him in his Catholic parish
or Jesuit college.

In 2000, a non-Catholic friend gave Lovell a set of tapes by
Scott Hahn, a Protestant pastor turned Catholic apologist. Hahn
elucidated Catholic beliefs on purgatory, Mary, and the saints. In
one lecture, Hahn said that for centuries none of the early church
fathers had disputed the Catholic belief of Christ's true presence
in the Eucharist. When Lovell read the early church writings, he
found himself wondering why his evangelical church had rejected
a doctrine that Christians had accepted for centuries.

"I thought, *Who are we to change it? How could it just change arbi-
trarily?*" said Lovell, who considered that the turning point of his
conversion back to Catholicism. "I was totally blown away."

A few months later, in the fall of 2000, Lovell attended an ecumenical conference for Generation-X Christians, where he heard
nearly a dozen stories like his own. He talked to Protestants
attracted to Catholicism because of Pope John Paul II's unflinching stands on moral issues and to Catholics who left the faith with
little understanding of church teachings, then returned after
receiving the catechesis they never had as children. Lovell said the
conference—and the kindred souls he met there—strengthened
his resolve to return to the faith. In 2001, he confessed his sins to
a Catholic priest and officially rejoined the church.

Many young Christians are drawn to churches that offer steadfast moral teachings or the authority of tradition, and some—like
Lovell and the Whitsons—are attracted to both. That attraction
often persists despite the weak or nonexistent religious instruction
many of them received as children.

Rosalind Moss—who received a Jewish upbringing before she became an evangelical Christian in the 1970s and then a Catholic apologist in the 1990s—says the lack of solid religious instruction may have cost the Catholic Church two generations of believers. What is bringing some of them back, Moss said, is the power of the gospel when it is preached with intensity by such figures as Pope John Paul II. The pope has consistently confounded media experts by attracting millions of young adults to his World Youth Day rallies, where he exhorts them to discipline themselves, embrace the gospel, and reject compromise.

"[The pope] deals with them not on the basis of what they are but what they're becoming," Moss said. "He assumes that they want God, that they want to fulfill their calling in life. He assumes they're up to the task."

Though the pope clearly publicizes official Catholic teaching on such controversial issues as abortion and homosexuality, many rank-and-file priests in the United States are not so bold. Some directly contradict the Vatican on such matters and encourage American Catholics to do the same. Others simply skirt controversial teachings to avoid alienating church members who might disagree. But their attempts at appeasement may actually be working against their mainline churches.

In 2001, the Hartford Institute for Religion Research released Faith Communities Today, the largest survey of U.S. congregations ever conducted. The survey showed a surge in new church development among evangelical Protestant and Mormon congregations, which are known for their conservative moral stands. The survey showed a decline in new church development among Catholic, Orthodox, and many mainline Protestant groups.

In its explanation of why some congregations thrive and others decline, the survey found a strong correlation between the vitality of a congregation and its commitment to high moral standards. According to the survey, "Two out of three congregations that emphasize personal and public morality also report healthy finances and membership growth. Congregations that place less emphasis on these standards are more likely to report plateaued or declining membership. A large majority of the most vital congregations report that they have a clarity of purpose and explicit member expectations that are strictly enforced."[7]

Moss—who works for Catholic Answers, a Catholic apologetics and evangelization organization—believes young adults naturally incline toward the demands of Christianity and toward churches that emphasize the challenge of the gospel.

"People think if we make it easy on [young adults], we'll draw them in," she said. "It's the very opposite. Youth are looking for a cause, a reason to live. They need something to give their lives to. A Christianity that says, 'Go to church on Sunday and be a nice person'—that's no cause. Christianity doesn't say go to church on Sunday. Jesus said, 'He who loses his life will find it.' In other words, 'If you don't love me above all things, you're not worthy of me.' But few people are given that message."

Indeed, that message is one Liz Sperry rarely heard while growing up in Norwich, New York, in the 1980s. Sperry (whose conversion is recounted in chapter 2) was baptized in a Methodist church as a child, but she did not embrace Christianity until she was a teenager. Her boyfriend at the time introduced her to the Bible after he attended an evangelical camp. Once she read it, she committed her life to Christ and resolved to return to her Methodist church. But its preoccupation with promoting self-esteem and affirming its members bothered her. She saw the adults at the church adapting Christianity to their lifestyles, rather than the other way around.

"They didn't really preach the hard gospel," said Sperry, who remembers her pastor dismissing the need for a disciplined prayer life and encouraging members to simply try to "fit God in" their lives.

When Sperry read Chuck Colson's book *The Body*, his criticism of such soft-pedaled Christianity struck a chord.

"It helped me to see how lazy those churches were," she said. "They didn't really convict people."

Sperry did not find a challenging Christian community until she entered Houghton College, a Christian school in Houghton, New York, the following fall. When she stepped onto Houghton's evangelical campus, Sperry met Christians who knew the Bible, lived their faith, and challenged her to conform her life to gospel standards.

"It was a whole new world," said Sperry, "exactly what I needed."

Like Sperry, John Chao encountered Christianity at an early age but did not commit to Christ until much later. Chao, a technology consultant in his midthirties, read the Gospel of John during the fall of his sophomore year at Carnegie Mellon University and was "really blown away by Jesus Christ." He committed to Christ while on a retreat that Christmas. A few years later, Chao moved to New York City for what he thought would be a brief stint on Wall Street before he moved to the West Coast.

Then Chao discovered Redeemer Presbyterian Church. The preaching of Senior Pastor Tim Keller convinced him to stay in New York.

"It's the gospel," said Chao, who added that Keller preaches the "dual truth" of human sinfulness and God's merciful love.

Redeemer's success in attracting young urban professionals to morally conservative evangelical Christianity has been noted in the *New York Times* and *Time* magazine. Each Sunday, the church—which holds most of its services in a college auditorium on Manhattan's Upper East Side—draws a crowd of several thousand with its vibrant worship style, small-group communities, and openness to spiritual seekers who are skeptical of Christianity. But for young Christians like Chao, Redeemer's greatest strength is Keller's preaching. The message is undiluted orthodox Christianity that does not equivocate about conventional morality. But Chao said Keller goes beyond the dos and don'ts of Christianity.

"It's not about the rules," he said. "It's about following the Lord."

For the members of the Carpenter's Company in San Dimas, California—a church affiliated with the International Church of the Foursquare Gospel, a fast-growing Pentecostal charismatic denomination founded in the 1920s—following the Lord led them beyond orthodox preaching into the heart of Eastern Orthodoxy. Their journey began with the 6 A.M. daily prayer meetings that the church had initiated under the leadership of Fr. Joseph (then Pastor Dennis) Corrigan in 1989. Corrigan had detected a lack of direction and a creeping worldliness in the church that he hoped the prayer sessions could combat. At first, the meetings consisted only of a recitation of the Lord's Prayer, but soon the church's mostly young-adult membership began to crave daily communion and other elements of liturgical worship not usually associated with Pentecostalism. A few years later, Corrigan picked up a copy of the sixth-century Rule of St. Benedict and brought it back to the leadership team of the church. The group devoured Benedict's writings—which effectively addressed problems they were dealing with in a way that contemporary authors had failed to—and soon moved on to writings of the early Eastern church fathers and more recent spiritual authors like Theophan the Recluse. By the end of 1995, Corrigan and his band of about a hundred church members were ready to convert. In December 1996, the Carpenter's Company became St. Peter the Apostle Antiochian Orthodox Church, and Corrigan—a fiftysomething former staffer for the evangelical Campus Crusade for Christ—became an Orthodox priest.

"It was a corporate obedience," Corrigan said, explaining the process that led his church to Orthodoxy. "We had decided to get serious about the gospel early, and toward the end of it, we found in the Orthodox Church the fulfillment of it."

Corrigan's church is not alone. Periodically in recent years, stories have surfaced in the national news about Pentecostal, evangelical, and, occasionally, Episcopalian churches converting to Eastern Orthodoxy and Catholicism. Many young evangelicals have converted individually to Episcopalianism, Catholicism, and Orthodoxy. When asked to explain, they often cite a desire to belong to churches that satisfy their hunger for tradition, self-sacrifice, and a more historical Christianity.

Douglas Law, a thirtysomething African American father of four, had spent time in outposts of the Vineyard Fellowship—an association of evangelical churches that emphasize informal and charismatic worship—before joining Corrigan's Foursquare-turned-Orthodox congregation. Like other orthodox converts at St. Peter's, Law said he had grown tired of churches that fixated on "getting saved and getting others saved" instead of cultivating spiritual depth and churches that focused on making Christianity appealing instead of stressing spiritual discipline. He knew there must be more to Christianity than that.

"There are a lot of people out there who want to hear about a life where the real demands of Christianity are part of your heartbeat and your breath," Law said. "I think every Christian knows it deep down—that it's a life of self-sacrifice. But we never had a place to fall down and die."

Now, Law said, he belongs to a church where he and his family practice obedience and sacrifice. His children's heroes are the Orthodox saints. His weekly routine includes participation in the divine liturgy and in the 6 A.M. prayer vigils that are now held in a converted Orthodox sanctuary. And his daughter recently confessed her sins to an Orthodox priest for the first time.

"I don't get emotional," said Law, whose eyes glistened with tears as he recalled the sight of his seven-year-old daughter standing with the priest before an icon, gripping a list of her sins that she had compiled with the help of her mother.

Seeing his little girl receive the sacramental grace of reconciliation, Law said, made all of the early mornings and late nights and demands of an Orthodox lifestyle worthwhile.

"That grace," he murmured, "that's *it*."

Holy Mysteries

For many young Christians, the trek toward Christian orthodoxy—and, in some cases, the attraction to its most historical churches—boils down to an encounter with God that defies description. Churches that preach the hard gospel or cling to time-tested teachings may capture the attention of seekers. But often it is the quality of a church's worship experience—and the degree to which it offers mystery and meaning—that makes them stay.

Few worship experiences match the mystery of eucharistic adoration, the traditional Catholic practice of reverencing the consecrated communion wafer that Catholics believe contains the body, blood, soul, and divinity of Jesus Christ. Catholics reared in the days before Vatican II remember devotion to the Eucharist as an integral part of the faith. But for those born after the landmark council—which collided with the social upheaval of the 1960s to trigger drastic changes in the way American Catholics approached worship, religious life, and catechesis—eucharistic adoration is another traditional devotion that few of them experienced as children. For that reason, and because of the intense spiritual experiences that young adults say they have had as a result of such adoration, the practice has sparked curiosity among many post–Vatican II Catholics, who are promoting it in their parishes and on their college campuses.

At St. Louis University in 2000, Jesuits-in-training Phil Hurley (whose conversion was recounted in chapter 2) and Christopher Collins, acting independently, introduced eucharistic adoration to students at the Jesuit campus. Collins spearheaded a traditional Friday afternoon service for students that featured long periods of silence, Latin hymns, incense, and solemn Benediction by a priest. Hurley modeled a Monday night Holy Hour after the charismatic adoration services he had experienced at Franciscan University of Steubenville, which blended the traditional devotion with contemporary praise songs, including many evangelical favorites.

Both Holy Hour services soon began attracting regular devotees. The evangelical adoration service on Monday nights drew so many students that the group had to move to a larger meeting space to accommodate the crowd. The campus ministry, which was known for its emphasis on social action, eventually took over organization of the Monday night assembly.

As students poured into the dimly lit dormitory chapel where adoration was held one Monday night in the fall of 2000, they could be heard lamenting their workload and reliving their weekends. But when Hurley unlocked the small tabernacle door and brought out the Eucharist for adoration, conversation ceased. Some students fell to their knees. Others sprawled on the ground under the candlelit altar where the host was displayed. One girl buried her head in her hands and quietly sobbed.

"It's amazingly personal," Hurley said, pulling his hands toward his heart as he recalled his first adoration experience in Steubenville, where hundreds of young Catholics sang praise songs, then knelt in reverence as a priest passed by them holding the monstrance that contained the Eucharist. "It was exactly what I needed."

Hurley and Collins know that many older Catholics associate eucharistic adoration with a rigid imposed piety that they happily discarded after Vatican II. For younger Catholics, though, adoration is unknown—and therefore, exotic and appealing.

"They don't have the baggage," Hurley said, referring to the hundred-plus college students who now flock to the adoration service. Instead, Hurley said, these Catholic young adults experience adoration as he first did: as a mystical encounter with Jesus that solidifies their identity as Catholics.

The phenomenon of eucharistic adoration among the young has spread to campuses across the country. From Harvard University and MIT in Cambridge to Thomas Aquinas College in Santa Paula, California, students in groups large and small have embraced eucharistic spirituality as a way to find serenity and connect with God.

"It's just so peaceful," said Danielle Rose Skorich, a student at the University of Notre Dame who regularly attends student-organized eucharistic adoration at a campus chapel. Adoration's appeal among her peers is part of a larger openness to tradition,

Skorich said: "You tend to see traditions as not big enough to hold your idea of faith for modern times. But this stuff was there before—so it is big enough, rich enough."

Skorich did not always appreciate traditional spirituality. When she was younger, the Mass seemed like an empty ritual. Then, as a college student, she took several trips to Medjugorje, the village in Bosnia and Herzegovina where the Virgin Mary is said to appear. The faith that she witnessed there impressed her, and traditional Catholic devotions took on new meaning. Now Skorich relishes eucharistic adoration, says the rosary every day, and attends daily Mass.

"If your heart is really in it, if you're just trying to respond in love, the grace just kind of jumps out at you," said Skorich, a bubbly woman with a dazzling smile, a nose ring, and straight brown hair that cascades down her back. "I feel a whole different level of trust in my relationship with God. I see a whole different beauty in the church. I'm just filled with joy in a whole different way."

Skorich said her favorite part of Mass in Notre Dame's Basilica of the Sacred Heart is when the priest holds up the round, white host and says, "This is the Lamb of God, who takes away the sins of the world. Happy are those who are called to his supper." After the congregation answers with words that mimic those of the centurion in Matthew's Gospel—"Lord, I am not worthy to receive you, but only say the word and I shall be healed"—the priest breaks the host.

"You hear [the breaking of the host] echo in the church," Skorich said. "Then we say, 'We're not worthy to receive you.' Then we go up there and receive it. I feel like we're called to be broken like that: called to love the world as Christ does, in a way that breaks our hearts, in a way that hurts. I feel like it all means something."

After Skorich receives communion, she hears the words "body of Christ" repeated to each subsequent communicant, like a mantra reminding her of Christ's sacrificial love.

"Sometimes I just get so overwhelmed that I have to start crying," Skorich said, her brown eyes shining. "He just gives and gives and gives, over and over. If you begin to contemplate what you're being given, how do you respond to that?"

An attraction to the sacraments is not limited to those who were raised in liturgical churches. Many young evangelicals are drawn to Catholic, Orthodox, and Episcopalian churches that emphasize mystery and tradition in their worship. Heidi Schneringer, a southern California native who grew up in nondenominational evangelical churches, never knew denominational divisions existed until she entered Whitworth College in Spokane, Washington. In the Whitworth chapel during the first week of school, Schneringer was exposed for the first time to a Presbyterian service in which participants said prayers that were written down, instead of composing them spontaneously. It rubbed her the wrong way.

"I thought, *Where's the heart involved?*" Schneringer recalled. "*Those are not her own words, those are someone else's words.* I went away mocking it."

In 1996, Schneringer spent the first semester of her junior year at a program for college students sponsored by Focus on the Family, a conservative evangelical organization based in Colorado Springs. She studied under a conservative Episcopalian who is now her boss at the Family Research Council in Washington, D.C. He introduced Schneringer to the Episcopalian tradition, using church visits, readings from the Book of Common Prayer, and explanations of Episcopalian beliefs. Later, she spent a semester in France and attended Catholic Mass each Sunday because she could not find any Protestant churches. By the time Schneringer moved to Washington, D.C., after college, she found herself more comfortable with liturgical worship and more interested in church history.

While shopping for a church in the Washington area, Schneringer and a friend visited Truro Episcopal, the theologically conservative, somewhat charismatic church that her boss attends in Fairfax, Virginia. They liked it enough to stay, though Schneringer continued to investigate other, nonliturgical Protestant churches. When she did, she noticed a stark difference between their services, where worship leaders did something new each week—often without any apparent reason for the changes—and services at Truro, where the rhythms of liturgy grounded her faith. She began to appreciate the way Truro's services required her to worship with her body as well as with her mind and heart.

"It's more than just an attitude of the heart," Schneringer said. "My faith must be more encompassing. It has physical realities. I mean, we kneel because it's a reminder of us before Christ the King. With all my being—my mind, my body, and my soul—I'm going to go and worship the King."

To her surprise, Schneringer also accepted Episcopalian belief in the Eucharist. Episcopalians do not embrace the Catholic and Orthodox belief that when the eucharistic elements are consecrated they become the body and blood of Jesus, keeping only the appearance of bread and wine. But the Anglican Church embraces a sacramental theology that says that in some mysterious way, Jesus is present in the Eucharist.

After reading about the sacraments, Schneringer said, she no longer accepted her childhood belief that receiving communion was a purely symbolic gesture. And the fact that she could not fully understand the Eucharist actually appealed to her.

"It may just be one of those holy mysteries," she said. "And that's OK with me."

Though Schneringer has not officially been confirmed into the Episcopalian Church—the church's national leaders seem too liberal and wayward to her—Schneringer happily attends the more conservative Truro, where many young "evangelical" Episcopalians like her have found a church that is quite different from the ones they once knew. Schneringer remembers being baptized as a child in an outdoor swimming pool. Now she attends a church where babies are baptized in the midst of a two-hour Sunday service that features scripted responses from the congregation, which pledges to raise each child in the Christian faith and sings a resounding alleluia after the babe is dunked in a traditional baptismal font.

"It's the pure celebration that it should be," Schneringer said. "This great celebration that begs a physical response is terribly powerful."

The Palm Sunday celebration at Christ Church of Hamilton and Wenham, Massachusetts, another conservative Episcopal church that attracts evangelical converts, was more solemn. A congregation brimming with teenagers and young adults silently processed around the courtyard of the church on this foggy morning in April 2001. Each person carried a palm as a reminder of Jesus' entrance into Jerusalem, where palm-waving supporters hailed him just before his betrayal, arrest, and crucifixion. A lone twentysomething man wearing a long blue robe played the trumpet as the worshipers filed back into the church for a somber two-hour commemoration of Christ's passion, which featured organ music, two choirs, and the sprinkling of holy water.

Near the end of the service, the choir's soft rendition of "Jesus, Remember Me" floated over the congregation. A young couple who looked to be in their early twenties swayed together in a pew near the front of the church. The man wore a beard and ponytail. Next to him, a lanky young woman in cargo pants and an oversized sweater leaned gently against him, her head resting on the nape of his neck. When it came time for the consecration of the host, they knelt in unison. The woman—half sitting on the pew behind her, half leaning against the pew in front of her—bowed her head as the priest said the eucharistic prayer. She seemed almost sunken between the two pews, her frame curled into a near-fetal position, her face intentionally hidden by the sea of her own hair. It was as if some invisible force had overshadowed her, and her only response was to crumple under its weight and divert her eyes from its splendor.

A few pews away, twenty-two-year-old Sarah Carlson assumed a similar posture, savoring the communion service that had grown to be such an important part of her Christian faith. Raised in Colorado Springs as a member of the Plymouth Brethren movement—a conservative Christian group that eschews liturgy, tradition, and hierarchy—Carlson's childhood experience of communion had been much less formal. The communion services she had attended consisted of tearing up bread and passing around cups of grape juice after men in the assembly spontaneously stood and repeated the words that they felt prompted by the Holy Spirit to say.

Carlson found it difficult to attend emotional, upbeat, and impromptu services on those days when she did not feel the fervor to worship. When she encountered liturgical worship as a student at Gordon College in Wenham and during a year in Oxford, England, she noticed herself gravitating toward the Anglican churches, where she could reaffirm her beliefs with a creed, regardless of her feelings. She also liked following a church calendar that connected the seasons of the year with the seasons of Christ's life. Now Carlson uses the Book of Common Prayer regularly and worships at Christ Church, a theologically conservative and highly liturgical Episcopalian church. The church has attracted throngs of students and faculty from Gordon, a nondenominational Christian school that has an evangelical flavor but a growing number of liturgical converts.

Like Schneringer, Carlson said she is reluctant to join the larger Episcopalian Church because of its national reputation for veering from biblical teaching. She added that she would more likely join the Catholic Church or the Orthodox Church than return to a nonliturgical evangelical one.

"I want to be more connected to history, the history of the Christian Church," said Carlson, who relishes the knowledge that she is worshiping the way Christians have for centuries. "There have been generations of people before me saying the same prayers."

The Generation Gap

The attraction of tradition, mystery, and ritual exerts a strong pull on many Generation-X worshipers—much to the surprise, and sometimes disdain, of the baby boomers attempting to reach them by more contemporary means.

In 1997, Fr. Willard Jabusch wrote a commentary piece for the Jesuit magazine *America* about the conservative bent of young Catholics. He discussed what he had seen as a priest who oversees Catholic campus ministry at the University of Chicago. Among other trends he had witnessed in the past decade, Jabusch noted student interest in the Latin Mass, the writings of Thomas Aquinas, and the early church fathers—as well as, in the words of one young convert, "a church that will not be shifting under my feet." Jabusch also noted that while today's young Catholics are not necessarily opposed to the ordination of women or a relaxation of priestly celibacy, those issues— which dominate the agendas of rapidly aging liberal Catholic groups like Call to Action—do not matter much to today's young Catholics.[8]

Jabusch did not expect the article to draw much reader response. So he was quite surprised when *America*'s readers roared with disapproval.

"The mere fact that I brought this up—it was heresy," Jabusch said, recounting the negative feedback he received from middle-aged liberal Catholics who expressed offense at his account of the next generation's conservatism. Considering himself a middle-of-the-road to liberal Catholic, Jabusch never imagined that his ideas would prove so controversial to other liberal Catholics. But their reactions were understandable, he said, because many baby boomers have spent their lives pushing for progressive causes that the next generation may dismiss: "When you've suffered like that, you take it all very personally."

For his part, Jabusch sees many of the students in his Catholic student center achieving a healthy balance between traditional and contemporary elements of Catholicism. As for those who trek across town to St. John Cantius, a parish that offers Latin Masses and Gregorian chant, Jabusch said, "I find it all rather bizarre, because it's a nostalgia trip that I don't want to take."

Fr. Zachary Hayes finds it worse than bizarre. A Franciscan priest and theologian at the Catholic Theological Union in Chicago, Hayes talks about the influx of conservative young seminarians and neo-Thomistic young Catholics with a mix of irritation and concern. He worries that their fascination with tradition is more about aesthetics than theology and that their idealized vision of the church is based more on 1950s-era piety than on the substance of true Catholicism. He also blames psychological factors—such as the yearning for stability in a world of rapid change—for the traditional leanings of many young Catholics.

"They want a safe harbor, religion to pacify and solidify," Hayes said. "There's a kind of nostalgia for a church that they've never experienced—and I have. And I know what that church is like, and so I don't have that nostalgia. I don't want to go back there."

Many young Christians acknowledge that tradition holds aesthetic and emotional appeal. During an after-dinner discussion on the campus of the University of Chicago in October 2000, several Protestant Generation-X graduate students and professors from nearby seminaries spontaneously quoted their favorite phrases from the Anglican Book of Common Prayer, laughing about the comfort provided by such regular recitations. The same group lauded the beauty of night compline services that featured Gregorian chant and snickered at the "happy clappy" services designed by baby boomers to appeal to their generation. Though several said they enjoy contemporary praise music, they wondered aloud why boomers seem preoccupied with justifying faith by reason, bringing political agendas into the church, and dismantling tradition.

"Boomers have a different agenda," said Scott Jackson, a twenty-nine year old pursuing his doctoral degree from the University of Chicago Divinity School.

One example, said thirty-one-year-old seminary professor Melody Knowles, is the boomer obsession with rationality. Look at the bookshelf of a typical boomer Christian, Knowles said, and there is a good chance you will find a copy of Episcopal bishop

John Shelby Spong's *Rescuing the Bible from Fundamentalism*—a title that sparked a chorus of groans from this group.

That book, Knowles said, represents the boomer attempt "to prove you can be a rational Christian. And my big thing is: Who *cares*?"

Today's postmodern young adults are not as concerned with having a purely rational modern faith, she said. Instead, young adults—including many young Baptists she knows who have joined the Episcopal Church—are "rebelling" by embracing traditional worship.

"It's sexy and exotic," said Knowles, who sees the trend as a backlash against boomers who discarded tradition in favor of rationalism and relativism. "The previous generation wimped out, and you want a challenge. It's kind of idealistic."

Contemporary and Conservative

Not all orthodox young Christians embrace traditional worship. Many are attracted to evangelical churches that combine contemporary worship with traditional teachings. Churches like Park Street in downtown Boston attract throngs of young adults to Sunday night services led by their peers. The church band members, clad in denim, play electric guitars and drums while the faithful sing lyrics projected onto a screen in the front of the church. The pews are packed with college-age students who are white, Asian, and African American. The church and its senior minister, Gordon Hugenberger, are thoroughly evangelical, as his personal testimony on the Park Street Web site affirms. And like the evangelical churches studied by Faith Communities Today— which showed that evangelicals founded 58 percent of all new church congregations between 1990 and 2000—this nondenominational, youth-oriented orthodox Christian church is thriving.

On the West Coast, the Abundant Life Christian Fellowship in Menlo Park, California, attracts a similarly young, diverse, and nonliturgical crowd. According to its Web site, Abundant Life offers "lively praise and worship, practical and dynamic Bible teaching, and great fellowship. At ALCF you'll find the young and old, professionals and plain ol' Joes, Ph.Ds and 'GEDs' all worshipping together."

The claims ring true. Though Abundant Life holds four Sunday services to accommodate the crowds, its overflow room—for those who cannot squeeze into its main auditorium-style sanctuary—still cannot contain the congregation. At one Sunday service in April 2001, worshipers clapped along to boisterous praise songs as a dozen teenagers formed a friendly mosh pit on the sanctuary stage. Later, a preacher offered an extended sports metaphor—thoroughly documented by Scripture—about the importance of "playing on God's team." Then the crowd heard the personal testimonies of several church members, including a young African American man who turned from crime after embracing Christianity and a middle-aged white man who told how his radical conversion to Christ helped him face a terminal illness. The service lasted nearly two hours, but its attendees—who spanned the racial and ethnic rainbows, from white to Asian to Hispanic to African American—participated with zeal to the end.

Protestant churches are not the only ones capitalizing on cravings for contemporary worship. The charismatic movement that swept the Catholic Church in the 1970s has found devotees in the new generation at places like the Franciscan University of Steubenville, which celebrates its "dynamic orthodoxy." And the evangelical praise songs that helped draw Catholics into Young Life, InterVarsity, and Campus Crusade for Christ fellowships have recently been finding their way into Catholic parishes. One example of the popularity of contemporary Catholic worship is the Life Teen program. Founded in a Mesa, Arizona, parish in 1985, the program organizes Masses set to contemporary music, complete with drum sets, and led by young-adult worship leaders. At the Masses, teenagers and young adults converge around the altar during the liturgy of the Eucharist. Afterward, the teenagers attend peer meetings devoted to Catholic faith formation. The vitality of Life Teen Masses has helped them spread nationwide, to some fifty thousand teens in about five hundred parishes.

Seeing the Unseen

After spending more than a dozen years in ministry to young Christians, author and pastor Dieter Zander appreciates the value of programs that welcome young adults and give them alternatives to traditional worship. He founded an evangelical church geared to young adults in 1986, and then he later joined the staff of Willow Creek Community Church, a nationally recognized megachurch in suburban Chicago. At Willow Creek, Zander pioneered the "church within a church" model, which gave Generation Xers their own contemporary worship service.

But Zander believes the key to reaching today's young adults is to help them grow—not just make them comfortable. Too often, young adults cycle through Generation-X services that are tailored to their worship whims yet leave them unchanged.

"It gets old to get pandered to for so long," said Zander, noting that services marketed only to young adults strike them as false. "There's something inside of them that says, 'This is not the way it really is.'"

Zander has since critiqued the model of generation-specific services that informed his work at Willow Creek. He now believes that youth ministers would fare better if they addressed the ideological shift between the rationality-oriented modern converts of yesterday and their mystery-craving postmodern children.

For many young Christians, worship shot through with symbolism and tradition offers an escape from niche-marketed, age-segmented, or strictly didactic church services. It also feeds the Generation-X craving for mystery.

"It connects with the yearning inside of them," said Zander, who added that liturgical church leaders must explain their rituals and symbols to young adults if they want these novice worshipers to participate. "You have to think about how to make your services accessible to people, because people don't want to feel stupid. Help a person see what they do not see."

That ability—to see with the eyes of faith—is what guides today's young orthodox Christians. Whether bucking a culture that sees their morality as reactionary or fellow believers who regard their traditions as retrograde, these young believers cling to the hard gospel and holy mysteries that, they believe, make those struggles worthwhile. And they gravitate to churches that help them reverence the intimate yet mysterious God to whom they have surrendered their imaginations, and their very lives.

4

FAITH COMMUNITIES
AND FELLOWSHIP

Behold, how good and pleasant it is
when brothers dwell in unity!

Psalm 133:1

The Bronx bustled as usual on this Wednesday afternoon, its pedestrian masses accustomed to the cacophony of car alarms, radios, and sirens. Young men bounded out of subway exits. Young mothers tugged toddlers past mobs of raucous teenagers. The crisp January air whipped through the crowd, brushing faces in every shade of white, brown, and black.

Threading his way through the swarmed sidewalk, a tall man in a long gray robe and sandals gave high fives to teenagers who looked just slightly older than he was. His infectious grin crowned a curly beard that extended well below his collarbone. On the street, a station wagon full of noisy children rolled by him, its driver sporting a similar gray garment, long beard, and broad smile.

All across the Bronx that day, bearded men in long robes and sandals were migrating toward St. Crispin Friary on East 156th Street, an outpost of the Franciscan Friars of the Renewal. Many disrupted their usual routines—of telling teenagers about Jesus, praying rosaries outside abortion clinics, bringing food to destitute neighbors—so they could greet Cardinal Christoph Schönborn, the fifty-six-year-old Catholic prelate of Vienna who was paying a visit to New York and wanted to meet the famous friars of the Bronx.

Founded in 1987 as a more ascetic alternative to the existing Franciscan Capuchin order, the Friars of the Renewal have captured the imagination of Catholics and non-Catholics alike with their austere lifestyle, abundant service projects, and burgeoning popularity among the young. In an era when young adults are said to abhor authority and resist commitment, the relatively new religious community already has welcomed some seventy priests and brothers whose average age is twenty-six. The friars take vows of poverty, chastity, and obedience—"no money, no honey, and a boss," as they like to say. They live in service and solidarity among the poor, in stark buildings lent to their community by the Archdiocese of New York. They spend several hours each day in prayer. Their model is St. Francis of Assisi, the thirteenth-century founder of the Franciscans, who renounced his wealthy family, traded his fancy clothes for those of a beggar, and embraced celibacy in imitation of Christ.

Francis might not have pictured station wagons, pickup basketball games, or an AIDS ministry when he assembled the first Franciscans some eight hundred years ago. But the activities of his modern-day followers in the Bronx—who painted a mural of the Virgin Mary on the wall of their Our Lady of the Angels Friary on East 155th Street and serve the poor and sick at all of their doorsteps—would likely warm the heart of the venerable saint. Those sights certainly impressed Schönborn, who marveled that so many young men had agreed to surrender so much for the sake of the gospel.

After following a throng of bearded young men into a former parish church that they had been given by the archdiocese, the cardinal genuflected before the tabernacle on the altar and joined the group in a spontaneous rendition of "Salve Regina," a traditional Latin hymn to Mary. As the last notes rang in the air, Schönborn surveyed the crowd of beaming young friars around him. Many had come to the community on the heels of a radical conversion, eager to lay down their lives in service alongside peers who wanted to do the same. Known for their medieval dress and reputation as "America's Mother Teresas," these young men seem to flout every stereotype about their postmodern, post-Christian generation.

"It shows that there are plenty of vocations," the cardinal murmured in a thick Austrian accent. "It's only the question of finding places where they can develop and grow. And this is certainly such a place."

A Quest for Community

Though Generation X is famous for defying labels and stumping sociologists, a few traits are commonly attributed to Americans born between 1965 and 1983. They are interested in spirituality, ignorant of tradition, and fearful of both commitment and abandonment.

Considering these conflicting characteristics, it is no wonder that religious leaders—including those seeking recruits for highly institutionalized forms of religious life—are not sure what to make of this generation. In some ways, these young adults look like a novice director's nightmare. They marry late, switch jobs and careers often, and move at whim. Deference to authority strikes many of them as odd, even laughable. And notions of self-sacrifice and obedience puzzle many young adults who learned from their parents, teachers, and cultural leaders to privilege personal fulfillment and autonomy above all else.

Yet the portrait of these young adults has another dimension. The same generation known for its struggles with short attention spans and commitment phobias has also shown an impressive desire to serve others, build stable families and communities, and avoid materialism and careerism.

Among this generation's most celebrated characteristics is its craving for community. Young adults themselves, not to mention the throngs of sociologists seeking to understand them, repeatedly refer to their quest for authentic, intimate communities. They long to come together around something bigger than themselves, something oriented beyond their own selfish desires and media-drenched lives. They exhibit a desire to spend themselves in community service. And sometimes—as in the case of the young men shepherded by Fr. Bill Wack into the flock of Holy Cross priests—they find their deepest longings addressed in Christian community.

"A lot of them are really concerned about, 'Will I live alone? Do you have community?'" said Wack, the associate vocations director for Holy Cross. Whereas priests twenty or thirty years ago assumed community was part of the bargain and came to Holy Cross in order to serve others, Wack said, today's young men assume the service but actively seek community life. "They seem to be isolated a lot. A lot of young people right now want to belong to something."

Experts often blame the isolation of today's young adults on the social forces that shaped their childhoods. America's divorce rate doubled between 1965 and 1977, and more than 40 percent of Generation Xers spent some part of their childhoods in single-parent homes.[1] Though experts disagree about the effects of divorce on children, many mention divorce when describing the jaded, world-weary persona of Generation Xers and their legendary longing for stable families and close-knit communities.

Franciscan Fr. Michael Scanlan, who presided over the Franciscan University of Steubenville from 1974 until 2000, has seen a surge in the last ten-plus years of young adults seeking guidance and reassurance from father figures. The change is not only among children of divorce, Scanlan said, but also among children from intact homes who have been affected indirectly by the decline in two-parent families and cohesive communities.

"They're really hungry for real fatherhood," Scanlan said. "It's an evident switch."

The childhood experiences that shaped today's young adults—both at home and in the larger culture—go a long way toward explaining not only their craving for community but also why many are attracted to Christian orthodoxy. Reared in a media culture that relentlessly lobbies for their attention and panders to their whims, many young adults find it refreshing when religious leaders demand sacrifice, service, and renunciation of consumerism. They feel strangely liberated by orthodoxy's demands of obedience and objective morality, which belie their culture's tendency toward individualism and moral relativism. And they are captivated by groups that stress stability, commitment, and integration—the very values they found wanting in their splintered, mobile families and fragmented, impersonal communities.

Fr. Thomas Brindley, an Episcopalian priest at St. Columba parish and retreat center in Inverness, California, sees "a great number of kids" embracing orthodoxy, both at his retreat center and at the Orthodox Church of America (OCA) monastery four miles away. They are attracted to tradition, coherence, and authenticity, Brindley said, and they often gravitate to orthodoxy's most countercultural forms—like the lifestyle of the OCA monks.

"They identify with that," Brindley said. "They say [to the monks], 'Wow, we don't like the world any more than you do.'"

A similar phenomenon, on a much larger scale, has been happening for four decades in Taizé, France. An ecumenical Christian monastic community situated in France's Burgundy region, Taizé attracts about a hundred thousand pilgrims a year, who come to participate in Taizé's prayer rituals, Bible studies, common meals, and chores.[2] Protestants and Catholics mingle with ease, and young adults flock by the thousands to spend their summers and spring breaks in a place where the rhythm of daily prayer sets the pace for the community.

Brother John, an American who joined the Taizé community in 1972, said he sees young adults attracted to the community's contemplative spirituality and uncluttered atmosphere.

"They're looking for something a bit more meditative or quiet," said Brother John, who also noted that Taizé communal prayer meetings near Chicago and San Francisco attract several hundred participants each month. As life gets more "crazy," he

said, young people crave more simplicity: "At a certain point, they
need to slow down."

The Power of Personal Witness

Interest in Christian community does not guarantee commitment
to it. Many young adults find traditional religion intriguing and
fellowship groups appealing but ultimately reject the accountability and discipline they require. Like the Generation Xers who
avoid marriage while pining for stable committed relationships,
young adults attracted to orthodoxy often feel conflicted when
faced with its demands. What often makes the difference between
a flirtation and a commitment is the personal witness of an individual or community that makes Christian virtues seem irresistible—and worth the work.

John Hart's appreciation of Christian community life sprouted
when he was a student at Kansas State University in Manhattan,
Kansas. Hart, an evangelical Christian in his late twenties,
accepted Christ at the age of seven and reaffirmed that choice in
junior high school. But it was not until he encountered authentic
Christian community in college—and noticed how his life in a
"Christian subculture" fell far short of that embodied ideal—that
he experienced the fullness of a life rooted in God and spent in
service to others.

Hart discovered the power of Christian community when he
became involved with the National Student Leadership Forum on
Faith and Values. The ecumenical event brings college students
together in Washington, D.C., to interact with political leaders,
discuss the role of faith in their lives, and examine "servant leadership," using Jesus Christ as a model. The forum grew out of the
National Prayer Breakfast, an annual gathering of diverse political leaders in Washington that student leaders participate in and
help coordinate. The people Hart met through his involvement
with the forum and the prayer breakfast embodied the sort of

Christian community he admired—and hoped to imitate. When he returned to Kansas State, he and a handful of his college buddies decided to think strategically about how to spread the gospel on campus, hold each other accountable as Christians, and live together in community.

"We just decided, 'Let's really take this thing seriously. Let's really be a community,'" Hart said. "So there's a level of intentionality that is definitely unusual. I think for community to be genuine, for it to bear fruit, there is a certain level of commitment and intentionality that has to happen."

The group began praying for the student-body presidents at their school. They worked to ease the divisions between believers on campus by organizing a weeklong campus event in 1995 that forced the leaders and members of competing Christian fellowships to work together. Their nucleus grew from five to fifteen and, eventually, to several hundred loosely connected friends around the nation who share the same vision for strategic evangelism.

Through his community-living experiences as a college student and, later, as a press secretary in Washington, D.C., Hart grew to appreciate the rewards and struggles of Christian community. He has learned to wash dishes that are not his, to keep a short account of the wrongs done to him, to turn the little frustrations of daily life into opportunities to love his neighbor. He has learned, in essence, to "die to self."

"It's so potent—you see the cost of it and you see the fruit," said Hart, who believes a commitment to some form of Christian community is essential to the faith. "I don't think I have any choice. We're not designed to live secluded, separate, independent lives."

Hart has experienced more than personal growth in community. He also has witnessed the conversion of his roommates—including a non-Christian friend who "was loved into the family of God." Christian language would have repelled that friend, Hart said, but the concrete example of roommates struggling to live gospel values led him to Christ.

"[Personal witness] is the best tool to bring people into the kingdom," Hart said. "But if the goal is to have a tool, then it probably isn't going to be very effective. If the goal is to evangelize yourself first and to really live out the Christ-centered life, then you have tools at your disposal."

For the generation weaned on Watergate and no-fault divorce, broken promises are a fact of life, and cynicism is a common condition. Lofty ideals of selflessness and sacrificial love can be a tough sell. But the concrete example of Christians who are happy, genuine, and radically committed to living—not just preaching—gospel ideals can cut through that suspicion and lead to conversion. Once those conversions solidify, young believers often join faith communities that help them stay committed. Eventually, many of them become witnesses to those very same gospel values that led them to conversion and that can, in turn, lead their peers to conversion.

That cycle of personal and communal witness has the potential to transform American Christianity and the face of a generation searching for substance.

Brad Wilcox, a postdoctoral fellow in sociology at the Center for Research on Child Wellbeing at Princeton, predicts that marriage rates and religious observance—cultural indicators of commitment and traditional morality—will continue to decline in the near future. But Wilcox also expects a corresponding expansion among faith communities that are fighting that decline.

"The ranks of the counterculture will grow," Wilcox said.

For believers like Hart, the number in those ranks matters less than the intensity of their commitment. After all, said Hart, Jesus staked his entire ministry on a band of only a dozen disciples.

"You don't need a whole generation. You need about twelve," Hart said. "There are all these people in our generation, and you can take a relatively small number of them. If they're committed to loving God, loving their neighbor, following Christ, it's stronger than the natural forces keeping us apart—alienation, self-centeredness, even religious differences. If we're able to overcome those things, then it's revolutionary."

Community and Its Counterfeits

Before the revolution begins, young Christians must find communities and fellowships that inspire and sustain them. Not every community fits that bill. Many churches, parachurch organizations, and religious orders struggle to attract young adults who seem hopelessly unresponsive. The attempts of these organizations to appeal to the next generation by diluting their message or softening their demands seem to backfire, leading many religious leaders to conclude that today's young adults cannot commit to Christian communities of any stripe.

The sociological sketch of this generation suggests exactly the opposite. Today's young adults are clamoring for community—but they are repulsed by its counterfeits. Weaned on Madison Avenue marketing, this audience knows when it is being pandered to, and it resists such manipulation violently.

"They have a very high nose for BS," said Christian author Os Guinness, who said young adults are searching for substance. "They want authenticity."

Authentic Christian communities—those that pass the sniff test of skeptical young believers and inspire them to lay down their lives—do not make it easy on young adults. These communities are sacrificial, demanding radical commitment, selflessness, and personal growth. They are incarnational, putting faith into action and emphasizing the connection between service and personal holiness. They are intimate, calling members to share their lives and hold one another accountable for their spiritual progress. And they are evangelical, spreading the gospel and engaging culture without selling out. Faith communities with those characteristics rarely want for members or momentum.

Rosalind Moss, a Jewish convert to Catholicism who works for Catholic Answers, identifies with today's young adults when she considers her own conversion to Christianity in the 1970s. Moss encountered the Jews for Jesus movement in California, and the fervor of that evangelical Christian community captivated her.

"Their faith just came out of every pore," Moss said. "They would die for it. They were so convinced, and they lived such an uncompromising life that I thought, 'I'll check this out.'"

Today's young adults are hungering for the same experience, Moss said, even if they are not actively investigating organized religion: "I would venture to say they're seeking God. They're seeking truth because God has put it within them."

Young adults want to surrender to something bigger than self and to share their spirituality with others, Moss said. And the groups that allow them to do that are the ones that flourish.

"They teach with Christianity that you're not your own," Moss said. "God did not design us to do our own thing."

Religious Life: A Radical Sacrifice

Few experiences of Christian community demand as much sacrifice and commitment as enrollment in a traditional seminary or religious order. Young adults who want to forsake their own desires and live for God alone often find freedom in a celibate, community-centered religious lifestyle that defies the conventional wisdom of their culture—and, often, the comprehension of their family and friends.

"[The young adults who join the order] are women seeking a purpose," said Sr. Gloria Therese Laven, assistant vocation directress for the Carmelite Sisters of the Most Sacred Heart of Los Angeles, an orthodox order that emphasizes contemplative prayer, loyalty to traditional Catholic teachings, and service in schools, hospitals, and retreat centers. "They come wanting to give themselves wholeheartedly to Christ in radical commitment. They're going the whole way. They don't want to hold anything back."

Laven, who is thirty-five, belongs to an order in which nuns wear ankle-length robes, gather several times a day for prayer and worship, and vow to spend their lives in poverty, chastity, and

obedience. The order has a surplus of nuns under forty, a handful
of nuns in training, and a steady stream of interested candidates.

When the sisters gather in their Alhambra, California, convent
chapel for prayer, they seem unified by their silence. They kneel
in pews before a simple altar, imbibing the silence before they
reach for their prayer books and begin to sing cherubic hymns in
perfect unison. On the left side of the chapel, a statue of the
nineteenth-century French Carmelite nun St. Thérèse of Lisieux,
wearing the same brown-and-white robe the sisters wear, presides
over the scene. The serenity in the chapel, and the abundance of
rapt young faces gazing at the Eucharist exposed on the altar
before them, is striking. Laven believes that the prayers said by
these women—who have forsaken wealth, marriage, and autonomy for the sake of loving God above all things—are powerful.

"We're living the gospel," Laven said, "transforming the
world through our life of prayer, in union with those Christ
calls us to serve."

The call to serve in religious life is not one that many Americans have heard or, at least, answered in recent years. The shortfall of religious vocations in the American Catholic Church is well
documented: the number of nuns in the United States has plum-
meted from 181,000 in 1965 to about 84,000 today, with the
median age for today's nuns near seventy.[3] Enrollment of young
men in U.S. seminaries has dropped from 6,600 in 1970 to fewer
than 3,500 today. Fifty years ago, there were 652 Catholics for
every priest; today that ratio is 1,257 to 1, and the average diocesan priest is fifty-seven years old.[4]

In the wake of Vatican II, many priests and nuns left religious
life, opting instead for marriage or the single life. Others stayed
but renounced their clerical clothes and religious habits, moved
out of community houses and into apartments, and shelved traditional devotions and rigid prayer schedules in favor of individual retreats and more informal or experimental prayer styles.
Still others remained in religious orders that never abandoned
the old ways—or they left their liberalized orders to found new

congregations that embraced the traditions of fixed-hour prayer, distinctive dress, and strict obedience to religious superiors.

Today, it is increasingly those hard-core, demanding religious orders and seminaries that are experiencing a surge in religious vocations. The Sisters of Life in New York, a conservative order whose nuns wear traditional habits and dedicate themselves to praying and working for an end to abortion, was founded in New York by the late Cardinal John O'Connor. The order started with eight members in 1991. Today, it has forty and a continuous influx of new recruits.

In Alton, Illinois, the Sisters of St. Francis of the Martyr St. George appeal to, as their Web site says, "young women who are seeking a more radical way of religious life in today's Church." The nuns gather as a community for daily Mass, fixed-hour prayer four times a day, eucharistic adoration, and the rosary. They recently admitted seven new postulants, welcomed five women into the novitiate, and witnessed the temporary vows of seven sisters and the final vows of sixteen sisters.

Another thriving order, the Dominican Sisters of St. Cecilia in Nashville, requires its members to live in poverty and wear floor-length robes. They rise at five o'clock in the morning for two hours of communal prayer and worship, then eat breakfast in silence and begin an eight-hour workday in the Catholic school system. The strictness seems to spawn vocations: the sisters welcomed twenty new postulants in 2000, the largest group in the congregation's 140-year history.

Orthodox groups for men, like the Legionaries of Christ and the Franciscan Friars of the Renewal, are similarly successful. The Legionary priests, who constitute one branch of the conservative evangelization-oriented Regnum Christi (Kingdom of Christ) movement within the Catholic Church, are known for their conservatism, fidelity to the Vatican, and strict adherence to traditional norms of dress and formation for priests. Critics say the movement, and its priests, are secretive, controlling, and retrograde. But many young men think otherwise: at present, more than twenty-five hundred seminarians from thirty-eight nations belong to the Legion, and their average age is twenty-eight.

The Franciscan Friars of the Renewal, who wear beards and medieval robes while serving the poor in the Bronx, have attracted so many young men that novice director Fr. Conrad Osterhout characterizes his community as "bottom heavy with young people." The order will need new houses to accommodate the influx of recruits, he said.

Enrollment trends in diocesan seminaries also reflect the attraction to orthodoxy among the young. In several dioceses where the local bishop stresses stability over progressivism and closely adheres to traditional Catholic practices and teachings—like devotion to the Eucharist and loyalty to Vatican stands against abortion and extramarital sex—seminary numbers have swelled. Consider the Archdiocese of Atlanta, which cycled through three leaders in as many years and had only a handful of seminarians before conservative archbishop John Donoghue arrived in 1993. Now seminary enrollment has climbed to fifty-eight. Similar trends have developed in cities like Fargo, North Dakota; Denver; and Lincoln, Nebraska, where Bishop Fabian Bruskewitz's modestly populated diocese leads the nation in the ratio of Catholics to seminarians.[5] In his book *Call to Action or Call to Apostasy?* Brian Clowes uses statistics from *The Official Catholic Directory* and the Vatican to substantiate his claim that dioceses where bishops are considered orthodox ordain nearly five times as many priests as those run by liberal bishops.[6]

The trend toward orthodoxy among young adults pursuing religious life has been widely noted in the secular and religious media in recent years. An article that appeared in the *New York Times* in September 2000 quoted baby boomer priests lamenting the increasingly conservative bent of their younger counterparts. The article cited surveys by sociologist Dean Hoge that revealed growing conservatism in the priesthood on such issues as priestly celibacy and women's ordination. Hoge's surveys also showed a clear split within the priesthood, with the oldest and youngest priests espousing predominantly traditionalist views and the middle-aged baby boomers between them tending to be more liberal.[7]

Critics of conservative religious leaders, and of their young fans, say orthodox seminaries are not inspiring the young as much as they are providing refuge for right-wingers who want an escape from the world and validation of their extremist views. These critics worry that the next crop of priests will be insulated, judgmental, and ill equipped to deal with the complexities of ministering to America's more moderate Catholics.

One such critic is Franciscan Fr. Zachary Hayes, a theologian at the Catholic Theological Union in Chicago who teaches students and seminarians from several religious orders and other countries. In Catholic circles, CTU has a reputation for being liberal, and Hayes said he eschews the traditional "handbook theology" formation popular with neoconservative seminaries. But he still runs across the occasional conservative student rankled by his presentation. In one introduction to theology class that he taught, Hayes said, a student angrily blurted out his objections to Darwinism after Hayes alluded to the "evolution" of theology.

"I'm not even remotely connected with Darwin," said Hayes, recalling the incident. "I was talking about the development of thought."

Seminarians who want to wear their long black robes and cling to a catechism-only formation are not experiencing the fullness of Catholic tradition, Hayes said. As for the conservative seminaries with growing enrollments, Hayes said that some of those seminaries are so eager for priests that they fail to adequately screen candidates—for psychological fitness, among other factors—before putting them into public ministry. He criticized one diocese for adding to its enrollment numbers by "importing" seminarians who were rejected by the seminaries in their home dioceses.

Bill Wack, of the Congregation of Holy Cross, has also noticed the increasing conservatism of young seminarians. As the associate vocations director for the Holy Cross order, Wack has received calls from prospective seminarians who immediately fire off questions about his order's orthodoxy: "Do the priests wear their black clothes and Roman collars?" "Are they apologists for the Catholic faith?" "Are they faithful to the pope and to the teaching authority of the Catholic Church?"

Wack believes that those questions, and the ostentatiously Catholic T-shirts and huge crucifixes that many young Catholics wear, are a reaction against religious pluralism.

"It's almost in-your-face," Wack said. "They want to make sure that we're proud of who we are and that we're public about it. They want things to be more clear-cut and straightforward."

Wack said Holy Cross is neither the most conservative nor the most liberal religious order, and Holy Cross seminarians are more interested in serving God and others than gauging the orthodoxy of others. Still, his order brims with seminarians who tend toward conservatism. On election night in 2000, the undergraduate seminarians took a straw poll that revealed that fifteen out of seventeen of them had voted for Bush over Gore.

Although Dean Hoge's surveys may trace the roots of young Catholic orthodoxy back to the 1980s, many young Catholics credit the enthusiasm generated by Pope John Paul II and his 1993 World Youth Day for the growth of the movement. That event—which brought nearly two hundred thousand young people to Denver to listen to the pope's message of salvation and sacrifice—is often mentioned in the conversion and vocation stories swapped by young Catholics. The stories frequently begin with references to the pope's Denver visit, lead into discussions of the communal faith manifested there, and end with excited declarations that "something has been happening" among young Catholics ever since.

For many, World Youth Day was the first time that they had seen so many young Catholics gathered in one place and had felt so much enthusiasm for the faith. The communal atmosphere of the event, and the pope's exhortation to young adults to lay down their lives in service to Jesus Christ and his church, left an indelible mark on many young Catholics.

Even for young Catholics who did not attend World Youth Day, Pope John Paul II is a central figure. Thanks to his extensive travels, he has been seen in person by more Catholics than any other pope. His use of contemporary media, including the Internet, has amplified his influence among tech-savvy Americans. And his fondness for young people—as evinced by the World Youth Day gatherings that he has convened since 1985 and by his continual references to the youth as the future of the faith and of the world—has endeared the pope to a generation hungry for a hero who believes in them.

Mike Floreth, a 1995 Notre Dame graduate who belongs to the Congregation of Holy Cross, said he never heard his peers labeling themselves "orthodox" until after World Youth Day in Denver. Since then, he said, he has gradually seen a rise in the attraction to orthodoxy and a growing tendency toward conservatism among his younger peers, many of whom were young teenagers when they attended the Denver celebration.

"I'm on the back of that wave," said twenty-seven-year-old Floreth, who sees younger seminarians soaking up Eternal Word Television, the twenty-year-old conservative Catholic network run by Mother Angelica, and worrying that baby boomer priests are not loyal enough to papal teachings and church tradition. Some seminarians, for instance, bristle when others fail to kneel during the consecration of the Eucharist at Mass—a reverential gesture mandated by Mass rubrics but abandoned by some parishes after Vatican II.

"That concern is definitely a very new concern," Floreth said.

While the older Holy Cross priests try to screen out seminarians who are excessively preoccupied with such matters, Floreth said, they also learn from the young Catholics who refuse to bend the rules or to dump tradition without good reason.

"The young guys push the older guys to think about the way they do things. Old liberals say, '[Do it] because we said so.' That's just not going to fly with these guys."

Mark Coomes, a Notre Dame undergraduate who was born in 1981, was accepted to Holy Cross's Old College program, which allows him to live among other seminary candidates while he discerns a possible call to the priesthood. Coomes knows that he and his classmates at Old College are considered conservative, but he says orthodox Catholicism—not conservative politics—is his guide. And Pope John Paul II, who embodies the life of sacrifice and commitment that Coomes aspires to, is his hero.

"He is very passionate about his beliefs," said Coomes, who believes that the demands of Christianity, as articulated by leaders like the pope, are what inspire young people to enlist in religious orders. "You don't attract people by lowering the bar, but by raising the bar."

The vocations shortfall certainly has left seminaries and religious orders less room to be choosy about applicants, conservative or liberal. But the religious communities making the most concessions to attract candidates—by emphasizing their decision not to wear religious clothing, the independence of their individual members, and sometimes, their dissent from controversial Vatican stands on such issues as women's ordination and homosexuality—often wind up with the fewest new recruits.

In their attempt to make religious life less demanding and more palatable to postmodern believers, some orders have even resorted to offering a "commitment-lite" approach to monastic life. One Benedictine order—in which middle-aged nuns wear sport coats instead of religious robes and describe their spirituality in such vague terms as "creation centered" and "open to the Spirit"—offers recruits a "new way to be Benedictine" in the want ads it runs in Catholic publications. The group's Web site features a picture of three temporary members, women who have agreed to join the community for one to three years while retaining the right to keep their cars and jobs.

Despite their accommodation to commitment-wary young adults, or perhaps because of that accommodation, these religious communities repel young orthodox Christians. Young adults who are seriously contemplating religious life want to embrace the challenge of committed community life—or not bother at all.

"If you're going to leave the world—if you're going to give up marriage, a job—why do it halfway?" said twenty-year-old Adrienne Rolwes, who left her family and boyfriend in St. Louis to begin formation in the consecrated life at the Regnum Christi motherhouse in Greenville, Rhode Island. "If you want to give yourself, then just go all the way."

Regnum Christi, a conservative movement within the Catholic Church that has fifty thousand members worldwide, includes laypeople and priests. The consecrated women of Regnum Christi promise to live in poverty, chastity, and obedience. Though they do not dress in religious habits or live in convents, consecrated women follow many of the same norms of formation, communal worship, and submission to authority as traditional nuns do. They wear long skirts, tailored suit coats, and heels in muted colors— all selected for them by their superiors. They travel in groups or pairs but never alone. They spread the gospel by teaching, counseling, giving spiritual direction, and working in missions or in the media. At the motherhouse, they gather at assigned places in assigned pews at assigned times for group worship. It's a life full of rigor and—according to several young women who spent Holy Week 2001 at the motherhouse—great rewards.

"God doesn't call people to half measures," said twenty-nine-year-old Ann Marie Bertola, who became a consecrated member of Regnum Christi in 1995.

Bertola knows that when the world looks at her life, it sees what she has given up—marriage, family, her independence. But she sees the bright side: a life of intimacy with God and support from other consecrated women.

"It's like going on a diet. You don't even notice you're losing weight. You just do. You feel healthier because you're becoming who you're meant to be as you get closer to Christ. Twenty years from now," Bertola said, grinning, "we'll be so happy!"

Michelle Hill, a vivacious, attractive twenty-four year old, was a successful chemical engineer who constantly found herself asking "what more" there was to life. When she discerned a call to consecrated life, she thought she had found the answer to her longing. But like Jesus in the desert, Hill said, she was tempted to abandon that call when she considered what the decision would cost her. She was a rising star in a top company that had enrolled her in a program for future CEOs. Corporate success—and all of its perks—was within her reach.

When Hill attended a retreat that allowed her time to pray about her decision, the answer became clear. She knew there was no comparison between the material rewards of her current career and the spiritual rewards that awaited her in religious life. Her boss cried when Hill told her the news.

"I think it impressed her that someone would make a decision like that."

Hill, in her first year of formation at the motherhouse, said she has finally found the "more" she always sought.

"Why am I so full here? It's the only thing that ever demanded everything of me."

The Call to Serve

Faith communities that attract—and sustain—committed young Christians do not demand sacrifice simply for its own sake. They cultivate disciplines of prayer, obedience, and commitment in members who are then encouraged to flesh out their faith in concrete action. They galvanize members around service but never divorce the call to serve from the quest for personal holiness. In so doing, they produce disciples of Christ—not social workers.

Sonia Moulard knows what a crucial difference that is. A Catholic campus minister in her early thirties, Moulard has experienced both types of service-oriented faith communities: those that focus on serving others as an end in itself and those that view service as a way to honor God and grow in holiness. When she spent a summer during college working with a liberal order of Catholic nuns and priests in Chicago whose sole focus was humanitarian service,

Moulard enjoyed her work with the low-income members of a Hispanic church. But she also found it challenging, and she received no spiritual formation from the religious community running her program. Instead, Moulard said, she came home at night to a chaotic coed living situation where she had to contend with "roommates sleeping around" and an atmosphere of constant bickering. Moulard cringes at memories of the nun who picked her up at the airport in skimpy shorts and a tube top, and of the priest who—upon hearing her mention St. Thérèse of Lisieux's spiritual autobiography, *The Story of a Soul*—laughed and told her not to "waste" her time "reading about dead people." Still reeling from a dramatic conversion, Moulard found the experience unsettling. And she saw her service work suffer from her lack of serenity.

"When you don't have that foundation, you can't give it to others," Moulard said. "That sense of service has to come out of one's peace."

After studying at the Franciscan University of Steubenville—a Catholic school known for its "dynamic orthodoxy" and fidelity to church tradition—Moulard again joined a faith community devoted to service. But this time, Moulard said, the community put first things first.

"It was like utopia," said Moulard, who lived, prayed, and taught in Nicaragua with a group of Steubenville graduates.

Unlike her previous community, Moulard said, this group relied less on its own ability to serve and more on God's providence. That attitude of total surrender to God's will, and of total confidence in his grace rather than their own efforts, paid off.

"Amazingly, our ministry in Nicaragua was more fruitful," she said, "because in striving for personal holiness we were letting God do the work. That's why so many programs don't work, because they're not allowing God to work."

Now, Moulard works at the University of Maryland's Catholic Student Center, where she tries to help students cultivate the personal holiness that fuels a desire to serve others.

"It's the interior conversion that has to take place, and out of that flows ministry," Moulard said, just moments after she welcomed the thirtieth student into the center's initiation program for Catholic converts. "I'm seeing this ministry here explode. I just love that God is blessing this place so much."

Faith-based service holds incredible appeal for the next generation of believers. In an e-mail poll of the campus chaplains at evangelical Christian colleges, fifteen of seventeen respondents said they had seen a significant rise in student interest in service projects and mission trips in recent years.[8] Short-term mission trips are particularly popular among today's teenagers and young adults: the number of people taking them has increased exponentially, from about 25,000 in 1979 to 120,000 in 1989. By 1995, the number of short-term missionaries had swelled to 200,000.[9] Faith communities that emphasize service and challenge young adults to express their faith in action are also experiencing rapid growth.

The Kairos ministry at The Falls Church (Episcopal) in Falls Church, Virginia, has seen its membership mushroom since its start with about two dozen young adults in 1996. The evangelical Christian fellowship emphasizes community, spiritual growth, and outreach to the nearby city of Washington, D.C. Kairos now attracts between 125 and 180 young professionals from across the Washington metro area to its Sunday night worship services—such a high turnout that the group had to move from the church's multipurpose room to its main sanctuary to accommodate the crowds.

Lauren Noyes, who has belonged to Kairos since its beginning, credits the group's service-centered ministry for its success. While other young adult groups often cater to the comfort of members, Kairos pushes young adults to look beyond themselves to the needs of others—an approach that appeals to idealistic young Christians who live in and around the nation's capital.

"It's challenging," said Noyes, a legislative director in her late twenties. "It's not just an insular group. It's a group that looks outward. People find that attractive. There's something very different about this group."

Another reason Noyes likes Kairos: it's not a couples club or a singles scene. It's a community of young Christians who are serious about living out their faith. The sermons delivered by founding pastor Bill Haley confront listeners with the demands of Christianity, and group events revolve more around corporate prayer and voluntarism than mingling and socializing. For Christians like Noyes, the group's clarity of purpose makes all the difference.

"People are tired of homogenous, fluffy groups," Noyes said.

The young-adult groups at some megachurches stress socializing over service and spiritual growth. They may draw larger crowds, Noyes said, but groups like Kairos at The Falls Church ultimately bear more fruit.

"If there's no depth going with those numbers, then I don't think they're successful. I don't know if Kairos is ever going to be a megachurch kind of group. I'm not sure that it should be. It's up to God."

Despite its relatively small size, the impact of Kairos and its outreach-oriented ministry is acutely felt in the southeast section of Washington known as Anacostia. At the Little White House, a home base for Christian outreach to the area, African American children and their parents frequently gather together with the mostly white, college-educated Kairos crowd for events and activities. On a crisp, sunny Saturday afternoon in October 2000, the group united for a fall festival that featured face painting, bobbing for apples, and oodles of Halloween candy.

At the picturesque house where they had gathered for the party, children and teenagers streaked through the yard, screaming and reeling from their sugar-induced energy spurts. Close on their heels were men and women in their twenties and thirties. Some wore Virginia Tech or Duke sweatshirts. Others wore outlandish Halloween costumes or T-shirts that had been soaked by water balloons that had been lobbed at them during earlier party games. Toddlers clung to their costumed mothers, older children showed off their carved pumpkins, and the Kairos young adults moved easily among them, hugging parents, painting the faces of children, and operating games to entertain the crowd.

Though only twelve miles separate Anacostia from Falls Church, the two communities are worlds apart. Anacostia is one of Washington's poorest neighborhoods, with an average income that hovers around $17,000.[10] Falls Church is the nation's sixth richest, with a median household income of $80,600.[11]

The ease with which the crowd mixed—across lines of race, class, age, and education—grew out of an intense, consistent effort by Kairos leaders to form bridges between these two communities and build life-changing, Christ-centered relationships. Several of the young Kairos members in the crowd have moved from their comfortable suburban addresses in places like Annapolis to Anacostia so they could interact more often with these children. One Kairos member, a thirty-two-year-old single woman who lives in Arlington, quit her job in July 2000 so she could devote herself full-time to caring for three young children from southeast D.C. whose single mother is in a drug rehabilitation program. To survive, she has relied on support from Kairos members, who helped raise funds to pay for the children's care.

"It will be hard to come into Kairos and not be challenged to give your life away," said Haley, the group's thirty-two-year-old pastor, who chose the Greek word *kairos* for the group's name because it means "the right time for action, a critical moment."

Haley is among those who moved to Anacostia. He now lives in the predominantly immigrant neighborhood of Adams Morgan in Washington, near the homeless medical facility where his wife works.

"Kairos is trying to lead people into vibrant relationship with God, to true community that leads to compelling witness and tangible action. There's a lot of pain in the world, and that's exactly why Christians are called Christians—so that we can follow Christ and meet that pain."

The Challenge of Intimacy

The paradox of finding peace in the midst of pain also applies to the challenges of life in Christian community. When young adults embrace that life—whether in the context of a religious order, a lay communal house, or a church-based fellowship group—they encounter unexpected struggles that can lead to unprecedented personal growth.

Max Finberg, a twentysomething native of upstate New York, had always been a loner in his Christian journey. Finberg's father was Jewish and his mother came from a Protestant family, but they raised him without any religion. While traveling through Israel with his Christian uncle during high school, Finberg decided there must be a God.

So he came home and read the Bible from cover to cover. His reading convinced him that Jesus was the Messiah, yet Finberg had no desire to attend church or embrace organized religion. During his college years at Tufts University, he began to seek out opportunities for Christian fellowship. But he did not experience intimate Christian community until he moved to Washington, D.C., after college to work on Capitol Hill.

Finberg's first experience of Christian community life happened in a house in Arlington where he lived for two years. Between eight and eighteen men lived there at any given time, sharing meals, playing sports, and studying Scripture together. Some were fresh out of college; some were fresh out of failed marriages. From that group, Finberg learned about the value of fellowship with other believers. And he learned about himself.

"I've always been full of pride, and I have a huge ego that bleeds over into arrogance," said Finberg, who works as a legislative assistant for Representative Tony Hall of Ohio. "What community offered was people who were willing to tell me that—and I could not just walk away. My sins and my ugliness were exposed, and I was forced to deal with that."

Eventually, the insights Finberg gained from living in close quarters with other Christians spurred him to take a bolder step. Finberg wanted to escape his "Christian ghetto" in Arlington and live out his conviction about the importance of achieving racial reconciliation through Christian community. So in the summer of 1994, he and an African American friend formed a mixed-race community in the historically black Shaw neighborhood of northwest Washington. Five core members moved in. Two were white; three were black. Two were male; three were female. Their occupations ranged from student to single mother to missionary. Spouses later joined the community as well.

"I knew the value of community, and I wanted to be for real about bridging the racial divide, and the gender divide," said Finberg, who joined an African American church in the neighborhood. "It put meat and feeling and experience to my ideals and beliefs. Being a privileged white male, I had to deal with that in a context that wouldn't have happened otherwise."

Living with people so different from himself forced Finberg to confront his "subconscious racist tendencies," his eagerness to argue others into doing things his way, and the natural tensions of living in a coed community. Now, Finberg said, the differences of race, gender, and class that divide so many Christians are ones he has tackled up close, at home. And the struggles that arose with his housemates have refined him as a Christian.

"A lot of my edges have been hacked away, filed away, worn away," he said. "I've had to change. They wouldn't live with me otherwise."

The prospect of living in an intentional, intimate Christian community appeals to many young believers. Veterans of such experiences say community life is tough and demanding. But most also argue that it's the surest way to practice the Christian ideals of loving one's neighbor and forgiving one's enemies.

For Andrew Witmer, the most instructive aspects of community life are the ones he never sought. Witmer graduated in 1998 from Taylor University, a Christian college in Indiana. After working in Charlottesville, Virginia, for a few years, he moved to Washington, D.C., and joined Jonathan House, an informal community of young Christian men who live together in a row house near Capitol Hill. Witmer arrived with vague intentions of making new friends and growing closer to God. He soon learned that sharing living quarters, meals, chores, and prayers with eight to fifteen housemates he had not handpicked demanded much more than he had expected.

"When you're living with that many guys in a limited space, there are stressors," Witmer said. "If you're a neat person, and you like order, you're going to be frustrated every day."

In those frustrations—a housemate's dirty dishes that demand washing, for instance, or a fight that requires forgiveness—Witmer found ways to imitate Jesus.

"I've had a lot of opportunities for servanthood. There's always a chance to do something for someone else," said Witmer, a Baptist who took on the job of structuring the house's weekly Bible-study and faith-sharing sessions. "In this place, you are placed in relationships with people that you might not seek out otherwise. I didn't really want the confrontation and the messiness, to be honest. It just happened that way."

Though Jonathan House is not utopia, Witmer said, it's a Christian community that has helped him grow.

"I'm learning about myself," he said. "It's messy. God uses that. A lot of the good things that happen here happen through God's grace."

Reliance on God's grace underlies the Jonathan House philosophy. The men who live there make a one-year commitment to stay. They agree to the house's eight-part covenant, which stipulates that they devote themselves to daily prayer and reading of Scripture, seek immediate reconciliation after a quarrel, and participate in house meetings, retreats, and workdays. They take turns cooking, frequently welcome new arrivals to Washington who need a place to sleep, and frown upon drunkenness. Witmer and his housemates know that outsiders may consider the demands of such a community life too strict and the challenge of living in close quarters with roommates they did not choose too unsettling. But for the men of Jonathan House, the trials of living in an intimate Christian community are what make it worthwhile.

Chris Socha, a twenty-four-year-old legislative correspondent and Jonathan House resident, said people in Washington tend to have many acquaintances and few friends. His relationships at Jonathan House may be more demanding than his interactions with colleagues on Capitol Hill, but they are also more rewarding. Socha said his housemates serve as "mirrors" to show him who he really is, faults and all.

"It's not a comfortable place to live, necessarily," he said. "But as Christians, it's imperative not to be comfortable with the status quo."

The discomfort of adjusting to a faith community is intensified for young Christians entering the priesthood or religious life. Not only must these young adults endure the typical trials of communal life—personality conflicts, messy housemates, demanding new rules and routines—they also must grapple with their own fears about committing the rest of their lives to a religious community.

Fr. Conrad Osterhout, who directs novices for the Franciscan Friars of the Renewal, sees young men enter his order brimming with postconversion zeal and a desire to make rapid spiritual strides. But settling into the routine of religious life and spending fifteen months with the same group of fellow novices often tempers that enthusiasm.

"Human relationships are messy, and we have that," said Osterhout, smiling as he surveyed a sea of gray robes in the kitchen of the Bronx friary where the novices had gathered one afternoon in 2001. "Imagine living with fifteen guys. It's not a frat house, and yet they're all guys."

The inevitable conflicts of community life can test the resolve of a novice. Many doubt their vocations, and some decide against their initial decision for religious life.

"Novitiate begins," Osterhout said, "when the first man leaves. That shakes them all. They came here to give their whole lives. They didn't come to consider leaving."

Around the time they profess their first set of vows, Osterhout said, "they come to a reckoning."

The men face the prospect of giving themselves totally to God and to the community for a lifetime. They confront the realities of lifelong celibacy and separation from family.

"Both extremes are there, in terms of breakdown and total commitment," Osterhout said, of that reckoning time.

Those who endure past those doubts—thanks in large part to their reliance on the sacrament of reconciliation, which allows them to regularly confess the mistakes they make in communal life—grow in compassion for themselves and others.

"They learn that one can be totally given and yet struggle, and that one can find forgiveness," Osterhout said. They also learn that "when you settle down to commitment, you'd better prepare yourself for the trial."

The challenge of intimacy extends beyond communal houses and religious orders. Young Christians seeking spiritual growth and support often gravitate to small groups run by churches and parachurch organizations. Those accountability groups—which regularly convene clusters of believers for Bible study, prayer, and mutual encouragement—have particularly flourished in nondenominational evangelical churches like Willow Creek Community Church, a nationally renowned megachurch in the Chicago suburbs that has about seventeen thousand people enrolled in its small groups.[12] Those groups also have sprouted from movements like the Promise Keepers, which encourages small clusters of men to meet regularly for fellowship so they can sustain the fervor ignited by such larger gatherings as the 1997 rally that drew an estimated one million men to Washington, D.C.[13]

The intimacy and honesty of a small-group meeting at New York City's Redeemer Presbyterian drew Pamela Brown-Peterside into that church in 1997. The thirtysomething research scientist had been shopping for a church since she recommitted her life to Christ in 1994. The first time she visited Redeemer, the service did not particularly move her. But the class she attended afterward about women and body image—one of many offered by Redeemer's School of Christian Community—indicated that this might be a church where she could grow.

Brown-Peterside recalled one woman who poured out her story of a lifelong struggle with eating habits and weight. The woman told the others that she was learning to love herself thanks to the love that God had given her. Though Brown-Peterside had not struggled with those issues, she found herself captivated by the honesty of the women assembled there.

"I was very touched by her story and her openness," said Brown-Peterside, a Nigerian native who later joined the church and found her small-group home in Redeemer's Racial Unity Ministry.

The Racial Unity Ministry group that she joined consisted of nearly a dozen Christians from ethnically and racially diverse backgrounds who came together to live out the gospel by celebrating their diversity and sharing their faith. Group members gathered regularly to study the Bible, cultivate community, and support each other. Over time, Brown-Peterside learned to let down her guard and share herself with people whose fellowship could bring her closer to Christ.

"It really challenged me to be as transparent as possible," said Brown-Peterside. "I learned that when we're really convinced of who God is, we can be totally honest and totally open about who we are."

Reaching Out with the Gospel

Once young adults experience fellowship and grace through Christianity, they want to share it with others. To do so, they seek the support of faith communities that are committed to evangelization and willing to dialogue with secular culture.

At All Angels' Church on the Upper West Side of Manhattan, a throng of twenty- and thirtysomething worshipers packs the upstairs sanctuary each Sunday. Many in the crowd are artists, writers, musicians, or actors. They wear everything from suits and ties to faded jeans and funky earrings. They are white, black, Asian, Hispanic. The rector is Indian. They are united by love for the Episcopalian liturgy, the contemporary music, and the theologically orthodox sermons delivered by their affable rector, who has a knack for learning their names. After swaying to the drumbeat of praise songs at the end of the service one Sunday in January 2001, they swarmed together for conversation. Many filtered downstairs for University Forum, a church-sponsored assembly that brings black-clad young artists, students, and professionals together to discuss the role of Christianity in today's culture. On this day, a professor from a nearby music school was leading a discussion about the integration of Christian principles in musical performance.

These gatherings give members of All Angels' a chance to think about how the creed they recite in church impacts the rest of their lives and the lives of those around them. At a similar conclave in Chicago's Hyde Park neighborhood in October 2000, about two dozen young Christians in their twenties and thirties met for a potluck dinner and discussion at the Disciples Divinity House of the University of Chicago. The participants came from evangelical fellowships, Orthodox churches, and Catholic parishes to talk about the most recent issue of *re:generation quarterly,* an ecumenical magazine for young orthodox Christians that organizes discussion groups in twenty-five cities. They laughed and argued, prayed and ate for several hours, swapping conversion stories and confessing faults. Many in the crowd of bright, articulate Chicago-area students and professionals had never met before that night. But the group quickly united around *RQ*'s tagline mission of "community transforming culture."

Kara Kirby, who grew up Southern Baptist, attended the meeting with her husband. She told the group about her desire to settle in a less insular place than the Christian enclave in Austin, Texas, where she lived before moving to Hyde Park.

"We were exactly like everybody else we knew," she told the crop of fellow Christians, several of whom were nodding in recognition. "We don't know any non-Christians—and that's tragic."

If Christians stick together too much and fail to interact with the broader culture and nonbelievers, Kirby asked the group, "are we actually being salt to the community?"

RQ editor Andy Crouch believes discussions like the one that took place in Hyde Park particularly appeal to young evangelical Christians who grew up in churches and homes that stressed detachment from the broader culture. Now those Christians want to bring their faith into the secular world where they live and work, with the help of peer faith communities that share their vision.

"Evangelicalism has tended to try to create its own culture rather than engaging the wider culture," said Crouch.

Adrian Walker, a thirty-two-year-old Catholic who teaches at the John Paul II Institute for Studies on Marriage and Family in Washington, D.C., recognizes the concern about integrating faith and culture among his Catholic graduate students. Though many have had potent conversion experiences that have pushed them to reject the values of the secular culture, they still must live in the wider world and, therefore, find a way to navigate it.

"Whether or not they're aware of it, integration is a problem for everyone," Walker said.

Once someone embraces orthodox Christianity and its philosophical implications, he said, "there is some inchoate sense that all of this needs to have some cultural form."

Integrating faith into daily life and sharing that faith with others takes tenacity—and assistance. In a pluralistic culture where all belief systems demand respect but none takes precedence, young orthodox Christians often gravitate to faith communities that send a clear message about what they believe. Campus fellowships with a blunt evangelical bent consistently attract more members than mainline groups that lack a distinct identity or hesitate to proclaim the universality of the gospel message. Even in Catholic circles, young adults increasingly are joining the fellowships and faith communities that unabashedly celebrate the particulars of the Catholic faith and encourage their members to proudly proclaim their beliefs.

In a suburb on the western edge of St. Louis, a cohort of young Catholics gathers each month for eucharistic adoration, confession, and charismatic praise-and-worship sessions. The group, known as the House of Prayer, is run by a handful of young adults brimming with enthusiasm for Catholicism and the desire to convert their peers. Attendance at meetings sometimes hovers around a hundred, and postmeeting conversations routinely include news of the latest conversion to Catholicism or vocation to the priesthood. Participants in the group also lead door-to-door evangelization blitzes and youth ministry events intended to invigorate the faith of Catholic teenagers.

William Portier, a professor at Mount St. Mary's College, said the popularity of traditional Catholic devotions and the willingness of today's young adults to proclaim their faith is "part of this evangelical culture of witness."

The Catholic subculture that allowed children to unquestioningly inherit the religion of their parents has dissolved in postmodern America, he said. Today's young Catholics must *choose* their religion and defend it confidently, with the help of other believers who share their convictions.

"Without any subculture to bond you to the church," Portier said, "religion—to survive—must be evangelical."

The passion for evangelization sometimes leads young adults into religious life. Overflowing with gratitude for their own experiences of God, some young Christians decide to spend their lives introducing others to Christ.

Michelle Hill, the chemical engineer who discerned a vocation to consecrated life with Regnum Christi, had been seeking a faith community that shared her sense of urgency about making disciples of all nations. She found kindred spirits among the consecrated women of Regnum Christi, who promise to live in poverty, chastity, and obedience so they can more completely devote their lives to God's service. For Hill, who reflected on her vocation during an interview at her Rhode Island motherhouse, those sacrifices—of lifelong celibacy and obedience to superiors—pale in comparison to what's at stake.

"When you know that six billion people are called to the exact same happiness you are," Hill said, her brown eyes widening as she leaned forward in her chair, "how can you possibly sit there and do something halfway?"

The Real Life of Christian Community

Whether embracing Christian community in the form of religious life, church fellowship groups, or informal lay alliances, today's young adults are attracted to groups that allow them to grow and serve. The celebrated idealism of youth—and the sacrifices it inspires—still endures today, despite cultural messages to the contrary. And the young orthodox Christians who defy those messages, by surrendering their lives for a cause that many of their parents and peers consider passé, still flock to the faith communities that challenge them to take a countercultural stand for Christ.

Laven, the soft-spoken young nun who helps direct novices in her California-based Carmelite convent, knows that a life of prayer and sacrifice often makes little sense to outsiders. She has heard the criticism that young adults who embrace life in orthodox faith communities are running away from the world and missing out on the sensual delights and material comforts of secular culture. But the way she sees it, young adults like her—who spend their lives for the sake of the gospel—are the lucky ones.

"We're living life to the fullest," said Laven while sitting in a rose garden behind the convent walls in Alhambra.

"This is not just quasi life or a false life. This is life. This is real life. Everything I do is an act of worship—everything. It's a preparation for what we're going to be doing for all eternity."

Laven paused, her eyes welling up with tears.

"You can't get much better than that."

5

SEXUALITY AND FAMILY

Blessed are the pure in heart, for they shall see God.

MATTHEW 5:8

The O'Hare Marriott ballroom in Chicago glittered with starry tiaras, sequined evening gowns, and thousand-watt runway smiles. Nearly a dozen beauty queens from seven states had gathered for a banquet on this October night, each adorned in movie-star makeup and presiding over her own table of admirers. They spent the dinner making pleasant conversation about their formative years and future hopes. Then one by one, they strode into the spotlight. Oozing glamour and poise, the young women celebrated the cause that united them: a commitment to sexual abstinence before marriage. They have proclaimed it from the rooftops—and the runways.

"The new sexual revolution is not being led by adults, but by young people," roared Mary-Louise Kurey, Miss Wisconsin 1999, top-ten finalist for Miss America, and author of a book about abstinence. "We are seeing a complete turnaround in young attitudes toward sex and relationships."

Kurey emceed this program for educators, which was sponsored by Project Reality—an Illinois-based abstinence group—and featured singing, poetry readings, and rousing faith-based personal testimonies like Kurey's.

"I knew that God was calling me to a life of chastity, as he calls each of us to chastity, purity," said Kurey, who wore a sleeveless black gown that matched her coal-black bob. "You know what? I'm twenty-six years old, and I'm a virgin. It's the best choice I ever made."

Kurey's choice has cost her. She has taken flak from some pageant directors who wanted her to tone down her abstinence platform to make it more politically palatable. Kurey, a Catholic, also has endured ridicule on national television's *Politically Incorrect,* a caustic talk show where she and her message of sexual purity are aberrations. Through all the derision and disbelief, Kurey has continued to share the message she believes today's young adults are dying to hear.

So has Jade Smalls, Miss Illinois 1999 and first runner-up to Miss America 2000. Smalls said she has seen teenagers despair when the bonds created by sexual intimacy are severed, and that led her to pair her faith-based abstinence message with an anti-suicide platform when she was Miss Illinois.

"Talk about it," said Smalls, the Christian daughter of a civil rights activist. "Because the kids are listening. The kids want to hear it because nobody else is saying it to them."

Again and again throughout the evening, beaming beauty queens bore witness to the benefits of sexual self-control and the faith-based rationale for their restraint. One evangelical Christian talked about her surprise at being named homecoming queen at her hard-partying college campus even though she abstains from sex, drinking, and smoking. She took the honor as a sign that fellow students admired her values. Another told the audience about the day that she accompanied a sexually active friend to the doctor and wound up ushering the wailing girl out of the office. Her friend was suffering from herpes and aching remorse. Virgins, the beauty queen explained, have no such regrets.

The evening's crescendo came when Miss Black Cincinnati, Lisa Miree, marched to the podium. Sporting a tiara atop her curly hair that seemed too delicate for her fiery prose, Miree bellowed out an original poem about the joys and struggles of being "Virginime"—a woman saving sex for marriage.

Miree, who later became Miss Black USA 2001, wagged her finger at suitors who might want to "defile" her. Gaining momentum as she reached her finale, Miree proclaimed that to be a virgin is to be carefree.

The audience rose and gave Miree a standing ovation.

In the back of the ballroom, Sue Davids smiled.

"The pendulum swings," said the Illinois high school teacher.

Whereas students thirty years ago fought for sexual liberation, Davids said, students today have seen the dark side of free love, and they want stability. She sees them responding to the Christian message of sexual purity, as articulated by the Baptist True Love Waits campaign and abstinence educators like herself. Davids recently asked her class, "Who wants to be married?" To her surprise, every hand shot up.

"That, to me, was stunning," Davids said, as she surveyed a ballroom brimming with young adults committed to the conventional values largely rejected by the baby boomers who preceded them. "Deep down, these kids want a committed relationship."

The Counterrevolution

Free love and casual sex were novel concepts to the young sexual revolutionaries of the 1960s and 1970s. But to many of their children, committed relationships—not casual hookups—are the novelty. Since 1970, more than one million American children a year have watched their parents split up, and one in every four Americans ages eighteen to forty-four is an adult child of divorce.[1] Premarital sex among teenagers, once considered taboo, has gained widespread acceptance since the advent of the sexual revolution. According to a study by the National Center on Addiction and Substance Abuse at Columbia University, less than 5 percent of fifteen-year-old girls and 20 percent of fifteen-year-old boys had engaged in sexual intercourse in the early 1970s. By 1997, that number had jumped to 38 percent of girls and 45 percent of boys.[2]

Teenagers of the 1960s and 1970s fought against the sexual "hang-ups" of their more conservative elders, and today's teenagers and young adults have reaped the results of that fight: they get free condoms at school and sex-saturated teen dramas on prime-time television. In most high schools and colleges today, it's the sexually inexperienced students, not the promiscuous ones, who are bucking the establishment—one that largely considers chastity a lost cause.

As the pendulum swings, a growing number of young adults are rebelling against their elders by embracing tradition in the way they dress, date, marry, and mate. Repulsed by the sexual license, moral confusion, and social chaos they see around them, these young adults are embracing conventional morality and an orthodox faith that gives meaning to their countercultural choices.

Consider these indicators: The 1998 UCLA survey of college freshmen found approval of promiscuity at a twenty-five-year low. In 1998, 39.6 percent of students said casual sex was acceptable, down from a record high of 51.9 percent in 1987. The same survey showed student support for legal abortion dropping for the sixth straight year, from 64.9 percent in 1990 to 50.9 percent in 1998.[3]

Data from the National Center for Health Statistics suggests that those attitudes may mirror new behavior: a study found that the number of high school boys who claimed to have had sexual intercourse at least once dropped from 61 percent to 49 percent between 1990 and 1997.[4] During roughly the same years, the Centers for Disease Control and Prevention found that the percentage of sexually active high school students aged fifteen to nineteen had fallen from 54 percent to 48 percent.[5]

In The Case for Marriage, authors Linda Waite and Maggie Gallagher cited a 1997 survey in which 94 percent of college freshmen "said they personally hoped to get married." The authors noted that more than 70 percent of young adults believe that children are better off with both parents; two-thirds said that children "develop permanent emotional problems" as a result of divorce; and 76 percent of teenagers said that divorce laws should be stiffer.[6]

A 1990 study of students who are now in their midtwenties, conducted by the University of Michigan's Institute for Social Research, found that a good marriage and family life ranked as a primary goal for 70 percent of students. Only 29 percent gave wealth the same ranking. The study also found that only 20 percent of students found it acceptable for a husband and wife to work full-time while caring for preschool-age children.[7] A survey in 2000 by the nonpartisan policy group Public Agenda uncovered similar attitudes: 80 percent of young mothers ages eighteen to twenty-nine said they would rather be at home than work full-time.

These attitudes are also visible in cultural trends, such as the popularity of books promoting old-fashioned courtship rituals, treatises on modesty, and Jane Austen novels and movies. In *The Rules: Time-tested Secrets for Capturing the Heart of Mr. Right,* Ellen Fein and Sherrie Schneider instruct postmodern single women in the art of playing hard to get. The book—which advises women to forgo casual sex and let men take the lead in romance—has sold two million copies since its 1995 debut and has sparked two sequels.[8] Joshua Harris, a homeschooled evangelical Christian who counsels his readers to reject dating in favor of platonic friendships and marriage-minded courtship rites, has sold nearly a million copies of his 1997 book, *I Kissed Dating Goodbye.* He, too, answered young fans' demands for a sequel.[9] And Wendy Shalit, who wrote *A Return to Modesty: Discovering the Lost Virtue* in 1999 at the tender age of twenty-three, created a national furor among feminists when she called for a sexual counterrevolution, led by young women insisting on sex-free dates, single-sex dorms, and old-fashioned, chivalrous suitors.[10]

Like the retro trend of swing dancing, covenant marriages and courtship rituals have taken off, as have virginity pledges. Since 1993, more than half a million young adults have promised to abstain from premarital sex through the True Love Waits campaign.

Much of the backlash against the sexual revolution has a distinctly religious character. A growing number of young evangelical Christians and conservative Catholics are embracing the concept of courtship—the conventional way of wooing that follows a strict protocol and aims toward marriage. The Promise Keepers movement has attracted more than 3.5 million men to ninety-eight stadium and arena conferences with its conservative Christian message of marital fidelity and moral integrity. Another religious group known for its conservative sexual morality and concomitant appeal to the young is the Mormons, who have watched their membership multiply more than tenfold since World War II.[11] Many young Jews also are joining the retro-revolution, by adopting the matchmaking and modesty mores of Orthodox Judaism, much to the chagrin—and confusion—of their liberal, secular parents.

Amy Kass, a literature professor at the University of Chicago, teaches a popular course on courtship with her husband of nearly forty years, University of Chicago bioethicist and humanities professor Dr. Leon Kass. The coursework revolves around readings from the courtship anthology they edited together, *Wing to Wing, Oar to Oar.*

Amy Kass said she sees her students becoming disillusioned with the moral relativism and promiscuity that pervade their campus and culture.

"There are so many young women who have had the experience of sleeping with someone only to discover that *that's* what he was interested in, not them. The purchase of sexual favors for attention—it just doesn't work. And they've been burned too many times."

She has been surprised by how warmly her ostensibly cynical students respond to the tales of conventional courtship they read in class. One selection, written by the sixteenth-century humanist Erasmus, recounted how a young woman refused the kiss of her beloved before marriage so that she could "deliver to you a virginity whole and unblemished." The Kasses expected their students to mock the passage and its antiquated mores. Instead, the students waxed poetic about the significance and implicit promise of a single kiss—not exactly the classroom comments the Kasses had expected to elicit from a crowd of postmodernists.

Amy Kass meets many students who fail to connect their desire for lasting love with their current dating habits, and she sees young adults so scarred by divorce that they doubt their capacity to build stable marriages. But she recognizes in her students an innate desire for intimacy and answers.

They want to know what it means to be married and why it matters if they sleep around, Kass said. "My trust is that it's only when people become really unhappy with their lives that they want to do something about it."

Against the Grain

For many young adults, the apex of unhappiness often follows a series of casual or failed sexual relationships. Reeling from the effects of a lover's rejection, an unplanned pregnancy, a sexually transmitted disease, or a nagging sense of emptiness despite frenetic sexual activity, they begin to examine their behavior and its consequences. They reconsider the moral messages delivered to them by parents, peers, and performers. And many find themselves captivated by the countercultural view of sex articulated by Christian orthodoxy.

Fr. Michael Scanlan, a Franciscan priest and former president of the Franciscan University of Steubenville, recalls giving a sermon to college students in the 1980s that boldly articulated church bans on everything from masturbation to premarital sex to contraception. Though he knew not many in the audience would disregard his advice, Scanlan laid down the law.

When he was finished, he said, "I expected silence. Instead, there was a standing ovation. Afterward, I asked them why. They said, 'Now we know. No one made it that clear before.'"

Of course, an attraction to moral absolutes does not guarantee conformity to them. And even if young adults observe traditional Christian embargoes on premarital sex, cohabitation, and childless marriages, they confront a culture that increasingly sides against them. The most recent national census found 72 percent more unmarried-partner households in 2000 than in 1990.[12] A survey of high school seniors in 1975 showed that 35 percent believed cohabitation before marriage was a "good idea"; two decades later, 59 percent agreed. The birth rate among unmarried thirtysomething women has climbed 15 percent since 1990, while the marriage rate among women has fallen one-third since 1970, according to the National Marriage Project at Rutgers University.[13] Married couples with children now constitute just over a third of the population, and they are outnumbered by married couples without children.[14] Over the last generation, the median age at which women marry has climbed to twenty-five from twenty, and among men it has risen to twenty-seven from twenty-two.[15]

Ryan and Emily Finnelly, an evangelical couple in their early twenties, know how it feels to buck cultural trends at their epicenter. The pair met at Trinity International University in Deerfield, Illinois, married after graduation, and moved to California to work in the entertainment industry. They soon learned that religious orthodoxy and conservative morality are rare in Hollywood.

Quite rare, in fact: a 1995 study comparing business, journalism, and Hollywood elites found that more than three out of every ten creators of television shows and movies identified with no particular religion, and Hollywood professionals were twice as likely as the other groups to embrace religions outside the Judeo-Christian tradition. Only one in four Hollywood elites said religion was important in life, and only one in five said they attended religious services at least monthly.[16]

As for sexual mores among their peers, Ryan Finnelly said, "Out here, no one even *thinks* about marriage."

His wife recalled a conversation she had at work with three colleagues, who were discussing marriage as if it were "a jail sentence." Though they knew she was married, none of them asked her opinion. Instead, they marveled that a middle-aged coworker had decided to take the plunge.

"We're just on a different plane," said Emily Finnelly. "It's kind of going against us, but we're trying to fight it."

Every so often, she catches glimpses of something other than disdain or disregard for her values. She recalled one conversation at her workplace about a Christian colleague who wears a gold ring to symbolize her commitment to remain sexually abstinent until marriage.

"It's astounding to them, truly astounding," Emily Finnelly said, of the surprise expressed by secular colleagues at the discipline that commitment entails. "Virginity is a huge issue to them. But what's amazing, what I was surprised by, is that they will openly admit that they admire that."

Another issue that divides young orthodox Christians from many of their peers is homosexuality. Like most young Americans, the majority of these believers say that gays and lesbians have an inherent right to be treated as equals and that they should not be mistreated or looked down upon because of their sexual orientation. At the same time, most of these young believers say that the Bible's exhortations against homosexual sexual relations are clear and irrefutable. So they overwhelmingly reject the legitimacy of same-sex marriages, noncelibate homosexual clergy, and public policies that confer on gay and lesbian relationships the same benefits afforded heterosexual marriage.

The majority of these young believers who reject gay rights describe their views as a sort of "tough love" approach to the question of homosexuality. They believe that God's plan for sexuality does not include homosexual relationships and that, while gays and lesbians may be oriented toward same-sex attractions against their will, homosexual activity ultimately will not make them happy or lead them closer to God because it is inherently sinful. While more liberal Christians contend for formal recognition of homosexual relationships and for the ordination of noncelibate homosexual clergy, these young adults believe instead that Christians must challenge gays and lesbians to live chastely. When it comes to homosexual sexual activity, they say, a follower of Christ must "love the sinner, but hate the sin."

Not all reject the gay rights platform with ease or certainty, and many struggle to reconcile their convictions with their desire to avoid offending gays and lesbians. They are painfully aware that their opposition is widely regarded as reactionary and intolerant.

For Emily Finnelly, the struggle to oppose homosexual sexual activity without alienating nonbelievers who are gay or lesbian is one that she has faced head-on in Hollywood. When one gay coworker asked her opinion on the matter, she had a frank conversation with him about her belief that the Bible forbids it. Afterward, she asked him if he was mad at her. He said no, that he simply wanted to know what she thought.

"I've spoken the truth as I understand it," said Finnelly, who saw the conversation as an opportunity to witness to her faith and values. "No lines of communication have been closed."

The Challenge of Chastity

In April 2001, a dozen adults, one toddler, and an infant squeezed into a comfortably cluttered living room on the outskirts of Harvard's campus, freshly fed and ready to dive into the evening's discussion. The handsome Asian man scheduled to lead it passed around typed sheets of paper titled "Case Study: Loneliness/Relationships." He stared silently at his own copy for a few moments, the embarrassment evident on his face. Then he plunged in.

"There's just that loneliness of wanting to be with someone," said the man, who sat cross-legged on a futon, wearing a blue button-down oxford and a bashful smile. "I honestly don't know if you guys can relate to this feeling."

If anyone could relate, it seems, it would be the people in this group. All were recent Harvard graduates and serious Christians. Most, like the young man, were unusually attractive and successful— the sort of twentysomething achievers their peers emulate. Twice a month, they gathered in the Cambridge home of Andy Crouch, their former InterVarsity campus minister, and his family. They took turns presenting case studies that documented their struggles to take the faith they cultivated in college into the real world.

Tonight, the discussion centered on relationships with the opposite sex. The big issues, for this group, are settled. Premarital sex is out of the question. So is seriously dating a non-Christian, someone they would never consider marrying. But how about flirting with non-Christians? Or stringing acquaintances along for an ego boost and reveling in their flattery? What about fantasizing about an unknown future spouse—is that harmless, or does it distract from doing God's will here and now? Scratch the surface of Christian sexual morality and, as these evangelicals discovered, it demands a lot more than just saying no.

The evening's presenter kicked off the conversation by explaining his dilemma. In college, he enjoyed plenty of female attention. But the working world offers him fewer interactions with women and fewer opportunities to date Christians. So he seeks affirmation from women whenever he can while worrying that his insatiable appetite for their attention is ungodly.

After he spoke, the group sat in silence for a few moments.

"There is some sort of fun to experiencing some sexual tension," said a young woman with a brown bob.

Laughter cut through the room, then another young man chimed in.

"The game is fun," he agreed. "It just doesn't seem honest about what you want and who you are."

Sometimes, the second man said, he struggles with the same unquenchable desire for attention. He finds himself sitting on the T, Boston's subway system, and wondering if the woman sitting nearby finds him attractive. It's easy to slip into a superficial mind-set, he said, and become consumed by concerns about your sexual appeal.

When that happens, he said, "I'm not even allowing my deep values to come forward. It's like I'm suppressing them."

An African American man with chiseled features nodded his head. In the hospital where he works, he had overheard a woman talking about his good looks. He found himself swaggering with satisfaction afterward.

"I'm turning somebody's head—that's pretty cool," he said. "But what does it mean? That's totally hollow."

The woman with the brown bob spoke up. She told the group how a male friend had confessed that he felt tempted to use her because she was attracted to him.

"That was just the ugliest thing anyone had ever said to me," she murmured. "If we are still using people to be sexually affirmed, then we do not fully hate that sin."

As the conversation proceeded, group members confessed their fears, their hidden vanity, and the way they deal with each. One explained how she conquered some of her compulsive flirting by cultivating more same-sex friendships. Another talked about the importance of waiting for the right person—and spending free time in the interim improving herself rather than chasing after flattery or flings. Crouch, the former InterVarsity campus leader who brought the graduates together, reminded them to keep their future spouses in mind when striving for purity and to keep one another accountable.

"Remind one another of your future," Crouch said as he locked eyes with his listeners. "Chances are very good you will find someone. You don't have these longings for no reason. It's going to happen someday. It's worth ordering your life around that."

When it comes to sexuality, young orthodox Christians order their lives in a drastically different way than their secular peers. Today's young Americans are renowned for their fear of divorce, cynicism about the sexual revolution, and longing for lasting love. But those who approach sexual morality from an orthodox Christian perspective are distinguished by countercultural attitudes that flout conventional wisdom—and sometimes persuade peers to do the same.

Heather Gallagher, a slim, pretty woman in her midtwenties, always believed sex should be saved for marriage. College convinced her to share that message with others.

Gallagher, who grew up in a suburb of St. Louis, lived in a sorority house while attending Butler University, a Christian college in Indianapolis. That's where she first noticed the difference between the chaste romances of a few sorority sisters and the sexual relationships of so many others.

"The relationships I knew where [the couples] were choosing chastity were strong, healthy relationships that were obviously different from the others," said Gallagher, a Catholic who started giving talks to teenagers about chastity during college. "I saw an element of respect in the chaste relationships. Then I turned around and saw a lot of girls that were really shallow in my sorority, and they were getting sex every weekend. And I was like, How does this interplay? I saw a lot of really good friends in my sorority who went through a lot of hard times, and they would turn to sex and relationships for love. I had a lot of friends in college who just had sex and didn't know why."

Christians like Gallagher like to stress the distinction between abstinence and chastity. Abstinence implies an avoidance of sexual intercourse, but chastity entails much more. It is a Christian virtue associated with purity of mind and body that can be practiced by the married and unmarried alike. Chaste people, in other words, must do more than save sex for marriage. They must also avoid dirty jokes, immodest dress, obscene language and entertainment, and sexual fantasies. They must strive to love others without using them for sexual satisfaction and to remain faithful to God and their current or future spouse in thought, word, and deed. It's a high bar for young Americans who are steeped in sexually explicit movies, music, and conversations.

"In a sorority house, you hear a lot of stuff," said Gallagher. "Girls telling me all these different things about sex, about that guy, this and that—a lot of it was just gross. I was like, I thought this was supposed to be special. We're throwing it around like it's nothing."

Back then, Gallagher said, she was too timid to defend chastity. But now she does—and that sometimes makes for stilted conversations with peers who swap dirty jokes and tales from the bedroom.

"I try not to get offended," Gallagher said, "but there's something inside of me that's offended. I don't really want to be listening to this. I don't want to be a part of this. I love the people, but it was really hard for me to sit around and listen to that when I'm trying to live a chaste life, I'm trying to have pure thoughts. It's so uncomfortable."

Gallagher now works full-time for the Archdiocese of St. Louis, giving chastity speeches and running retreats for teenagers and young adults. She tells audiences to preserve or reclaim their virginity, to scrutinize media messages that might lead them astray, and to pray for self-control. Since she often is talking to a crop of sexually active students, her message has the potential to tank. Teenagers sometimes fire off hostile questions and accuse her of naivete. Others applaud enthusiastically or commend her for sharing her personal testimony.

"A lot of people are just shocked that I'm still a virgin. They're like, 'What's wrong with you?' When they find out that there are no major problems in my life, that in itself is kind of a witness for God. I never say that I can do it on my own. It's always through God's help."

Chastity, said Gallagher, "is the answer to all of the questions and fears that young people have about themselves and relationships."

A *Los Angeles Times* article in 1994 spotlighted the enthusiasm for chastity among the young and the rise of virginity pledges. The article—which noted that True Love Waits organizers have filled sixty-three thousand requests from pastors and youth directors for their chastity curriculum—quoted a Los Angeles psychiatrist who said that chastity helps young Americans resist unwanted sexual pressure.

Sex frightens most teenagers, psychiatrist Mark Goulston told the *Los Angeles Times,* and chastity vows "give kids permission to be innocent."[17]

Chastity educator Jason Evert adopted the cause in college after seeing the pain and remorse that accompanied premature sexual activity as he conducted retreats, chatted with women friends, and counseled pregnant women outside abortion clinics. A twenty-five year old from Arizona, Evert now travels the nation talking to teenagers and young adults about chastity. He uses plenty of humor and tailors his message to the gender of his audience. If he is talking to men, he challenges them to live up to the tasks of remaining pure and protecting the purity of the women around them. With women, he emphasizes how precious they are in the eyes of God and how much God wants them to enjoy the lasting, pure love that blossoms from chastity. In Catholic settings, he quotes the Bible and Pope John Paul II's *Theology of the Body*. In public schools, he simply talks about the dignity of the human body.

"I don't take the fear approach and try to scare them," said Evert. "It's not about repression, but about romance without regret, the goodness that comes from knowing you're using sex according to God's plan."

Once, Evert prayed feverishly for an opportunity to address the students at an all-girls Catholic high school run by an order of nuns known for resisting male images of God and challenging church teachings against abortion and contraception. When he got his chance, Evert spoke to the school's 725 girls, emphasizing such traditional Catholic teachings as the image of God as Father and the intercessory power of the Blessed Virgin Mary. He walked through the school gym cradling a baby as he spoke, to drive home the image of a heavenly father who treasures his daughters. The message hit home.

"The girls just started crying and crying," Evert said.

After his speech, Evert said, the crowd swarmed around him. He doled out Miraculous Medals—small silver medals that bear an image of the Blessed Virgin and are revered by traditional Catholics—and allowed the girls to sign his Bible so he could remember to pray for them.

A few weeks later, Evert traveled to San Francisco to train ninety-one teenagers and young adults in the art of talking about chastity. "The young people are wanting a cause to make their own and to fight for," said Evert, who sees the crusade for chastity as countercultural enough to energize young adults. "They're saturated with sex and unhappy."

Conversion and Consuming Love

Sexuality often plays a central role in the conversion of young orthodox Christians. Some find themselves attracted to Christian orthodoxy because its strong sexual morality addresses their deepest concerns in a way that secular values do not. Others experience radical Christian conversions that force them to evaluate their sexual morality and bring their behavior in line with the creed they now confess. Most fall somewhere in between, finding themselves drawn to the idealism of traditional sexual morality while also unsure about their ability to live up to its daunting standards.

Miguel Buckenmeyer was raised in a Protestant home and attended Catholic schools, where he found himself drawn to the countercultural quality of conservative Christianity. After he broke up with his high school sweetheart in college, he and his best friend pledged on a Bible to shun premarital sex.

Buckenmeyer spent the next several years following the letter of that promise but not its spirit. He still "hooked up" with girls, though he did not sleep with them. He wrote commentaries for his college newspaper supporting conservative Christian causes like the fight against abortion. But his heart was not converted.

"We used to like to talk the talk but not walk the walk," said Buckenmeyer. "I really abused the gifts God has given me, all to the glory of Miguel. There wasn't anything compelling me, absolutely no introspection. I just acted. And the culture allows you to act like this."

In January 1998, Buckenmeyer ran into an ex-girlfriend at a Catholic Mass on the campus of Georgetown University, where he was attending graduate school. The encounter crushed him. She was with another man, and Buckenmeyer realized he wanted a woman like her—someone who loved goodness and God. As he fled the church in despair, Buckenmeyer realized he was not someone with those qualities. So how could he expect to find a woman who fit the bill?

Buckenmeyer made a resolution on the spot: From that day forward, he would attend daily Mass and confess his sins frequently. He would try to become the sort of Christian he wanted to marry. Buckenmeyer spent that spring in deep thought and prayer—about his sins, his parents' divorce, even his half-Spanish, half-German heritage. Through those periods of silent prayer, Buckenmeyer realized what it was he had been seeking all along.

"I'd been trying to fill myself with self-love," he said. "I was trying to find God in women and in relationships. I realized then that what I'd really been looking for was God."

After three months of soul-searching, Buckenmeyer found himself saturated with regret and despair. He could not study. He cried often in church after attending 8 A.M. Mass each day. One morning, an elderly man approached him and said gently, "God loves you." Buckenmeyer dismissed the platitude and returned to his mournful prayer: "Lord, whatever it is you want to show me, please tell me."

Each day for two weeks the man returned, always with the same message. One Sunday, Buckenmeyer hit bottom. He lay down at home and wept, overwhelmed by his hopelessness. Then he prayed.

"For the first time in my entire life, I said a Hail Mary of my own volition."

Suddenly, the old man's message came flooding back, as if God himself were speaking.

"It just dawned on me: 'I love you,'" said Buckenmeyer. "It's incredible. After three months of emptiness, I was just filled with hope."

Young orthodox Christians often refer to the inflow of an over-powering divine love when explaining their ability to embrace strict moral standards and forgo the affections of lovers who impede their relationship with God. They credit God's consuming love for freeing them from past sins, addictions, and compulsions. And they say that it is through God's love—not their own willpower—that they can reform their behavior and love others unselfishly.

Still, sticking to their convictions can be tough over the long haul, even after a powerful conversion experience. Anne Beaudry was a twenty-eight-year-old actress and fallen-away Catholic when she first felt the jolt of divine love. She was attending a charismatic conference at the Franciscan University of Steubenville with her family, utterly uninterested in the proceedings and still reeling from the recent suicide of a close friend.

"There was a part of me that was sorry that she beat me to it," said Beaudry. "I was cruising until I figured out a way to get off the bus."

At the conference, Beaudry heard Fr. Scanlan, the college president at the time, give a sermon about sin. One by one, she matched the sins on his list with her own deeds and noted indifferently that she had committed them all. The talk did not faze her—not yet.

"Then he gets into the 'God loves you' little speech," Beaudry recalled. "At that moment, something enveloped me. It was like something came from behind. It was pure love."

She started to weep. Sitting in a back row amid her astonished family, Beaudry felt overpowered by the cleansing racking sobs. She slipped away from the tent where Scanlan was speaking.

"Then there was like this, 'Oh shit, he's real,'" Beaudry said, recalling her thoughts as she stood outside the tent. "'So many things are going to have to change.' I was living a highly immoral life."

Beaudry's life did change—drastically. She canceled an audition in Canada because her only prepared piece was packed with French swear words that ridiculed the Eucharist and other elements of

Catholicism. She told her agent and colleagues about her conversion. She told her unmarried friends that they could no longer bring their lovers to sleep in her apartment. She abandoned her pro-choice stand on abortion and became pro-life. And she moved to Steubenville, Ohio—the site of her conversion—to immerse herself in classes about the faith. Eventually, Beaudry earned a master's degree in theology from Steubenville, taught theology at the school's Austrian campus, and studied for two years in Rome.

After several years of studying theology, Beaudry's zeal began to wane. Her theological questions had been answered. She no longer felt intellectually challenged. And she detected a discrepancy between the faith she confessed and the issues she faced in daily life.

"I knew a lot about God," Beaudry said. "But I didn't know *him*. It was becoming increasingly empty, reduced to a lot of Catholic busyness."

So Beaudry took a break. She moved to Canada and met a man who seemed to be everything the Catholic men she had met were not. He was simple, kind, happy—and uninterested in her faith. Beaudry asked God to change the situation if this man was not right for her. But she grew impatient, and her boyfriend wanted them to be living together. Within four months, she said, "we practically were."

"The day we started sleeping together is the day I went to war with God," said Beaudry. "I lost the faith."

Beaudry stopped believing in the Eucharist, in Christianity, in the changes she had made in her life up to that point. She told her Catholic friends to stay away if they intended to preach to her. It all seemed like a waste.

"When it snapped," said Beaudry, "it was fury. I was angry that I had invested that much time and was seeing no return on it. I was angry that God had picked me out of the lineup and wished he had left me alone."

Two months after Beaudry and her boyfriend started sleeping together, she realized the futility of the relationship and she ended it. But still she kept her distance from the church.

"I just couldn't stay [in the relationship]," she said. "That was too meaningless. But so was the church."

The connection between faith and sex is a powerful one. Pastors often say that transgressions of Christian sexual morality lead young believers away from the faith faster than any other moral lapses. Their explanation: sexual intercourse is an intimate, potent experience, and the desire for sexual activity often clouds moral judgment. Christians who engage in extramarital sex while at the same time professing to believe it is wrong often feel a tortuous sense of guilt and hypocrisy that eventually estranges them from the church.

Even for those who resist sexual temptations, the strain of sexual self-denial can lead to bitterness or doubts about God. Mary Beth Bonacci, a national chastity speaker and syndicated columnist, wrote about that phenomenon in a 2001 column.

"I've received numerous letters from single men and women who told me that they were taught to live chastely because, if they did, God would reward them with a loving husband or wife and a wonderful marriage," Bonacci wrote. "If they did their part, Christ would do his. Now it hasn't happened, and they're experiencing a faith crisis."

Bonacci said single Christians—encouraged, at times, by chastity educators eager to tout the practical benefits of saving sex for marriage—forget that "morality is not a quid pro quo arrangement."[18]

In Beaudry's case, the path back to Christian morality was a meandering one. After she left the church, she decided to test the unconditional love of God that she had heard so much about, the love that she felt so strongly that night, years ago, in the conference tent.

"I decided, 'I'm gonna just *be*,'" said Beaudry, explaining that she gave up trying to please God and live by his rules. "That's when the relationship really started to grow. By my doing nothing—just being—I got a stronger sense of his presence. Things would happen, and he was there."

Gradually, Beaudry found her way back to the church. She began to attend Mass and confess her sins to a priest. Finally, her belief in the Eucharist returned. This time, though, Beaudry knew she must rely on God's love—not her own strength—to keep her faithful to her convictions.

"It was a really hard time, but I was really blessed," said Beaudry, who is now a full-time actress working on a stand-up comedy routine that introduces audiences to the Christian virtues. "I had a lot of people who loved me."

Marriage and Mutual Support

Support from like-minded peers often helps young orthodox Christians sustain a conversion and adhere to Christianity's countercultural moral standards. A spouse can be the greatest help of all. Those seeking a marriage mate with similar values may congregate at church singles functions or turn to Christian dating services, but such venues can be disappointing for devout young adults. Many serious believers complain that church events can be as tacky as the bar scene, packed with nominal Christians more interested in securing their next date than glorifying God. The singles scene at churches often attracts not the most ardent young Christians but the most desperate. Because of this, many young orthodox Christians look elsewhere or plead for divine intervention.

Anthony Buono, a husband and father, remembers how it felt to wander through the singles scene as an orthodox Catholic committed to church teachings on sexuality.

"I just hated it," said Buono, who lives in Front Royal, Virginia. "It's very needle-in-the-haystack to find this level of Catholicism."

Buono eventually met his wife at a church function, but it was "a fluke thing." The struggle to find her made him wonder, *Is this how it has to be?* He knew many single Catholics who felt alone in their opposition to premarital sex and contraception and hopeless about finding spouses who shared their values. He wanted to heed the pope's call to help build strong Christian families in the new millennium.

So in May 1998, he launched Single Catholics Online—now known as Ave Maria Single Catholics Online since its purchase by billionaire Catholic Tom Monaghan. The Web site links orthodox Catholics to one another for a $60 fee. Before they can join, applicants must complete a questionnaire that gauges everything from their opinions on the authority of the pope to the frequency of their Mass attendance. A year and a half after its start, the site boasted 23 marriages, 24 engagements, and 78 serious relationships, with a membership of more than 2,700 that was growing at a rate of 250 members per month.

"We really tend to attract serious people," said Buono, who tries to keep recreational daters off his site. "We don't make any bones about it: We're a marriage service. There are people who are repelled by it, but we don't want them anyway."

For many young Christians, marriage is a primary means of spiritual support. Fr. David Burrell, a Holy Cross priest and professor at the University of Notre Dame, said many of his students are seeking romantic friendships rooted in faith that will lead to marriage and allow them to spend a lifetime growing together.

"They really are looking for an anchor," said Burrell. Students reared in a culture of divorce, he said, "are scared to death of that. They have this sense that our society is falling apart."

Todd and Zena Dell Schroeder know how it feels to need an anchor. An evangelical Christian couple in their late twenties, the pair met in 1994 at the American Academy of Dramatic Arts in Hollywood.

"We were the only two Christians at the school," said Zena Dell Schroeder, a willowy actress from Montana. "There were others—but we were vocal."

The decadence that surrounded her in Hollywood scared her.

"I realized this business was going to eat me alive," she said, recalling the pervasive drug use and promiscuous sex among students at the acting school. "I started really praying that God would bring me a Christian friend."

She found that friend in Todd Schroeder, who was in the same position. When the couple spent time together, she said, "we both acted a little better."

She lost touch with Todd Schroeder after graduation. While working as an actress and tending bar in Studio City, Zena Dell Schroeder felt torn between her bouts of heavy drinking with others in the entertainment industry and her deepest Christian convictions.

"I loved Jesus. I just didn't know how to stop sinning," she said. "I was trying not to sin, and I could not do that on my own."

One night, a friend offered to set her up with a Christian actor he knew. He showed up with Todd Schroeder, whom she had not seen in eight months. They resumed their friendship and started attending church together. Zena Dell Schroeder began immersing herself in theological questions and debating them with Todd Schroeder. Those conversations centered her attention on Christ instead of her sins.

"It was forcing me to look in the Word and study," she said. "My focus changed to really finding the truth about Christ, and those other things just sort of disappeared."

In December 1996, after a six-month courtship, the couple married. Now they host a weekly Bible study in their home, attend an accountability group for Christian couples, and support each other's attempts to glorify God through acting and writing for Hollywood.

"Our focus is really on our spiritual life first," said Zena Dell Schroeder. "Our focus is on Christ."

Many young orthodox couples say that focusing on Christ—rather than simply on each other—strengthens their marriage and inspires them to trust each other more. A mutual faith allows a couple to pray together when making major decisions and to orient their lives around what they believe God is asking of them.

For Paul Cranefield, the Christian convictions he shares with his wife allowed the evangelical couple to make a major move from Boise, Idaho, to Hollywood. In 2000, Cranefield was working for a television station in Boise and chipping away at a screenplay in his spare time, hoping to move to Hollywood in a few years to pursue a screenwriting career. Both he and his wife liked Idaho and the house they had recently bought there.

"We planned on being there awhile," Cranefield said.

God, it seems, had other plans. Cranefield attended a conference in Los Angeles for Christian screenwriters where he made several key contacts with film producers. He felt the tug of the Holy Spirit prompting him to take the plunge and move to Hollywood, to try to impact the world by writing scripts that glorified God. So he called home and left a voice-mail message for his wife that said, "Honey, I think it's time."

When he and his wife first discussed the idea, she balked. She had grown up in Idaho and had never lived far away from her family. Cranefield said he did not try to convince her—he "left that to God"—and a few days later, she was laid off from her job. The couple took it as a sign of God's will and hunkered down to pray together. Within twenty-four hours, they had decided to make the move, with no jobs or living arrangements lined up. During a subsequent trip to Los Angeles that spanned only five business days, his wife found a job and they landed an apartment.

"That's a God thing," said Cranefield, who started working as a production assistant in a television studio a few months after they moved to Los Angeles.

Cranefield said he is not sure that God called him and his wife to Hollywood so he would succeed in screenwriting. But he is sure that God called them there, and he is grateful to have a wife who is supportive enough to heed that call with him.

Indeed, heeding the call of the Holy Spirit—in decisions big and small—is a central goal for orthodox Christian couples who see marriage as a divine institution. And they see love that grows between spouses as a reflection of the love God has for his people.

In his letter to the Ephesians, St. Paul compares the relationship between husbands and wives to that of Jesus and the church. He also reminds them of the Genesis command that "a man shall leave his father and mother and be joined to his wife, and the two shall become one flesh."

In Catholic theology, marital unity is sealed by the sacramental grace conveyed to couples who marry in the church. Catholics believe that grace helps them love each other more and stay unified in their service to Christ.

Pope John Paul II, a moral authority for many young Christian couples, has said that the future of humanity depends on strong Christian marriages and families. In his apostolic exhortation *The Role of the Christian Family in the Modern World,* the pope cites this description of the beauty of Christian marriage, from Tertullian, an early Christian theologian:

> *How wonderful the bond between two believers, with a single hope, a single desire, a single observance, a single service! They are both brethren and both fellow-servants; there is no separation between them in spirit or flesh; in fact they are truly two in one flesh, and where the flesh is one, one is the spirit.*[19]

Being Fruitful

A mutual focus on God—rather than simply on each other—defines the marriages of many young orthodox Christians. And mutual dependence on God often leads Christian couples to submit everything to divine providence, including decisions about when to have children and how many to have.

In an age enamored with sexual license, the historic Christian stand against artificial contraception is a radical one. Most Christian churches have backed away from that ban in the past century, but Catholic and Eastern Orthodox churches still maintain it. Statistics have estimated that as many as 93 percent of American Catholics believe one can use birth control and still be a "good Catholic."[20] But small and growing numbers of young Catholics—and some Protestants—are embracing the countercultural view of reproduction and contraception that is articulated most publicly by Catholic leaders.

Catholicism teaches that sex has two functions: bonding and babies. When couples block one of those functions, the church teaches, they cut God out of the equation and short-circuit the total gift of self that sex should be. Artificial contraception also carries broader social consequences, according to the church: it encourages extramarital sex, undermines marriage and the family, and allows people to more easily use each one another as a means to an end. Dissenters from those teachings—whose ranks include the majority of American Catholics—say the church's birth control ban impedes believers from relying on their own consciences when making family-planning decisions.

Though they remain solidly in the minority, an increasing number of American couples have embraced natural family planning (NFP), a process developed in the late 1960s that allows a woman to predict her fertility by monitoring her body signals. The method boasts a 96 percent effectiveness rate[21] and a sounder scientific basis than the notoriously unreliable rhythm method. NFP has gained popularity among Catholic couples seeking to follow church bans on contraception and among other Christians with medical and moral misgivings about artificial birth control. According to the doctor-run Couple to Couple League, one of four major groups that certify family-planning teachers, the number of Americans in League-sponsored classes rose 17 percent in 1999, to about fifty-two hundred couples. In 1995, the Center for Disease Control and Prevention's National Center for Health Statistics found slightly fewer than one million women ages fifteen to forty-four using periodic abstinence as a form of contraception.[22]

Couples who use NFP admit that it tests their sexual self-control, since they must abstain from sex for several days each month, when the woman is ovulating. But NFP fans say the method also forces couples to talk daily about such intimate issues as the woman's fertility cycle and their decision about how many children to have.

"What other form of birth control includes both people in communication?" asked Joshua Scott-Fishburn, a newlywed in his twenties who lives in California and recently converted to Catholicism.

When they first entered the Catholic Church, Scott-Fishburn and his wife resisted the teaching against contraception. But soon, he said, they came to value NFP and the way it brought them closer to each other.

"It put things on the table that would've taken us years [to discuss]," he said. "The last few months have been the best ones of my entire life."

Sarah Schloss, a Catholic convert in her midtwenties, married a fellow Cornell student who was raised Catholic. Since their wedding in June 2000, Schloss and her husband have grown together in their faith and have reversed an earlier decision to use contraception.

At first, she said, they were "looking for excuses" to disregard the ban on birth control. A priest gave them what they needed by telling them to discern the matter for themselves.

But shortly after their wedding, Schloss forgot to take one of her birth control pills.

"We were just terrified," she said. "I think that both of us realized: This is so silly. We know in our hearts that this is not what we're supposed to be doing. It's difficult and it's expensive. It's just silly."

So they contacted the Couple to Couple League for information on NFP, and Schloss tossed out her pills. Now, she said, they chart her fertility together every morning, and she no longer bears the burden of birth control alone.

"It's just a world of difference," said Schloss.

Critics of natural family planning say the method is too demanding for the average couple to use effectively. In a 1999 article on the practice, the *Boston Globe* quoted an obstetrician and gynecologist whose criticism of NFP summarized the attitudes of many health-care professionals.

"In a very select people who are very motivated and aware and intelligent and reliable, sure it works," Dr. Raymond Haling of Pittsfield, Maine, told the *Globe*. "[However,] people don't have time to fiddle around with these types of things. They are too busy to be concerned intellectually and physically when there are other reliable methods to depend on."

Schloss sees it differently. Rather than lamenting the lack of sexual spontaneity and the sacrifice that NFP entails, Schloss focuses on the ways NFP brings her and her husband closer together.

"That time [of abstinence] can even be more special than any other time during the month. I think it really forces you to focus on each other, to talk more."

The backlash against artificial birth control has reached some Protestants. In November 2001, *Christianity Today* published an essay by Sam and Bethany Torode, a Protestant couple who argued that artificial birth control is not a biblical choice for Christians. They wrote:

> *We've heard it said that since artificial birth control is not explicitly forbidden in the Bible, it's fine for Christians to use it. But the contraceptive mentality—treating fertility as an inconvenience, danger, or sickness—seems to go against what the Bible has to say about the goodness of creation and children. The Bible teaches us to approach sexual intimacy and the possibility of conception with awe and reverence. The womb is the place where God forms new life in his image, not a frontier to be invaded and conquered.*[23]

The essay sparked a host of critical letters from the magazine's mostly evangelical readership. But its authors are not alone among Protestants in their reconsideration of artificial contraception. At a fall 2000 gathering of the Vine, an assembly of Generation-X Christians sponsored by *re:generation quarterly* magazine, young adults in their twenties and thirties packed a panel session on sexual ethics. Presenters in their twenties and thirties talked about everything from chastity to body image in a discussion dubbed Today's Sexual Retro-Revolution. Jenell

Paris, a young anthropology professor at Bethel College, a Christian school in Minnesota, spoke on "Fertility Management as Christian Stewardship" and encouraged her audience not to interpret NFP simply as "Not for Protestants."

"When we accept contraception, we're really living in disharmony with most of Christian history," Paris told her largely Protestant audience.

Instead of evaluating birth control methods solely by their effectiveness, Christians should also consider their moral, spiritual, and marital implications, Paris said.

One Vine attendee, Matt Dorn, cited the ban on artificial contraception as one of the reasons he converted to Catholicism.

"[The ban] was so contrary to conventional wisdom that it made me want to think about it," said Dorn, who belonged to the Calvinist Reform Church of America before slipping into agnosticism in college. "I've seen a lot of churches just become overly accommodating to a modern technological mind-set."

The Catholic Church teaches that every part of the human person—mental, spiritual, physical, and sexual—is unified. According to the church, an action that intentionally disables one component of a person, like his fertility, goes against human dignity and God's will.

That sense of unity within the human person appealed to Dorn. He also liked the social consequences of the Catholic teaching. Though he understands that following that teaching—and having larger families—is tough in America, Dorn believes larger families could propel a return to a less materialistic, more community-oriented culture.

Large families hold great appeal for some young orthodox Christians, particularly for Catholics who oppose contraception. Many see large families as another way for them to buck a selfish culture, imitate Christ's generosity, and surrender to God's will—even if it entails having more children than they intended to have or getting by on fewer luxuries because they have more mouths to feed.

Large families also can serve as a source of support for young Christians. Joseph Griffin, a tanned and lean Hollywood actor, touts his wife and six children as the secret to his spiritual survival in Hollywood. Griffin said he strives to maintain his integrity on the job because his family is watching his work. And he derives inspiration from day-to-day encounters with his children, encounters that strengthen his Catholic faith.

The power of those encounters became clear when Griffin discovered that his eldest son was autistic. Griffin, who grew up as a popular, athletic boy who never considered the plight of the disabled, suddenly found himself recognizing the vulnerability of his child, and of himself. He began to pray more, sacrifice more for his children, and rely more on God.

"My son really has been instrumental in changing me," Griffin said. "The children break everything down. They break down barriers because they're real, they're tangible, they're not a philosophy."

Children also bring rewards for Christians like Griffin, who view them as blessings, not burdens. Even when they are not with him, Griffin said, he feels their support as he steps into the secular realm of a Hollywood set.

"When I walk into a room, I walk in with my family," Griffin said. "It's a strength."

Patrick Madrid, editor in chief of *Envoy* magazine and author of several books on Catholic converts, sees a bright future for orthodox Christians who want to embrace large families, natural family planning, and conventional sexual teachings. After all, statistics are on their side: those who reject artificial contraception are more open to children and, therefore, will have larger families. In a few decades, the liberal Catholics who support birth control will be dying out, he said.

"The only way that side can perpetuate itself generationally is by converting people," Madrid said. And while orthodox Catholicism appeals to young adults, liberal Catholics "are converting no one. Their theology is sterile. It's a relativistic cult of self."

Homeschooling to Hand On the Faith

For orthodox Christians who want to pass on the faith to their children, homeschooling has emerged as a popular alternative to public, private, or liberal parochial schools. The ranks of home-schooled students in America—which are growing by 7 to 15 percent each year—now number between 1.5 and 1.9 million. Those numbers may portend a rebirth of the conservative sexual values of orthodox Christians, who hope to protect their children from the moral relativism that left them confused and craving orthodoxy.[24]

Silvio Cuellar is a thirty-one-year-old Catholic who works for the Diocese of Providence in Rhode Island. He and his wife homeschool their four children, blending lessons from Seton Home Study School—a Catholic academic publisher that serves an enrollment of about ten thousand students—with their own ad hoc field trips and meetings with other area homeschooling families. Cuellar said his wife first wanted to educate their children at home when she saw their oldest son becoming bored and distracted at his parochial school. Private schools were too expensive, he said, and the local public school was "not even an option." Now his children find their Catholic faith woven throughout their school day, and Cuellar notices that they relate well to people of all ages—a common refrain among parents about their home-schooled children.

"God is the center of our life," said Cuellar, who added that he and his wife practice NFP instead of using artificial birth control. He said the family lives simply—with used clothes and little money in the bank—but things always seem to work out: "We are faithful to God; God is faithful to us."

Allan Carlson, a historian and president of the Howard Center for Family, Religion, and Society, believes homeschooling parents like Cuellar could be crucial to a renaissance in American family life. In a 2000 article for *World* magazine, Carlson said parents seeking stronger families should "move into homeschooling, thereby reclaiming a central purpose of the natural family. The option of home education is not only good academically and morally for the children, the evidence suggests that it also strengthens the family by focusing all of its members on a critical common task."[25]

Homeschooling also allows parents to inculcate values in their children that they might not get from secular, or even religious, schools. But far from producing automatons, supporters say, homeschooling creates students who can recognize and critique the values of the dominant, relativistic culture. Homeschooling creates its own countercultural heroes. Among them: author Joshua Harris, a homeschooled evangelical who wrote a best-selling book on courtship, *I Kissed Dating Goodbye*; and Grammy-winning pop singer Rebecca St. James, an evangelical homeschooler whose song to an unknown husband, "Wait for Me," urged young fans to save sex for marriage. Homeschooled students can also attend colleges geared to their worldview. Patrick Henry College, a new evangelical school in Virginia, was founded specifically for homeschooled students. Several small orthodox Catholic schools also attract a large number of Catholic homeschooled students seeking an education that entwines faith with reason and steeps them in classical thought.

Critics of homeschooling—including many young believers themselves—worry that isolation from secular peers and schools is harmful to a child's intellectual, emotional, and even spiritual development. Some say that it could fuel a backlash among the next generation of believers. Zealous young Christians who rebelled against secularism may accidentally produce the opposite effect in their children: by sheltering their children from the world, they may drive them to reject orthodoxy and lead a pendulum swing back toward secularism. The solution, say many young orthodox Christians, is to protect their children from harm while still giving them enough freedom and experience to navigate the pluralism they will inevitably confront as adults.

The future remains unseen, but young adults who adhere to traditional standards of sexual morality and family life and who raise children trained to do the same are well positioned to influence the culture and the church. In the meantime, young orthodox Christians like Cuellar and Griffin, the Hollywood father of six, say they are already enjoying the peace that comes from living out their deepest convictions, even when those convictions demand sacrifice and countercultural choices.

"When you're living with that peace—not as the world knows peace—it's a great gift," said Griffin. "It all works out for the good. It really does."

6

THE CAMPUS

If you are really a product of a materialistic universe, how is it that you don't feel at home there?

C. S. LEWIS

On a temperate Friday night in April 2001, young adults swarmed the streets of Cambridge, imbibing the sights and sounds of Harvard Square. They streamed out of chic ethnic eateries, ducked into dark congested pubs, and swarmed around sidewalk musicians. Any distraction they wanted—from the intellectual to the experiential, the sublime to the ridiculous—beckoned from the square's colorful corners. Some awestruck pedestrians simply plopped down on benches, content to spend the evening watching an endless parade of punks, professors, and hobos pass them by.

At the heart of the campus was the packed auditorium and overflow room of Harvard University's Science Center, just off Harvard Yard, where a standing-room-only crowd had gathered for a lecture. More than five hundred young adults, mostly students, remained engrossed in the presentations despite the late hour, the countless diversions that awaited them outside, and the fact that most of them had spent an entire week sitting in academic lectures.

This one was voluntary, and it showed. Sitting next to young men in button-down oxford shirts furiously punching notes into their Palm Pilots were young women with shocks of dyed hair and multiple piercings. The crowd laughed with the speakers, furrowed their brows at the lectures' tough lessons, and strained to hear over the lingering applause after each salient point. The standing ovation that followed the lecture—a spontaneous, prolonged, and thunderous answer to the arguments offered that night—seemed to surprise everyone, including the audience.

Welcome to Jesus Week at Harvard.

"Nothing here lasts forever, but you do," said Boston College philosophy professor and author Peter Kreeft during his lecture, "The Philosophical Merits of the Christian Faith." "And therefore, every single human individual is an end and not a means."

After University of Georgia chemist Fritz Schaefer spoke on the connections between cosmology and theology in his lecture, "The Big Bang, Stephen Hawking, and God," Kreeft took the stage and spent the better part of an hour outlining more than a dozen major philosophical puzzles and the way Christianity solves each of them. Whether unpacking the "primal mystery of subjectivity" or the law of noncontradiction, the aging philosopher kept his audience hanging on his every word. One young man, who looked to be in his late teens, spent the lecture leaning forward in his seat, a living replica of Auguste Rodin's *The Thinker.* His chin rested on his hand and his eyes squinted in concentration as he listened to Kreeft pose, and then answer, such questions as "Why is reality consistent?" and "What in the world does Christianity have to do with that?"

Earlier in the evening, about two hundred young adults had filled another Harvard lecture hall to hear a panel of distinguished Christian professors, politicians, and professionals talk about the integration of faith and career. Audiences also packed a student debate on God's existence, a Christian music concert, a compline prayer service, a Christian festival, and several other lectures and discussions through the course of Jesus Week, which lasted six days and attracted nearly two thousand participants.

The events marked a revival of the Veritas Forum, a Christian grassroots movement that began at Harvard in 1992. Kelly Monroe, who worked at the time as a chaplain to the evangelical Harvard Graduate School Christian Fellowship, cofounded Veritas with a group of Christian Harvard students, alumni, and professors. They conceived of it as a way to help the campus community come together to explore the truth claims of the religion that their school's founders had embraced. Indeed, the forum took its name from Harvard's motto, "Veritas: Christo et Ecclesiae," which stresses fidelity to truth as found in Jesus Christ and his church.

As Monroe recounted in the epilogue of the 1996 best-selling book that she edited, *Finding God at Harvard: Spiritual Journeys of Thinking Christians,* her inspiration for working on the Veritas Forum came largely from her own experience at the notoriously heterodox Harvard Divinity School, where she enrolled as a graduate student in 1987. At the school, she found that anything goes— except orthodoxy.

"Ironically, all seemed tolerated except that for which Harvard College was founded—Truth for Christ and the Church," Monroe wrote. "Any earnest believer seemed like a real threat to prevailing relativism, deconstruction, and mysticism." [1]

Monroe and fellow Christians at Harvard wanted to see Jesus Christ and orthodox Christianity taken seriously in an intellectual setting. So they convened the first Veritas gatherings in the Ames Courtroom at Harvard Law School in 1992. Students and alumni led the seminars and events, which were organized around the purpose outlined in Monroe's book, of examining "the truth and relevance of Jesus Christ by raising the hardest questions of the university, society, and the human heart."

Planners expected the first annual Veritas gatherings to draw about a hundred participants. Instead, more than seven hundred participated, and the idea quickly spread across the nation to some seventy-five colleges and universities. As a grassroots initiative, the movement is organic to each school and is designed to unite the campus Christian community. So rather than welcoming a traveling tour of speakers, local organizers draw from their own academic communities to structure the event around local interests and to connect participants with local campus fellowships. They glean ideas and inspiration from the Veritas Web site and from Monroe, who now works as an adviser to the Veritas Forum and travels to schools across the nation to help campus Christians get their Veritas gatherings off the ground.

At Harvard, the Veritas Forum fell dormant for a few years—something Monroe attributes to a lack of support from the traditional Christian structure at the school. But students at its alma mater revived it during Holy Week of 2001, which campus planners dubbed Jesus Week.

During an interview in October 2000, Monroe explained why the Veritas movement has caught fire on secular campuses.

"I think [students] are getting back to the first and most important questions," Monroe said. "The problem is, they're not really allowed to ask them in the classroom."

Today's students have been trained to reject absolute truth, but a part of them still seeks it, Monroe said.

"People have feelings that go deeper than they have words to express. They've been programmed to think relativistically, but their longings are not that way."

Relativism and Revolt

American universities have always been incubators for new ideas and for the resurgence of dormant ones, just as American college students have long been regarded as the heralds of new cultural trends. In the 1960s, the political and social upheaval manifested by students on college campuses prefigured sweeping changes in American culture—the sexual revolution, the civil rights movement, the widespread suspicion of government and organized religion. Those changes crystallized into new cultural patterns and values, ranging from greater racial equality to a decline in traditional sexual mores and the rise of new gender roles.

Among those changes were shifts in the reigning ideology of the academy itself. The once prevalent assumptions of modernity—that progress is inevitable and that reason alone, not religious faith, leads to truth—have gradually given way to a postmodern rejection of reason and embrace of relativism, the idea that objective truth is not knowable. So a secular academy that once taught students that religious tradition was irrelevant to the quest for truth and moral absolutes now teaches them that neither truth nor moral absolutes even exist.

Today's academy is not a monolith, of course. It is fractured into a myriad of specialized disciplines and racked in many departments by turf wars and ideological battles. Colleges vary according to the administrators, professors, and students they attract. But relativism and postmodernism, both in and out of the classroom, are pervasive at many schools. Students often are encouraged to tolerate one another's religious differences but to avoid debate about them, lest the debate give offense. Many professors and administrators instill in students their own values—which often entail a rejection of traditional religion and morality—and remind young adults not to judge others according to moral codes that cannot possibly apply to everyone.

Given this atmosphere, the odds of Christian orthodoxy flourishing on college campuses seem slim. Orthodoxy opposes religious and moral relativism at every crucial point, insisting that its adherents accept as universal its rigorous moral standards and unflinching truth claims.

Despite the obvious obstacles, a growing number of college students in recent years have been embracing orthodoxy on campus, often while attending secular schools where relativism is most entrenched. Their decision is by no means a furtive one, either: campus fellowships that proclaim a bold, evangelical faith or distinguish themselves with the most distinct trappings of tradition are attracting the most young adults, as are religious colleges that confidently assert their Christian identity. The trend has many puzzled, including some baby boomer professors and campus administrators who expected the next generation of college students to turn out like them—liberal, secular, and suspicious of tradition.

Robert George, a political scientist who has taught at Princeton University for about fifteen years, has witnessed the evolution of a student-centered movement that has united conservative students across the Judeo-Christian spectrum. Secular Jews are embracing orthodoxy, Catholics are becoming "orthodox and enthusiastic," and many other students are joining Princeton's burgeoning evangelical Christian movement, he said.

"It's partly a reaction to the secularism of the professoriat," said George, a Catholic. These children of baby boomers also are rebelling against "the permissiveness of the '60s."

The result is an ecumenism of orthodoxy that unites students and allows them to collectively challenge the secularist liberalism of their school and its professors.

"Students in all of these various movements feel a kinship with each other that, I think, is unprecedented," George said. "These kids feel a certain comradeship with each other even though they're not in the same religion."

In his constitutional law and civil liberties classes, George sees evangelicals, Catholics, and Orthodox Jews arguing "arm in arm against secularist liberals."

Today's classrooms are a far cry from those of the 1960s, when students were more leftist than their professors, he said. Now many students regard the professors as too liberal.

Many young orthodox Christians have found their faith invigorated—not expunged—by the experience of defending their Christian principles in secular schools where objective truth and conventional morality are routinely dismissed as cultural constructs.

James Kovacs, a Catholic and recent graduate of Harvard Law School, said he has always been someone who hesitated to "go with the flow" of popular opinion. That quality came in handy when he arrived at Harvard: "When I encountered the difficulties and the culture [at Harvard], it just reinforced my desire to stand firm."

On secular campuses like Harvard, Christian students gravitate toward vibrant fellowships that offer them sustenance and support for their battle against the liberal, secular establishment that once waged its own war against conservative authorities.

"Christian students feel called to challenge the general culture of the school," said Kovacs, who said the witness of outspoken Christians—like those in his InterVarsity law school fellowship group at Harvard—emboldens others to defend the same values. "To see someone who displays some level of courage, to see that example, was helpful for me."

Evangelical campus fellowships, which are known for their unapologetic defense of Christian orthodoxy, have boomed in the past decade. About a thousand graduate students belonged to the e-mail list of Harvard's InterVarsity Christian Fellowship in 2000—twice the number that were signed up four years earlier.[2] InterVarsity serves some thirty-four thousand Christians on more than 560 campuses across the nation. Other evangelical ministries, such as Campus Crusade for Christ—which nearly doubled its student ranks between 1995 and 2000—also draw hearty numbers of college students on secular campuses with their uncompromising message and fervor for evangelization. And where Catholic campus ministers proclaim church teachings without apology, they, too, have enjoyed a revival among students steeped in secularism.

"There is an increase in the number of students in fellowships almost across the board," said Mike Woodruff, of the Ivy Jungle Network, a national association of campus ministers.

Woodruff said many students are attracted to campus fellowships not only because of spiritual hunger but also because they want to surround themselves with other students who are concerned about living good, moral lives. On campuses where moral relativism is the norm and conventional morality is an oddity, students seeking to buck the tide have fewer choices for companionship. So they gravitate to groups that take a strong countercultural stand for traditional values.

"Christian fellowships," Woodruff said, "represent one of the last bastions of good."

Christian worldview programs, organized by such strongholds of conservatism as Focus on the Family and the Family Research Council, also are gaining steam. The semester-long programs are designed to help Christian college students integrate their faith into their studies and career training so they can learn to see the secular world through a Christian lens. The worldview concept appeals to many young adults because it offers them a holistic way to look at the world, a grand system of thought through which they can make sense of everything they learn in college.

The worldview approach stands in strong contrast to the prevailing ideology in many corners of the secular academy. Many of today's academics focus on specialized disciplines and dismiss any grand systems of thought as biased or oppressive. So students must assimilate a vast amount of disparate facts and theories, but they have no overarching worldview to help them make sense of that knowledge. Into that void comes organized religion.

Andy Crouch, who spent most of the last decade working as an evangelical campus minister at Harvard, credits the collapse of the "impressive modern consensus" that dominated academia in the 1960s and 1970s for the growth of conservative and evangelical fellowships since the early 1990s.

Today, he said, the secular certainty of modernism is out, and the pluralism of postmodernism is in. Academics often brawl over issues of race, class, and gender. Many wage turf wars to protect increasingly narrow, specialized academic interests. Secularist professors who once united to assail the "irrationality" of religion now fight amongst themselves—and leave students too confused to glean one overriding message from the clash of viewpoints around them.

"You're in the midst of a sort of multicultural civil war, a guerrilla war," Crouch said. "You've stepped into this cacophony of voices and you're one of the voices."

Crouch compared yesterday's modern academy to a river that forced Christians to swim against a strong current of disbelief. Today's postmodern academy, he said, is more like a flood:

everyone is drowning in confusion, and "you just want to find something to hold on to."

Herman Sinaiko, a seventysomething University of Chicago professor who chairs the school's Committee on General Studies, knows that he is in the minority among humanities professors because he eschews postmodern philosophy and prefers to teach classics like Aristotle's *Poetics*. But he finds his students hankering for tradition.

"They're hungry for solid, substantial stuff," said Sinaiko. "When you dangle classics in front of them and say, 'I'm going to show you things that have been around three thousand years that are really terrific. But it's going to take a lot of work on your part because you're going to have to learn how to read, how to learn, how to think, how to write.' They're real excited about that."

Dr. Leon Kass, a University of Chicago bioethicist and humanities professor, advises several dozen students in a three-year interdisciplinary program that allows them to organize their studies around a central question of personal or intellectual concern. When the program began in 1983, Kass said, students wanted to investigate issues of political or aesthetic interest. Now more are choosing religious topics. In recent years, a few graduates have even opted to attend seminary or divinity school after college.

"That simply would not have happened in the beginning," said Kass. "The students weren't interested in those things."

In recent years, Kass has seen 250 students pack a lecture on Darwin and creationism sponsored by an evangelical fellowship. He has watched a growing number of Jewish students embrace serious religious study at the campus Hillel. And he has witnessed the emergence of young orthodox Catholic thinkers who sponsor campus lectures on the connection between faith and reason.

"It's not the church militant, but it's not the church in hiding," Kass said. "They feel comfortable being public on campus, which is new."

Christian colleges and universities, which allow students to integrate faith and reason inside the classroom as well as outside, also are enjoying renewed popularity. Enrollment rose 24 percent between 1990 and 1996 at the ninety-five schools that belong to the Council for Christian Colleges and Universities (CCCU). The council's roster consists mostly of evangelical colleges that remain committed to their founding principle of bringing biblical faith to bear on every aspect of education, and students at those schools are expected to adhere to strict norms of traditional morality. That enrollment spike contrasts sharply with the 5 percent rise at nonreligious private schools, 4 percent increase at public universities, and 11 percent growth at nominally religious schools during the same time.[3]

The students flocking to CCCU schools are not intellectual slouches, either: while 35 percent of freshmen at other private colleges earned A averages in high school, 47 percent of freshmen at CCCU schools got the top grades. At Wheaton College, an evangelical school in Illinois that belongs to CCCU, the class of 2003 boasted sixty-one National Merit Scholars, and its 1999 rejection rate topped the University of Chicago's.[4]

In Catholic circles, students seeking immersion in orthodoxy often choose one of the "Big Six" schools: Christendom College in Virginia, Franciscan University of Steubenville in Ohio, Magdalen College in New Hampshire, Thomas Aquinas College in California, and the College of St. Thomas More and the University of Dallas in Texas. Several of these schools have reported enrollment surges in recent years, which students and staff attribute to the schools' unflinching devotion to the Vatican and focus on classical works by such thinkers as Aquinas, Aristotle, and Augustine.

"They want to come back to the faith," said Tom McFadden, a Christendom College graduate who handles public relations for the school, which employs a strict dress code and offers plenty of pre–Vatican II piety. "They're kind of rebellious in some way."

According to the National Center for Education Statistics, schools with religious affiliations enjoyed a 12 percent enrollment growth in the 1990s—about three times the enrollment growth of all institutions. In the Associated Press article that carried those statistics, a spokesman for the American Council on Education, which represents some eighteen hundred colleges and universities, attributed the popularity of religious schools to a search for meaning.

"I think we have a lot of students looking for answers outside of themselves, outside of today's popular culture," council spokesman Timothy McDonough told the Associated Press in 2000.[5]

Although Christian colleges offer students a more structured way to integrate faith and scholarship, critics worry that they breed students who are ill prepared to navigate a pluralistic society and who are missing out on the intellectual and social benefits of spending their college years in a more diverse setting. Many young Christians take this view and refuse to sequester themselves in religious schools or construct spiritual niches on secular campuses. They prefer the ultimate rebellion against the postmodern professoriat: a career in academia that allows them to infiltrate the secular system and change it from within.

These young adults take their cues from the Christian intellectual revival that is percolating among high-profile Catholic and evangelical scholars. They are inspired by *Faith and Reason,* Pope John Paul II's 1998 encyclical that called for a repair of the relationship between philosophy and theology. In the encyclical, the pope asked academics to take metaphysical truth into account in their work:

> *Different philosophical systems have lured people into believing that they are their own absolute master, able to decide their own destiny and future in complete autonomy, trusting only in themselves and their own powers. But this can never be the grandeur of the human being, who can find fulfillment only in choosing to enter the truth, to make a home under the shade of Wisdom and dwell there.*[6]

Aspiring Catholic scholars draw from a rich and renowned intellectual tradition. Many of today's young orthodox Catholics are ardent neo-Thomists eager to dust off the gems of classic Catholic philosophy and reintroduce them to a secular academy otherwise consumed by the deconstruction of texts and tradition. Evangelical Christians, who largely withdrew from the secular academy in the last century, have made great strides there in recent years, as exemplified by the work of such scholars as Harry Stout at Yale, Stanley Hauerwas at Duke, and George Marsden and Nathan Hatch at Notre Dame.

The secular academy that today's young orthodox Christians seek to penetrate lives by the postmodern maxim that all ideas are valid but none are universally true. While these budding scholars abhor that relativistic mind-set—believing that their religion is either true for everyone or not true at all—they recognize that postmodernism gives them entrée into the academy in a way that modernism never did. If all ideas merit discussion, then Christians constitute another minority that deserves its due. Suddenly, the theological tenets tossed out in the Enlightenment reclaim intellectual respectability because, at least theoretically, they are entitled to as much consideration as Marxism, feminism, queer theory, or any other ideology.

Christian author Os Guinness sees young evangelicals who are "lunatic in their enthusiasm" for postmodernism, because it gives them more freedom to express themselves than modernism did. But that enthusiasm worries Guinness.

"Postmodernism gives you a place at the table," he said. "But it reduces everyone to a preference."

One happy by-product of the academic culture wars is the ecumenism of orthodoxy that has united Christians across denominations in the fight against secularism and moral relativism. Anti-Catholic sentiment has abated in recent years among evangelical academics as they find common cause with Thomists who defend the essentials of the Christian faith. Conservative Catholics, too, are finding that they often have more in common with evangelicals on campus than with liberal Catholics. One example of the new ecumenism is Evangelicals and Catholics Together, the 1994 declaration of a Christian worldview that sprouted from an ecumenical alliance led by Chuck Colson and Fr. Richard John Neuhaus. Another example is the popularity among orthodox intellectuals of Neuhaus's ecumenical and neo-conservative journal, *First Things*.

To handle the challenges of a postmodern academy, the realities of life on a licentious secular campus, or the perils of seclusion on a conservative religious one, today's young orthodox Christians rely on faith, fellowship, and a countercultural self-image. Though they sometimes disagree about the place of a Christian in the academic world and the best way to educate and intellectually fortify believers, they concur in their desire to integrate faith and reason. These young adults seek to unify the life of the mind with that of the soul. And they believe that such unity is not only possible but is also essential to their spiritual and intellectual survival.

Faith and Reason

The University of Chicago is the sort of place where students weave through sidewalk traffic with their noses tucked in worn copies of Plato's *Republic*. They sport T-shirts that say "The University of Chicago: Where fun comes to die" and "Hell does freeze over." They quote surveys like the 1993 magazine poll that rated three hundred American colleges according to their fun quotient and academic laxity. Chicago, its cerebral students note with pride, ranked dead last.[7]

Given their reliance on rationality, Chicago students might be expected to shun the supernatural emphasis of Christian orthodoxy. Indeed, many do.

But not the students connected to the Lumen Christi Institute. The institute, which was founded in 1997 by young academics seeking to revive Catholic intellectual tradition on their postmodern campus, sponsors lectures, small study groups, and vespers services. Its events attract students of various Christian denominations who want to reconcile their academic and spiritual selves. Their attitude is one of "faith seeking understanding"—meaning that faith is the starting point for, and is implicit in, their intellectual inquiry.

Paul Griffiths, a Lumen Christi founder and former University of Chicago professor, said the popularity of the institute and of similar movements among lay Christians is a sign of something new.

"The recovery of intellectual tradition is, for the first time in the history of the church perhaps, not being led by clerics. That's interesting, and no one knows what it means."

Converts and highly educated young Catholics are blazing the trail that leads back to Catholic tradition, said Griffiths, who is himself a Catholic convert from the Anglican Church. In 2000, Griffiths moved from the University of Chicago to the University of Illinois at Chicago, where he has launched a Catholic studies program. The program is one of several that have developed in recent years at public and private universities.

At a Lumen Christi gathering in October 2000, about a dozen students and professors assembled in the cozy basement of the University of Chicago's Catholic Student Center. They sang a brief, a cappella doxology—a traditional hymn of praise to God—then dove into a candlelit dinner of vegetarian lasagna and Greek salad.

The crowd was an interesting mix. Most, but not all, were Catholic. A few were Jewish. One was Presbyterian. An aging Catholic priest talked about his informal class on church history, which attracts some forty undergraduates to its meetings. Next to him, a young professor explained his involvement with Communion and Liberation, an international Catholic movement with an active contingent of young intellectuals in Hyde Park. A pretty, blond-haired woman in her second year at the university grinned as she ticked off her spiritual supports at this secular school: weekly Lumen Christi meetings, Friday night campus worship sessions with Asian evangelicals, and Sunday morning services at a popular Protestant church in Chicago's Lincoln Park neighborhood. Across from her, two young Catholic men debated the merits of various religious orders, while other diners discussed the genesis of postmodern thought and the connection between academic and religious tradition. After the meal, students and professors washed dishes side by side. Then they strolled across campus to a lecture hall, where they heard a

Lumen Christi—sponsored speech on "Fallen Angels and the Book of Genesis" that attracted about seventy-five students—a full house.

After the lecture, University of Chicago senior Rory Conway lingered in the next room to chat with friends from Lumen Christi.

"This university's mantra is 'The life of the mind,'" said Conway, as he tapped the side of his skull. "It's all located up here."

Lumen Christi, Conway said, gives him an opportunity to intellectually engage the Catholic faith he has known since his birth in Ireland and childhood in New York City. Conway attended Regis High School in Manhattan, which offers a rigorous tuition-free education to academically gifted Catholic boys. He felt prepared for the intellectual challenge that awaited him in Chicago. But freshman year shook his faith.

Conway's professors taught him to question everything, including his belief in God. Though he continued going to Mass, the fragmentation of the intellectual universe around him—where his three majors of history, philosophy, and physics seemed utterly unrelated—left him scrambling for coherence.

Conway's exposure to nihilistic philosophers and relativistic professors at Chicago made him yearn for more. He realized that he still believed in good and evil, and he began to doubt the objectivity of secular academics who operated under an a priori assumption that God did not exist. When he compared their cold rationalism to the reality of love and self-sacrifice he had seen among Christians as a child, Conway took a second look at his faith.

"Christ was the most true thing I could believe in," said Conway, a soft-spoken man with an intense gaze who wore wing tips and a denim jacket. "That truth spoke to me in ways and on levels that went beyond the university's idea of knowledge."

Conway realized he needed help to explore his faith and its moral implications, and to learn more about God. So he attended a conference of the Intercollegiate Studies Institute, a nationwide organization that promotes Judeo-Christian morality and conservative thought on campus. He found an intellectual home in Hyde Park with Lumen Christi. And he began gathering with other students to read, contemplate, and discuss various Christian texts, from the writings of fourth-century theologian Augustine of Hippo to the New Testament's first epistle of John.

Now, Conway said, he has found the unifying truth he sought as a freshman.

"Christianity is the lens that enabled me to make sense of everything. It provided a richness that the university's approach to truth was lacking."

The holistic quality of Christianity can be attractive to students in the secular academy because, unlike specialized academic disciplines, Christianity offers a comprehensive philosophy that applies to every aspect of life. If "all truth is God's truth," as the age-old Christian maxim goes, then everything Christian students learn in the secular academy can teach them about God and God's creation. And Christianity, in turn, can help them assimilate secular knowledge into a coherent framework. C. S. Lewis, a famous modern defender of orthodoxy, summed up the appeal of Christianity this way: "I believe in Christianity as I believe the sun has risen, not only because I see it but because by it I see everything else."

Chris Vreeman, a Los Angeles engineer on the cusp of his thirties, still remembers the confusion that swirled around him during his undergraduate days at the University of California at Los Angeles. Vreeman, who had been baptized Catholic but had received no religious training, said an experience during his freshman year in college helped steer him toward atheism. He met a fellow student in his dorm who was a fundamentalist Christian. The man asked Vreeman if he had been saved. When Vreeman said no, the student launched into his case for God's existence, one that Vreeman found laden with gimmicks and faulty logic.

"If this is what all Christians are basing their faith on, this is pretty pathetic," said Vreeman, recalling his reaction to the pitch. "I remember really clearly after that deciding I was an atheist."

Vreeman spent the rest of his college years surrounded by friends who, like him, had no interest in religion. His secular liberal leanings blended in well with the campus climate. But as time wore on, he grew tired of the ubiquitous protests by secular liberals who he thought were more interested in inflaming emotions than arguing facts. As a budding scientist who prided himself on sticking to the facts and seeking the truth, he became bothered by their tactics and began to question the moral relativism and rejection of objective truth that pervaded their arguments and the campus atmosphere.

When Vreeman enrolled in the graduate mechanical engineering program at Purdue University, he started working with a Catholic Ph.D. student who became his mentor and friend. For more than two years, the pair spent hours together, working in the lab and debating philosophy, politics, and history over lunch.

"I started developing a lot of respect for his faith, but [I was] still kind of clinging to the idea that I was an atheist," said Vreeman.

One day, Vreeman's friend told him about Thomas Aquinas's theory of natural law, which the Catholic philosopher and saint expounded in the thirteenth century. Aquinas argued that laws are just when they are based on the way God designed the universe. So certain moral actions are right or wrong in their very nature, depending on their conformity to God's law. And human beings instinctively know it.

Natural law flies in the face of the moral relativism that pervades most secular schools. Moral relativism argues that there are no universal moral standards, and thus, morality can be adapted to fit particular circumstances or personal preferences. When natural-law theorists take on moral relativists, their argument runs something like this: If natural law does not exist, and if there is no absolute standard against which humans can measure their behavior, then how can anyone say anything is right or wrong? How can society have order? How can people measure degrees of goodness or evil without assuming the existence of an absolute standard? While relativism allows people to construct or change morality, natural law requires them to adhere to absolutes.

The distinction between the two philosophies hit Vreeman hard. Both could not be right, he realized. Suddenly, which one was right mattered to him—a lot. He began reading voraciously, eager to learn what various religions taught and why. While working as a thermal engineer for Boeing, he chatted with religious friends and pored over such C. S. Lewis books as *Mere Christianity* and *The Abolition of Man*. Vreeman decided he had to make a decision. And he realized he believed in God.

"The alternative," Vreeman said, "is not rational."

In contrast to the specious arguments he had heard from the fundamentalist student he met at UCLA, and the emotional appeals he had witnessed among protesters there, Vreeman said his was an intellectually defensible position because it was based on an honest search for the truth.

"I was excited because I felt I had approached it with my logic," Vreeman said.

For Eve Tushnet, the seeds of faith were sown during her first year at Yale University in New Haven. Tushnet was raised Reform Jewish but considered herself an atheist and a moral relativist. In an e-mail interview, she recounted her campus conversion:

A few weeks into my freshman year in college, a friend told me about a weird right-wing debating society at Yale. Supposedly they would give you free mixed drinks if you went to one of their debates. I'd never had a mixed drink and never seen a right-wing debate, so I was intrigued. I went, mostly to make fun of the debaters.

Instead, I was totally hooked. That night I decided I would join the thing, even though I was about as leftist as possible (maybe more). The people debating seemed to know each other really well and be concerned with one another . . . and used words that only children's books take seriously anymore—honor, vengeance, duty, sacrifice, awe.

Over that year, I got to know these people. Many (including people who are now close friends) were and are atheists. But I also met the first orthodox Catholics I'd ever spoken seriously with. They

answered some of my questions ("What's the deal with the church's
teaching on homosexuality? How does that make any sense at all?")
and threw out intriguing fragments of Christian thought.

Tushnet began to probe the writings of Aquinas, G. K.
Chesterton, and St. Anselm—giants of the Catholic intellectual
tradition. By the fall of her sophomore year, she had started taking classes at a Catholic church. She was confirmed that Easter.

After her reception into the church, Tushnet began to have
doubts. She worried that her conversion may have resulted from
"wishful thinking." But her exposure to the philosophical alternatives—including the dark vision of Friedrich Nietzsche, whose
writings she pored over that summer—eventually confirmed her
decision. The hopelessness of those writings contrasted sharply
with Catholic thought and led her to believe that she must choose
either Catholicism or despair, since she saw no rational middle
ground between the two.

Reading atheist philosophers, Tushnet wrote, "briefly shocked,
but ultimately strengthened, my faith."

Christian Fellowships: A Refuge from Relativism

Young adults who embrace orthodoxy amid the guerrilla-war atmosphere of academia still must contend with secular campus life.
Whether taking courses from professors who actively undermine the
foundations of orthodoxy or living with students who mock their
morality, Christians on campus quickly find that their faith cannot
survive without spiritual support. So they turn to fellowship groups
and campus ministry organizations for sustenance and strength.

At a weekly meeting of Stanford's Campus Crusade for Christ
in April 2001, about fifty students streamed into a lecture hall on
a typically warm and sunny California day. After pulling the
shades down on the windows, they opened the meeting with

fifteen minutes of singing. The students in the multiethnic group seemed lost in adoration, raising their hands up, casting their eyes down, singing along with such evangelical songs as "Come, Now Is the Time to Worship."

"One day every tongue will confess you are God," they sang as a student guitarist accompanied them. "One day every knee will bow / Still the greatest treasure remains for those / Who gladly choose you now."

When the music faded, they bowed their heads for prayer, then settled in to watch a film about Stanford students who spent their spring break spreading the gospel in Mexico City. Next, a recent Stanford alum talked to them about how to pray in the midst of chaotic campus life. Then the group sang another song before bowing their heads for a closing prayer.

"When you come to college, you have to make your faith your own," said Alex Polk, a junior, after the meeting ended. This Campus Crusade fellowship, he said, gives students "fundamentals that you'll take with you for a long time."

Though Polk and his fellow worshipers expressed gratitude for their campus Christian community, most also said that facing secularism head-on at Stanford had solidified their faith.

"I was very purposeful when I came to Stanford," said Vanessa Padgett, a senior majoring in English.

Admidst grappling with the temptations of freshman-year parties and the attitudes of relativistic professors, Padgett learned how to integrate Christianity into every part of her life at Stanford.

"Coming to a place where you have to make a stand makes you stronger. My faith has taken off."

Despite their rewards, secular schools like Stanford pose formidable threats to a student's Christian convictions. Several at the Campus Crusade meeting talked about the unspoken code on campus that students can harbor religious beliefs but should not proclaim them publicly or label them as universally true. One student mentioned a philosophy class that allowed students to probe contrasting ethical systems but not compare them—presumably to avoid offensive value judgments.

Alan Klug, a sophomore studying aeronautical and astronomical engineering, said relativism abounds at his school.

"The whole concept of absolute truth is lost on 99.9 percent of people here," he said. At Stanford, Klug explained, "we're not going to pass judgment on *anything.*"

After a college career spent in that atmosphere, senior Brenna Peterson noticed herself adopting that relativistic posture, almost unconsciously, in the way she considered ideas.

"It's this kind of disengagement," Peterson explained. "I hadn't really realized how much I was picking it up."

Relativism and postmodern attitudes occasionally even permeate orthodox Christian circles. Those influences were apparent at a Campus Crusade meeting in St. Louis in March 2001, when about five dozen undergraduate students at Washington University in St. Louis met to discuss the concept of objective truth.

On the blustery Thursday night, the students packed the multipurpose room of a campus dorm. The campus minister introduced their guest speaker—a lanky middle-aged professor with a crisp British accent—who embarked on a fact-heavy lecture on the rationality of Christian truth claims.

Early into his talk, though, the students started to fidget. They cast knowing glances at one another beneath baseball caps pulled purposely low. Midway through the speech, several shot out pointed questions: How can I know that what is true for me is true for everyone else? Is it my place to apply moral absolutes to others? And why do I need Jesus to be a good person?

The audience—which consisted mostly of Christian students, with a few seekers sprinkled in—was challenging some basic tenets of Christian teaching. They seemed to dismiss his rational, modern arguments while pressing him for details about *his* conversion, about what Jesus had done for *him,* about what had made *him* believe in the truth of the gospel.

The professor answered their questions with aplomb but seemed slightly flustered by their lack of interest in his impressively argued apologetics. Clearly, these students who clutched Bibles and surrendered several hours of their free time each week to prayer and Bible study believed in the Christianity they confessed together. But equally clear was the way they had been affected by the relativism and postmodernism that dominated their campus and culture.

Jeff Barneson, who runs the InterVarsity Christian Fellowship graduate ministry at Harvard University, said he has seen signs of young believers' hunger for stories and lack of interest in purely rational arguments in Harvard's fellowships. He cited a group of several dozen graduate students who meet weekly at Harvard's Kennedy School of Government for an after-class Bible study session.

"They hold [Scripture] up like it's a lens and ask, 'How does this story relate to our story?'" Barneson said. "It's a very postmodern approach."

Some Christians believe that approach is as valid as any other way of reading Scripture or examining the Christian faith. But as the professor who lectured at Washington University found out, students steeped in relativism and postmodernism often have trouble accepting the moral absolutes and universal truth claims of Christian orthodoxy.

When campus culture seems aligned against orthodoxy, Christian fellowship groups help believers combat relativism and attacks on their faith. And groups that serve specific constituencies—like medical students, for instance, or Koreans—offer extra solace for battle-weary believers.

At the Massachusetts Institute of Technology in Cambridge, the Black Christian Fellowship is one of about twenty Christian groups on campus. Its members share the double distinction of being Christian at a bastion of scientific veneration and being African American at a school where fewer than 4 percent of students are black. On Wednesday and Friday nights, they gather for Bible study, worship sessions, and plenty of lighter moments.

"We laugh a lot," said Baptist Terrell Bennett, who is studying electrical engineering and computer science at MIT. "Sometimes it's just comforting to know that other people are going through the same things."

Members of the Black Christian Fellowship occasionally unite with other campus Christian fellowships for a joint meeting. But mostly, BCF members like to gather on their own, at more intimate meetings where they feel comfortable enough to pray aloud, sing without instruments, and call out responses to their speakers. During those meetings, members say, they can escape the competitive, secular atmosphere of MIT and relax with people like themselves.

BCF makes members feel comfortable, Bennett said, because it allows them to worship in their own way. The group is an oasis of support where members help one another figure out what God wants them to do at MIT.

"There's definitely a reason that we're here," he said. "Figuring out what that is—that's not always the easiest thing."

Students at the University of Chicago formed the Asian American Students for Christ—a branch of the multiethnic InterVarsity Christian Fellowship—about a decade ago, in response to the rising number of Asian Christians on campus. At a Friday night meeting in the fall of 2000, about sixty students converted a dimmed lecture hall into a concert venue. Two Asian students led the worship, one strumming a guitar as the other tinkered with the lighting. The group sang, broke for intermittent prayer set to music, then sang again. After the worship, they turned up the lights for a Bible study session led by Christine Kim, a campus minister who shepherds the group. At the end of the session, the throng—which was mostly Asian, with a few white students— spilled out into the corridor to laugh, flirt, and sip soda.

Kim said that many of the Asian American students who attend the meetings come for the sense of camaraderie, not the Christian doctrine. Some of the non-Christians never convert, and some of the Christians continue their drift from the beliefs that their parents instilled in them.

But for those drawn by the group's unapologetic evangelical message as well as its social benefits, Kim tries to instill in them a desire to integrate their faith into their studies and extracurricular activities. While evangelical students involved with the main InterVarsity group are participating in the wider campus culture more and more, Kim said, Asian Christians often are more reticent to do so because of their minority status. They also may struggle with issues that are particularly prevalent in their culture, such as fear of failure and of dishonoring one's parents. She tries to encourage members of the fellowship group to boldly live out their Christian faith, using God—not other people—as the standard for their behavior.

Asian students in particular have gravitated toward campus fellowships that nurture an evangelical faith. In 1999, the national office of InterVarsity reported that the past fifteen years had produced a 267 percent rise in the number of Asian Americans involved in its fellowships, from 992 participants to some 3,640. The surge in Asian involvement has made many campus fellowships boom and has precipitated the birth of new fellowship groups that cater specifically to Asian Americans at schools like Chicago and Harvard.[8] Experts say these fellowships reflect the rising numbers of Asians on campus, the attraction of young Asians to groups that address their specific concerns, and the popularity of evangelical Christianity among young Asian Americans.

Christian students gravitate not only to those groups that seem tailored to their needs but also to groups that have a clear identity and strength of conviction. In some cases, these elements even override denominational differences.

Fr. Willard Jabusch, director of the Catholic ministry at the University of Chicago, sees the campus groups that have a clear identity—evangelicals, Catholics, and Jews at the campus Hillel, which now has an orthodox rabbi—drawing large crowds. Meanwhile, the mainline Protestant groups that promote "vague" or "feel-good" theology tend to attract smaller numbers. And among orthodox believers, Jabusch sees overlap and cooperation. Some

Catholic students attend evangelical events, he said, and a well-attended campus speech given by a conservative Jewish professor on the topic of euthanasia struck many of the same chords as would a Catholic take on the topic. When it comes to topics like abortion, Jabusch said, conservative Catholics, evangelicals, and orthodox Jews often are united by their similar stands.

Michael Eades, a Catholic student at the University of Notre Dame in Indiana, said he finds more common ground with conservative Protestants on campus than with liberal Catholics.

"They're very true, I think, to the gospel," Eades said, of the Protestants who share his opposition to abortion, for instance.

Eades is active in Iron Sharpens Iron, an interdenominational Christian group at Notre Dame that gathers evangelical and Catholic students for worship, teaching, and prayer. Its members can join single-sex small groups for peer support and attend large-group meetings that are alcohol free. Eades believes Catholics are attracted to groups like Iron Sharpens Iron, and to orthodoxy in general, because they offer moral absolutes based on the gospel and a clear identity amidst a swirl of disparate ideologies. The moral relativism that has crept into some corners of the church is unsatisfying, he said, and young Christians are looking for strong, definitive answers.

"I think people are kind of realizing that what we're being told is good is empty," said Eades.

Orthodox Catholic students at Notre Dame struggle to find peers and professors faithful to church teaching, even though they attend a Catholic school, Eades said: "You have to fight. You have to seek it out."

Once an orthodox Christian has sought out a religious niche on his or her larger campus, new questions arise. Chief among them is this one: How can Christian students transform the world for Christ, as the gospel commands them to do, when they are confined to Christian cliques? The insularity of some campus fellowships, particularly those groups whose members feel embattled by a hostile campus culture, can lead to isolation, defensiveness, and other ills unbecoming a campus evangelist.

Barneson, of InterVarsity at Harvard, said that most of the students he sees active in campus fellowships are also active in the larger campus community. But some Christian students are disengaged from campus life and using fellowships as a refuge.

"It's the holy huddle," said Barneson, who believes Christians at Harvard need not be fearful of boldly proclaiming their faith in the public square. "My intuition tells me it's safe."

Perceptions of the outside world can become skewed when students spend too much time lamenting its evils, something Harvard law professor William Stuntz, a Christian, occasionally has seen happen during his years on college campuses. Some Christian fellowships attract students who are unhappy with campus life and blame their problems on perceived persecution they have suffered as Christians.

"Those tend to be pretty unattractive groups," Stuntz said.

Like Barneson, Stuntz said that most of the students he has met in Harvard's vibrant fellowship groups are happily engaged in the rest of the school. And those students—the joyful ones—are the ones most likely to attract others to orthodoxy.

Catholic Campus Ministry: Evangelizing with Tradition

For the Catholic Church, the overlap between Christians on campus—and particularly, the attraction of Catholics to the evangelical message—has sometimes been costly. Students surrounded by relativism and secularism naturally notice the clarity and conviction with which evangelicals on campus preach the gospel. When the Catholic campus ministry is not as vibrant, or when Catholic campus leaders downplay church teaching in order to blend in with a liberal, secular campus culture, cradle Catholics seeking orthodoxy may drift into evangelical fellowships. Some continue to attend Catholic Mass on Sundays and simply rely on the evangelical groups for sustenance in the campus culture wars. Others leave Catholicism altogether. Some Catholic campus ministries are realizing that in order to attract—and keep—young Catholics in the church, they must imitate the boldness of evangelical fellowships while emphasizing what makes Catholicism distinctive.

Curtis Martin, a Catholic in his early forties who discovered evangelicalism in college, said his search for a solid Bible church led him back to Catholicism—but not before he acquired an appreciation for the evangelical emphasis on Scripture and Christ-centered fellowship. Martin's experiences led him to launch the international Fellowship of Catholic University Students, or FOCUS, which appropriates many traits of evangelical fellowships in its attempts to supplement the work of Catholic campus ministries. FOCUS offers small-group studies of Scripture and the writings of the early church fathers, formation for student leaders, help for students who want to communicate Christian principles on campus, and large-group events that allow Catholics on campus to witness to their friends. As of January 2001, the three-year-old program had about six hundred student participants and twenty-seven staff members active on ten college campuses. Martin said demand for the group's services continues to grow.

"We just can't train staff fast enough," he said.

Martin said the program is successful because it trains top students to become "campus missionaries." At the University of Colorado at Boulder, for instance, Martin said FOCUS students are "some of the brightest, sharpest, most attractive young people you'd ever want to see"—and their enthusiasm for the faith is contagious.

In his work on the campuses of Princeton, Columbia, and Yale, Fr. C. John McCloskey often focused on evangelizing campus leaders—the students most likely to influence others. It's an approach often taken by the lay Catholic group to which McCloskey belongs, Opus Dei. To reach those students, the priest pushed the hard truths of the Catholic Church: the demands of the gospel, the bans on birth control and premarital sex, the requirement that serious Catholics do more than trudge to church on religious holidays. McCloskey rejects the "conservative" label for his message. It's not liberal or conservative, he said; it's simply church teaching. And students deserve to hear it.

"A lot of people are afraid to tell the truth about the church because they're afraid the students will go away. Well, that's always the risk."

McCloskey believes the benefits outweigh the risk. Though campus culture and liberal professors seem to grow more hostile to Christian morality each year, McCloskey said, many students reject relativism when given the alternative of orthodoxy.

"College campuses are the refuge of the sixties liberals," said McCloskey, who is in his late forties. "Now, *they* are the old fogies who say, 'Gee, [the students] are not like we were.' Thank God for that."

Mitchell Muncy, a Catholic in his early thirties, encountered McCloskey during his freshman year at Princeton. Though Muncy had attended secular schools his entire life, his parents had thoroughly formed him in the Catholic faith. He attended Mass each week and confession each month.

But the spiritual direction that Muncy received from McCloskey pushed his faith to the next level. The priest challenged him to attend daily Mass, confess his sins weekly, and set aside time each day for prayer and spiritual reading. Muncy began to adopt the Opus Dei attitude of turning his work into a sort of prayer and seeking to glorify God in everything he did. The habits Muncy cultivated at Princeton led him to integrate his faith more fully into his current work as the executive vice president of a book publishing company—a position he landed at the age of thirty-two. Those habits also attracted the attention of his friends. Muncy remembers his secular friends being more accepting of his devotion than the lapsed Catholics he knew.

"[Catholics] see it as a standing criticism of their way of life," said Muncy, who is now a married father of three. "There's this presumption that orthodox Christianity in general is really unrealistic and to try to incorporate your faith [into your life] is so unrealistic that it's almost absurd to try."

When students at secular schools do try to live their faith—and succeed—they often inspire others. At the University of Maryland at College Park, where new leadership has sparked renewal at the campus Catholic center, dozens of students pack the center for Benediction services that reverence the Eucharist and for the casual meals that follow. Fr. Bill Byrne, who became the director of the center in the fall of 1999, said about 480 students were involved his first year. By 2000, student participation had topped 700, and about 30 students were enrolled in a class at the center that prepares converts to join the church.

"It's not me; it's God," said Byrne, a rosy-cheeked priest in his late thirties, when asked to account for the success. "Quite frankly, I think it's because we started the eucharistic adoration. The Eucharist is the source and summit of the Catholic faith. It's about acknowledging the centrality of Christ."

Students at the center rave about Byrne and his fidelity to church tradition and teaching.

"He's kind of been like a breath of fresh air," said Allyson Hudak, a Maryland student who complained that the previous campus ministers were "like pre–Vatican II."

"It's funny you should say that," said Ray Bossert, a Maryland graduate student who noted that the older campus ministers who preceded Byrne were actually more liberal. "He's conservative. He's funny and all, but he doesn't pull punches."

Bossert said he liked that Byrne returned the tabernacle to a prominent place in the chapel, encourages students to bow their heads in reverence when reciting the Nicene Creed, and incorporates the feast days of Catholic saints and the traditional Angelus prayer into his Masses. Those traditions attract students like Bossert and Hudak, who see them as integral parts of Catholicism that they want represented on their secular campus.

"I love the tradition," said Hudak. "That's why I would never leave the Catholic Church."

The countercultural attraction to tradition is not limited to students at secular schools. Students at Catholic colleges and universities—including several schools run by Jesuit priests, who are known for their engagement of and, some would say, accommodation to secular culture—complain about the waning Catholic identity of their schools. They tell stories of fighting professors and campus ministers for permission to stage eucharistic adoration, practice traditional devotions, or promote conservative Catholic morality.

Young Catholics are working to revive the Catholic identity of their schools. A group of orthodox Catholic students known as the Children of Mary has organized eucharistic adoration and rosary devotion at the University of Notre Dame. At St. Louis University in Missouri, a handful of students—led by a young Jesuit scholastic—launched a weekly eucharistic adoration session that now attracts more than a hundred students each week. At Marquette University in Wisconsin, a small band of Catholic students has worked to revive the campus Knights of Columbus chapter, a men's fraternity dedicated to "faith, family, and fraternity" and known for its loyalty to Rome. And Catholic University of America in Washington, D.C., has experienced a renewal of its campus ministry program since the arrival of Fr. Bob Schlageter, a Franciscan priest who has instituted a popular eucharistic adoration session and sent out mass mailings to Catholic students on campus urging them to attend confession.

Georgetown University, a Jesuit school in Washington, D.C., has come under fire from Catholic students in recent years for removing crucifixes from classrooms, allowing *Hustler*'s Larry Flynt to speak on campus, instituting mandatory safe-sex sessions with condom demonstrations, and allowing the formation of a campus abortion rights group.[9]

Brother Jonathan Kalisch, a Georgetown graduate who is studying to be a Dominican priest, belonged to the campus chapter of the Knights of Columbus in the early 1990s. The group had restarted its Georgetown chapter in 1990 despite the dismay of campus administrators who feared lawsuits from women who would be excluded from the all-male group.

"Joining the Knights—it was like you were taking a stand against the administration," said Kalisch. "We saw ourselves as being the orthodox defenders of the faith."

Despite opposition from students and staff, the Knights attracted about thirty active members during Kalisch's time. A few years later, the group united with some non-Catholics on campus to push the university to bring crucifixes back to its classrooms. Now the group boasts about a hundred members, who organize frequent eucharistic adoration services and invite pro-life speakers to campus.

In an e-mail interview, Stephen Feiler, who presided over the group during the 2000–2001 school year, said the Knights "have thrived in recent years."

Feiler wrote:

> There is a large number of Catholic males who are seeking a way to express their faith in an authentic manner. Particularly on college campuses, campus ministries are really into "interfaith" and ecumenical initiatives, which, while important to an extent, shouldn't be at the expense of authentic Catholicism. Young men see in the Knights a proudly Catholic group that doesn't pick and choose what elements of Catholicism we practice.

Many of the most vibrant Catholic campus ministry initiatives—the ones that attract committed students and help those students grow deeper in the Catholic faith—are grassroots efforts. Though many in the Catholic campus ministry establishment downplay the traditions and distinctiveness of Catholicism, Catholic students themselves often show great enthusiasm for groups that are unabashedly Catholic and unapologetically orthodox.

The Growing Popularity of Religious Schools

The movement toward orthodoxy and tradition among the young has fueled another phenomenon: the rising popularity of explicitly religious schools. Orthodox Catholics and evangelical Christians who want to avoid the divisions and culture wars on secular or liberal campuses are increasingly choosing to attend colleges where Christian convictions are woven into the curriculum and campus life.

"The spiritual life pervades everything we do here," said Merrill Roberts, a student at Thomas Aquinas College, a Catholic liberal arts college known for its Great Books program and fidelity to the Vatican. "Theology comes up in everything—even math."

Roberts wore flip-flops and T-shirts to his high school classes in Key West, Florida. Now he wears slacks and a collared shirt at a college where the entire population—about three hundred students—roughly equals the size of his senior class in high school.

Roberts's life at Thomas Aquinas is different in other ways, too. As per the protocol of his school, his classes open with a prayer, and he addresses fellow students by formal titles ("Mr." or "Miss") and last names in class. The size of his classes usually hovers around fifteen students, and the reading list contains no textbooks—only original texts from such thinkers as Aristotle, Augustine, Euclid, and Kant. Three full-time campus chaplains are available to minister to his spiritual needs, and their three daily Masses are jam-packed with devout students who march in lockstep toward the altar rail to receive communion on their knees, the old-fashioned way. At night, Roberts checks into his all-male dorm, content to meet its curfew of 11 P.M. on weeknights and 1 A.M. on weekends.

Roberts admits that he initially recoiled at the prospect of a strict dress code, and he knows that curfews and single-sex dorms are increasingly unusual on modern campuses. But he has grown to love the traditional style of life at his college.

"You realize how good it is," said Roberts, who explained that the restrictions help him concentrate on his studies. "I wouldn't want to live in a dorm with girls. It's a respect issue."

California native Seana Morgan gave up a volleyball career to attend Thomas Aquinas because she liked its atmosphere and academic approach.

"It teaches you how to reason logically in steps," said Morgan, a slim woman with long brown hair who, like many students at the college, was homeschooled for part of her education.

At Thomas Aquinas, Morgan said, men open doors for women, couples avoid overt public affection, and women feel safe.

Shannon McAlister, a 2000 Thomas Aquinas graduate, concurs. The restrictions actually liberate students, McAlister said: "They are freeing you to be happy."

Christendom College, another conservative Catholic college devoted to the classics of Western thought, draws a similar crop of students who find freedom within the confines of orthodoxy. When discussing life at his Virginia school one night in October 2000, senior Ben Suer said he came to Christendom because the students were nonconformists.

"I was tired of people who were always trying to impress you," said Suer, a Georgia native who wore a suit and tie to dinner with his professors and fellow students that night. "Over here, people aren't afraid to show you who they are."

Christendom students do conform to some standards, including a strict dress code and mandatory attendance at speeches like the one Suer was preparing to hear, by an elderly nun who came to defend the legacy of Pope Pius XII. Most students live in single-sex dorms, typically attend daily Mass, and make frequent visits to the old-style campus chapel, where the Eucharist is reserved and sometimes exposed. A steady stream of Christendom students enters the priesthood and religious life each year.

Lisa Kirchner, also a senior in the fall of 2000, said that older people think she is "crazy" for attending a school as strict as Christendom, where the opportunities for typical college partying are severely curtailed. Sometimes, Kirchner said, she feels strange when visiting friends at state schools who live in coed dorms or partying on campuses where students walk through the streets carrying cups of beer.

"I kind of wouldn't mind going to a school like that," Kirchner said, grinning. But then her expression sobered: "I don't think I would be good at all."

Kirchner—who said she follows the church's authority more closely than her parents do and that her parents are "more tolerant of a lot of things than I am"—sometimes worries about life after Christendom. Will she have the strength to follow the teachings and traditions she has learned on her secluded campus?

"That's what I'm worried about," Kirchner said. "I have no idea."

Still, Kirchner hopes to someday send her own children to Christendom.

"We're sheltered," said Kirchner. "But at the same time, we're not."

Often, it is precisely the sheltered atmosphere of religious colleges that appeals to young adults. Tired of fighting the tide of promiscuity, partying, and postmodernism in the secular culture and eager to scrutinize their faith in the classroom, young orthodox Christians often choose schools that they hope will help them gain spiritual and intellectual maturity. Many who choose these religious schools are homeschooled students, who now number about 1.2 million and consist largely of the children of evangelical Christians and conservative Catholics.[10]

Patrick Henry College in Virginia, an evangelical school that opened in the fall of 2000, is designed specifically for homeschoolers. Its students study the principles of government with an eye toward impacting the culture when they graduate. In the meantime, they must pledge to forgo alcohol, cigarettes, and premarital sex while enrolled at the school. Strict rules do not seem to deprive Patrick Henry of quality students: in its first year, the school attracted eighty-plus students with SAT scores that easily outranked the national average.[11] Regent University, an evangelical graduate school with a similar vision for inculcating Christian values, started with seventy students in 1977. Now the Virginia Beach school founded by Pat Robertson has nearly twenty-five hundred students and a $319 million endowment. In the past five years, its enrollment has climbed 60 percent.[12]

Another bastion of orthodoxy, Ave Maria College in Michigan, opened in 1998. Domino's Pizza founder and Catholic philanthropist Tom Monaghan founded the school for Catholics seeking a liberal-arts school with a clear Catholic identity. In 2001, Ave Maria College had 135 students. The Ave Maria School of Law, which Monaghan envisioned as a way to blend faith and reason and produce principled attorneys, opened in August 2000 with 77 students and a faculty that included such legal celebrities as conservative judge Robert Bork.

Cesar Reyes, a graduate of the evangelical Wheaton College in Illinois, admires the way religious schools such as his alma mater blend "longtime traditions and liberal-arts open-mindedness." In an e-mail interview, Reyes recounted the challenges and rewards of studying at a school where Christians were forced to reconcile faith and reason:

> *Once I had to write a paper on how the Incarnation was possible without using direct Scripture as my source of argument. It seemed impossible! But it got me thinking about how to be strong-minded and still have deep faith. I think there's a large tradition of thinkers like this, for example, Augustine, Aquinas, Erasmus, Kierkegaard. . . . However, this kind of curriculum can be sometimes dangerous because if one does not have strong faith going into some of these classes, one can find it overwhelmingly difficult to still think that faith is a viable option in our world.*

While the professors at Christian colleges may challenge students to think more deeply about their faith, some alumni of religious schools say that the piety of their peers can make intellectual inquiry difficult. While studying to be a Christian apologist at Wheaton College, Daniel Gallaugher found himself questioning the beliefs he was preparing to defend. The evangelical subculture and worship style began to repel him, and Gallaugher wanted answers to the tough questions he was asking about Christian theology and the Bible's authority. But he felt too confined by the school's religious atmosphere to seek them out.

At Wheaton, Gallaugher said, "doubters would take the easy way out, one way or the other. They would accept evangelicalism and refuse to question it or throw the whole thing out. Neither one of those was a real possibility to me. I was questioning, but the one thing I was sure of was there was something real there. It was almost a decision of the will, a decision of faith: 'God, I don't know what is going on, but I'm not going to let go of you.'"

Gallaugher's search outlasted his time at Wheaton. He eventually found the answers he had been seeking in the Catholic Church, which his Protestant parents had left years ago. His was a meandering path, but the intellectual aspects of Catholicism appealed to him, and he came to treasure the very tradition that had repelled his parents. Now Gallaugher is studying theology and preparing for the priesthood. He harbors no resentment about his experiences in evangelicalism, Gallaugher said, but he looks forward to helping students who are struggling with the intellectual aspects of the Christian faith, as he once did.

"I'd love to help anybody going through a college questioning period like I did, particularly because I didn't seem to find much help."

Students at religious colleges face other dangers to their development. The same insularity and defensiveness that plagues some members of campus fellowships at secular schools also surfaces among some students at religious colleges. Students who have spent their college years scrupulously avoiding the temptations of the outside world face a reckoning on graduation day, when they must leave their evangelical or Catholic subculture and tackle pluralistic American society head-on. The transition can be painful.

Fr. Dave Pivonka, a Franciscan priest who directs Christian outreach for the Franciscan University of Steubenville, said he receives calls from Steubenville graduates who want to know how they can cultivate faith communities and find support after leaving the Christian confines of their college.

"It's very sad sometimes," said Pivonka, who has seen some graduates become frustrated and discouraged when parish life does not offer the same intimacy, sense of community, and charismatic brand of "dynamic orthodoxy" that they experienced on campus. "It's tough out there."

Faced with the prospect of entering pluralistic society, many alumni of religious colleges never leave the subculture, and some raise their children in the same tight-knit circles. Others may assume a defensive posture that pits their piety against the pluralistic masses or, in the case of conservative Catholics, against more liberal Catholics. Many Christian students at religious colleges are determined to avoid that pitfall—and do. But just as orthodox believers on secular campuses constantly run the risk of adopting the relativistic attitudes around them, so do students at religious colleges face the imminent danger of losing the ability to empathize with, evangelize, and learn from people who do not share their faith.

Inside the Academy

Many young believers are attracted to secular campuses and callings that allow them to witness their faith to others in the academic realm. Though living a Christian life on a secular campus can be difficult, these young adults are eager to embrace that challenge. They want to transform culture by influencing its intellectual roots in the secular academy.

James Seward, an evangelical Christian who grew up in Wheaton, Illinois, considered attending a religious college where he could receive encouragement and training in his faith. But he ultimately opted for its polar opposite: the elite, secular University of Chicago in Hyde Park. Seward knew a group of Christians who were seeking to "plant" a church near the university, and he wanted to help. He also wanted to put his faith into action.

"I was well aware of the need on secular campuses for Christians who are proclaiming Christ," said Seward, who saw the good grades he earned somewhat effortlessly in high school as a sign that the University of Chicago might be the school God wanted him to attend. "God had kind of put together a high school career that got me into this school."

Seward followed the prompting of divine providence and gained admission to the university. He quickly found fellowship among his fellow church planters and a small group of Christian men at the university who shared his convictions.

The religious pluralism that rattled some of his friends never unsettled Seward, but it inspired him to pray for them. In the summer of 2000, before his third year at the university, Seward and other Christians at the university began to fast and pray for a fruitful next year at Chicago. When they returned to school that fall, four of them—including Seward—decided to live in the same area of the dorm. They soon launched an informal prayer ministry, gathering nightly in a dorm room to pray for their friends, their campus, and unbelievers they knew. As word of their ministry spread among students, Seward received supportive responses, even from agnostics. The little flak he drew was from more liberal Christians. But Seward persevered.

"I was coming to this school to proclaim Christ," Seward said. "I wanted to do what I set out to do, not waste time. I'm only going to be at this school four years."

Already, Seward has seen results. By November 2000, the prayer meetings had spread to five dorms on campus, and the Christians Seward knew seemed to be gaining confidence and momentum.

"That excitement spreads, especially at our age," said Seward. "It's contagious excitement."

Like Seward, Chinwe Osuji considered attending a religious college before she opted to enroll at Harvard Law School. A Catholic and native of Nigeria, Osuji attended City College of New York and almost joined the inaugural class at Ave Maria School of Law, Tom Monaghan's new orthodox stronghold, when she graduated. But she decided that a Harvard degree would give her more leverage to influence the world.

"It was really hard for me to decide," said Osuji, a tall, bright-eyed woman. She saw Harvard as a place where her own faith could grow as she witnessed to others: "There's something about being in an environment where people don't necessarily agree with you. It helps you ask yourself the basic questions."

At City College, Osuji said, she defended orthodoxy and traditional morality at every juncture. But as a first-year student at Harvard, she found herself staying mum more often.

"It's not always easy," she said. "You really have to pick your battles. Otherwise, I think people label you too quickly."

Osuji and other supporters of pro-life causes united in April 2001 for the annual Society for Law, Life and Religion symposium, featuring conservative columnist Ann Coulter. The society is an anti-abortion organization for Harvard Law students composed mostly of orthodox Catholics.

"I can't imagine this existing years ago," said Roger Severino, a society officer and Catholic law student who hopes to eventually get into politics.

Severino said he takes classes from secularist liberal professors who used to be campus protesters in decades past. Moral relativism dominates the school, and though students can talk about the ideas of Karl Marx, "you would get weird looks if you would mention Jesus."

Still, Severino senses a growing desire among his peers to challenge the hegemony of secularism and relativism in academia.

"This generation is a lot more vocal and willing to say, 'We're going the wrong direction.'"

At Harvard Medical School, Christians like Michael Turner are issuing such challenges. Turner, an outspoken, enthusiastic medical student from California, organized the singing of Christmas carols at the school to recall Christ's birth during the holidays. He also has considered promoting the pro-life cause by putting a poster of an infant in the student lounge, and he speaks out when classmates talk about a doctor's duty to facilitate abortions for patients.

"It's a little bit edgy," said Turner, who gets support from a group of fellow evangelical Christians who pray together in the medical school's dorm. "But it's the truth. The truth is the truth."

Another way to impact the campus for Christ is a career in campus ministry. Many young orthodox Christians are choosing to spend their lives leading college students to the faith. Evangelicals may sign up with InterVarsity or Campus Crusade for Christ, or a number of other campus organizations, if they want to spread the gospel at secular schools. Orthodox Catholics dedicated to campus ministry—who are often outnumbered by more liberal Catholic campus ministry staffers at secular and Catholic schools alike—may seek employment at a school's Catholic campus ministry office or take an alternate route. One choice for Catholic men intent on campus evangelization is the Brotherhood of Hope, a religious community of brothers and priests founded in 1980 that mixes orthodox theology and traditional community life with enthusiastic evangelization of the young. The order's brothers and priests work with students on such college campuses as Florida State University in Tallahassee, where they focus their efforts on educating fallen-away and nominal Catholics and other young adults who have questions about Catholicism.

Twenty-seven-year-old Brother Gregory Szot is a Naples, Florida, native who has worked with the Brotherhood at Florida State, spreading the Catholic faith to college students. Szot said he was drawn to the community because its members—many of whom are young—share his passion for reaching other young adults on college campuses.

"I saw excitement and joy," said Szot. "Our mission is evangelization."

Many young orthodox Christians conclude that the best way to beat the secular academy is to join it. They reason that few callings could make more of an impact for God than the vocation of teaching, which would allow them to lead others to conversion or, at least, a deeper understanding of the Christian worldview.

"I can't imagine a better relationship for communicating wisdom, truth, and faith than the professor-student relationship," said Andrew Witmer, a twenty-five-year-old Baptist who is working toward a doctoral degree in American history at the University of Virginia.

In an e-mail interview in 2002, Witmer expanded on his vision for his vocation.

> *It's about much more than communicating information, though that's a big part of it. I think good teachers can shape the way students feel about and interpret the information. . . . My classes at the University of Virginia have not been hostile to religion, but they don't really take it seriously either. One of my professors, wondering about my beliefs, jokingly asked me in class if I was a "throwback." Our class discussion of American revivalism in the eighteenth century was entirely naturalistic, proceeding on the assumption that supernatural explanations were neither plausible nor appropriate for mention in an academic setting. I'm excited about helping to shape a "community of discourse" in my own classroom some day. I'm not sure yet what it will look like, but I know that I want it to include respectful treatment of religious belief and an awareness that we really won't understand much of history until we take religion and religious motivation seriously.*

Josh Good, Witmer's former housemate in a Washington, D.C., house for Christian men, has a similar trajectory. He graduated in 1998 from Covenant College, a Christian college in Georgia. He then worked for two Washington think tanks on issues of religion and public life before enrolling in 2001 at Harvard. Now he is pursuing a degree from the divinity school and is taking courses at the Kennedy School of Government. Good expected the divinity school to live up to its reputation as a bastion of liberalism and pluralism where evangelicals like him find themselves outnumbered. So far, he said, it has.

"The more biblically motivated follower of Christ is definitely in the minority," said Good, who added that many of his classmates dismiss the idea of objective truth. "I'm challenged by a lot of that right now and trying to really discern, and witness, what it means to pursue biblical truth."

Those challenges, though, are exactly what Good was seeking. He wants to make an impact on secular culture and figures he cannot do it as effectively from within his evangelical subculture.

"I'm excited about that," said Good. "To be in the ring, not on the sidelines."

Some are finding institutional support for their academic aspirations. The Civitas Program in Faith and Public Affairs, sponsored by the Pew Charitable Trusts, brings Christian doctoral students from leading universities to Washington, D.C., for a five-week summer institute. Once there, they study the connection between Christianity and public affairs and pair up with Christian academic mentors under the auspices of the Center for Public Justice, the Brookings Institution, and the American Enterprise Institute. The program is designed to produce Christian public intellectuals in the mold of Abraham Kuyper, a Dutch Reformed theologian and political leader who blended Christian orthodoxy with social reform.[13]

Many Christian academics see reasons to be hopeful about their impact on students. Tim Muldoon, a Catholic theologian in his early thirties, said the students he encounters at Mount Aloysius College in Cresson, Pennsylvania, spout many of the same relativistic ideas as students on secular campuses. Even though the school is Catholic, students there often reject the value of an inherited religion. Still, Muldoon connects with them when he argues that wisdom traditions that have endured thousands of years deserve their attention.

"Younger folks get this right away," said Muldoon, who chairs the college's department of religious studies, philosophy, and theology. "Organized religion provides us a place to encounter horizons that are different than our own. We're not the sole arbiters of ultimate truth."

William Stuntz, the law professor at Harvard, said outspoken Christians are more accepted in the academy than when he attended the University of Virginia School of Law in the early 1980s. Back then, Stuntz said, Christian academics mostly kept quiet about their personal convictions.

"Finding anybody who was out of the closet about their religious opinions—it was hard," said Stuntz. "That has changed markedly. Students at places like this are definitely wary about religion as a topic of conversation, but the degree of reticence has noticeably changed."

Stuntz credits the crumbling of secular modernism and the rise of postmodernism for the shift. Outspoken Christians, particularly evangelicals, are no longer dismissed as intellectually inferior, he said. And students who see Christian peers and professors speaking out no longer assume that an embrace of religious orthodoxy means confinement to religious ghettos or intellectual suicide.

"Instead of being stupid, they're odd. And odd, in universities, is kind of a good thing to be," said Stuntz, of Christians on campus. "I have to believe that God is at work in this generation in universities. I see signs that he really is at work powerfully."

7

POLITICS

I am the king's faithful servant, but God's first.

ST. THOMAS MORE

Smiling and singing, chanting and praying, the throngs of teen-agers and young adults came from every direction. They swarmed the city's sidewalks, streets, and subway stops, moving with cheerful resolve toward its epicenter. Once there, they seemed oblivious to the biting January wind and the mud swallowing their shoes. Instead, they exulted in the sun that shone down on them and in the hint of a springtime that they believed would surely come soon.

Twenty-eight years after the landmark *Roe* v. *Wade* decision legalized abortion on demand in America, anti-abortion marchers might be expected to slouch grimly through the streets of Washington, their faces worn with age, their ranks thinned by almost three decades of defeat. But it was not so on January 22, 2001. The annual March for Life looked—as it has for years now—more like a youth rally than a protest. Tens of thousands of mostly young marchers, who had converged on the nation's capital from across America, rejoiced at their solidarity and at the inauguration two days earlier of President George W. Bush, whose evangelical faith and opposition to abortion gives them hope. Grinning college students swayed arm in arm to religious hymns. Gaggles of high school boys recited rosaries on their way to the Supreme Court. Priests and nuns stood next to red-and-green-haired young women wearing Rock for Life T-shirts. Groups from Cornell

University, Massachusetts Institute of Technology, Williams College, and the University of Notre Dame rambled alongside Greek Orthodox priests in long black robes who carried icons of the Virgin Mary and baby Jesus. Boisterous teenagers with "Protect Life" stickers plastered across their backpacks and down jackets scampered through a crowd that blanketed the National Mall. Ignoring the sleep deprivation brought on by all-night cross-country road trips and makeshift beds in church basements, the young activists chanted in unison: "Hey, ho, hey, ho, *Roe* v. *Wade* has got to go!"

When a congressman announced that afternoon that President Bush had decided to cut off U.S. aid to international groups that provide abortion services, the crowd erupted with enthusiasm. Everywhere, young religious adults—most of whom were Catholic, with plenty of evangelicals and conservative Protestants in the mix—reveled in what they prayed would be the beginning of the end of legalized abortion. Many told stories of feeling alone in their Ivy League schools and secular offices. But their battle scars seemed to disappear here, replaced by sheer excitement at this movement that seemed so young, so vibrant, and so diverse.

"We get everyone from the Young Republicans who couldn't live without a tie to the hippies who come barefoot—literally," said George Paci, a 1993 Cornell graduate who stood on the curb of Constitution Avenue watching masses of young adults march past him.

Paci serves on the board of the American Collegians for Life (ACL). He said membership in ACL, a national student-run group that unites college abortion opponents, has been "steadily increasing" in recent years.

Just then, a handful of students from Paci's alma mater rolled down the street. As Paci turned to watch them, a middle-aged woman in the thick of the crowd spotted them, too.

"This is wonderful," she said, after scurrying through the crowd to get a closer look. "Cornell. I never would have thought so."

"There are only eight of us," said one of the Cornell students, a young woman who had traveled seven hours from Ithaca, New York, for the march.

The woman ignored the apology, her eyes twinkling at the group's pro-life placards and windbitten cheeks. Gazing at them with a mix of wonder and delight, she smiled.

"God bless you."

A Lived Philosophy

After the march, many participants set off on red-eye road trips back home, departing on the same rented buses that they had arrived on. For those who stuck around, there was the Dubliner, an Irish pub just off the National Mall where pro-life placards rested beside bar stools, chilled marchers warmed up with pints of Guinness, and fathers danced with their rosy-cheeked babies.

In the midst of the happy chaos sat David Schindler, a theology professor at the John Paul II Institute for Studies on Marriage and Family in Washington. Schindler laughed and ate with a band of graduate students from the institute who had attended the march. All were devout young Catholics who want an end to abortion, but their interest in politics and culture does not stop there. As Schindler has witnessed while teaching such courses as Faith and American Culture, many young orthodox Christians are not content to separate themselves from a society rife with unwanted pregnancies, addiction, violence, and divorce, protesting only occasionally at rallies with like-minded peers. Instead, they want to actively engage secular culture.

"There is a perception among young people that there are a lot of problems in the culture," said Schindler, in a later interview. "They are intensely interested in trying to understand the roots of the problems."

Young believers often reject the separation of sacred and secular that marks modern political thought. Instead, they see the two as inextricably connected, and they hope to transform the public square with the same faith that has transformed their personal lives.

To do that, many young adults are turning to traditional Christian theology and philosophy and are listening to such traditional religious figures as Pope John Paul II. More and more, Schindler said, he sees young Catholics coming to the institute who want to embrace orthodox Christian values while still remaining active in secular politics and society.

"They realize that they're going to have to live in an uneasy tension with the culture," said Schindler.

Adrian Walker, who joined Schindler at the Dubliner after the march, is a Catholic in his early thirties who also teaches at the institute. He sees young converts to orthodoxy reacting in one of two ways to politics and culture: either they take a "moralistic" approach and try to avoid contamination by secular culture or they take an "incarnational" approach and try to understand and change that culture while still avoiding assimilation to its values. Walker said many young Catholics and evangelicals fall somewhere between those two extremes. Many also begin in the first camp—thanks to the initial fervor of a radical conversion—then slowly drift into the second as they consider the cultural implications of Christianity.

For Christians in the second group, Walker said, "culture is an incarnation. It's like a lived philosophy of life."

The young orthodox Christians interviewed for this book fall largely into the second category of believers. They insist on integrating their faith into every aspect of their lives—including their political lives—and they reject claims that they should simply remove themselves from secular culture in order to protect their faith. Emboldened by tenets of both Catholic and Protestant theology that call Christians to work for peace, justice, and redemption of the social order, these young Christians are striving for a political approach that balances active participation in this world with devout preparation for the world to come.

A Tale of Two Activists

At first glance, University of Notre Dame graduates Sheila Moloney and Sheila McCarthy seem to be worlds apart.

Moloney, a pretty, pearl-clad policy wonk on Capitol Hill, has a résumé that could double as a roster of the Religious Right. She has worked for the Heritage Foundation, the Family Research Council founded by James Dobson, and as executive director of Phyllis Schlafly's Eagle Forum. Her current employers are a group of socially conservative congressmen known as the Republican Study Committee. The outspoken twentysomething founded a conservative newspaper at Notre Dame and now makes occasional appearances on TV's *Politically Incorrect,* a caustic national talk show where she debates liberal rivals on such topics as abortion, contraception, and sex education.

McCarthy, a quiet young woman with sparkling eyes and the intentionally sparse wardrobe of a peacenik, spends her political capital elsewhere. She did not vote in the last presidential election. Instead, she spent her time organizing pacifists in the school's chapter of Pax Christi. She coordinated a hunger awareness day in the campus cafeteria that gave students a firsthand look at the volume of food they were throwing away. After graduating from Notre Dame in 2001, she joined the Catholic Worker movement, founded by her heroine, Dorothy Day. McCarthy now lives in a Catholic Worker house in Los Angeles, near a run-down part of the city known as Skid Row. She and her housemates serve six meals a week on Skid Row and tend to the sick and dying people who live with them. They pray, work, and study as a community, advocating for the rights of the poor and against violence and war in any form.

As different as Moloney and McCarthy are, they have more in common than Irish surnames and Notre Dame degrees. Both are staunch Catholics who see their political activism as an outgrowth of their faith. Both trust the teaching authority of the church on issues like abortion, which they oppose. Both grew up less religious than they are now and saw their devotion swell in college.

For McCarthy, pacifism and abhorrence of materialism preceded her adolescent conversion. But her discovery of Catholic social teaching—which reserves a "preferential option for the poor," defends the rights of immigrants and laborers, and critiques the excesses of capitalistic consumerism—gave her political opinions theological grounding. When she took a class from Fr. Michael Baxter, a fortysomething Holy Cross priest and Notre Dame professor renowned for irritating both conservatives and liberals with his staunch defense of social justice and traditional morality, McCarthy was hooked. Baxter's class convinced her that it was radical to take the teachings of Christ and the Catholic Church seriously in a culture that often ignores both. His articulation of "Catholic radicalism" changed McCarthy's image of the Catholic Church, which she once regarded as oppressive.

"All of that stuff just started fading away," she said. "Every day after class I'd just pick his brain."

McCarthy found the countercultural ideology she had been seeking in the last place she had expected: the Catholic Church of her childhood. She began attending daily Mass, often in the company of young conservatives who loved Baxter because of his defense of traditional morality and church authority. Now McCarthy sees the Eucharist and Catholic liturgy not as antiquated, irrelevant traditions but as the sustenance for and driving force behind her embrace of pacifism and rejection of materialism. And she sees her political convictions—which range from conservative to liberal to radical, depending on the issue at stake—as consistent with her faith.

"Catholicism doesn't line up with any political party," said McCarthy, who pairs opposition to abortion with opposition to the death penalty, for instance. "If you take your Catholic identity seriously, then you'll have a very different understanding of yourself as an American."

Like McCarthy, Moloney—who calls herself "a hard-core, smells-and-bells Catholic"—saw her faith deepen in college and inspire her grassroots political activism, which in her case centered on the fight against abortion. But unlike McCarthy, Moloney's activism led her to embrace conservative causes on Capitol Hill. Now she fights for school vouchers and against abortion and government funding of controversial or blasphemous art. When she appears on television to argue politics, Moloney draws from Catholic theology to make her points. On one show, she mentioned the importance of "avoiding the occasion of sin," though she did not refer directly to Catholic teaching. Though she worries that her appearances on *Politically Incorrect* lend legitimacy to a show that veers toward the tasteless, Moloney also rejoices that she can explain her faith-based political convictions to such a large audience.

"I can't say I normally get six million people to listen to my discussion about avoiding the occasion of sin."

Allegiance to God

Though Moloney and McCarthy have applied their orthodox Christian faith to politics in drastically different ways, the Gospels arguably support the political philosophies of both women. Christian orthodoxy entails a defense of traditional values in the areas of sexuality, marriage, and family—the issues that occupy much of Moloney's energy on Capitol Hill. But that same orthodoxy is rooted in the Gospel passages that inspire McCarthy, parables that praise the poor and peacemakers and rail against the dangers of money and power.

Consider the debate among Christians in 2001 over how America should respond to terrorism. After the attacks on the World Trade Center and the Pentagon, young orthodox Christians huddled in university halls and at cocktail parties to hash out the meaning of the gospel in the context of modern war. Some argued that the gospel outlaws all violence. Many others pointed to the Christian theory of just war, which says that governments seeking to preserve order and defend their citizens can legitimately engage in battle, as long as they avoid intentionally harming innocent civilians.

Working out a political ideology that is compatible with Christianity, and applying the gospel to today's political debates, is no easy task. Increasingly, young orthodox Christians are not content to wholeheartedly align themselves with one political party. Many see their religious principles—not their party allegiances—as the key to the way they approach politics.

One example is the dichotomy between traditional moral values and a concern for the poor and oppressed. That separation may be pronounced in America's political discourse, but it is increasingly intolerable to young believers who see the two as inextricably linked. Like Moloney and McCarthy, these young orthodox Christians may disagree on political strategies or party affiliations. But they repeatedly affirm the political principle they hold in common: that Christ reigns supreme in their lives, and loyalty to his agenda—not to a secular political platform—guides their conduct in the political arena, and in every realm of life.

This political independent streak is particularly prominent among young Catholics who revere Pope John Paul II, a leader known for blending concern for traditional morality with progressive critiques of consumerism and capital punishment. Like the pope, these young believers often confound conservatives and liberals alike, who cannot easily classify their political convictions. Liberal baby boomers who equate the fight against abortion and same-sex marriage with intolerance and knee-jerk conservatism often express shock when they see young opponents of abortion and gay rights working for racial reconciliation or opposing the death penalty. Older conservatives may find themselves equally stumped when a young Christian joins them to battle condom distribution at schools and pornography, then critiques trade agreements that may endanger human rights. How, they ask, can these young adults be so inconsistent?

Young orthodox Christians say their political philosophy is consistent. In fact, they say, it is more defensible to conform one's political ideology to Christianity than to force Christianity into political categories. Though the debate still rages among many orthodox believers about the truly "Christian" approach to such issues as stem-cell research and federal funding for faith-based charities, these young believers are increasingly charting an independent political course and using their faith to guide their political activism.

"It's just a new generation," said Baxter, the theology professor at Notre Dame who taught McCarthy. "They're working out of a different paradigm. These kids don't fit those categories of liberal and conservative."

Baxter said today's young Catholics do not necessarily make the same connections as their parents did, between social activism and liberal theology or between traditional devotions and conservative politics. His Notre Dame students will pray the rosary while protesting an execution outside a prison, for instance. At St. Louis University, a Jesuit school, student activists gathered for a night of eucharistic adoration—a traditional devotion normally associated with conservative Catholics—before heading to Fort Benning, Georgia, to protest outside the School of the Americas, a rally largely attended by political liberals. Many of those same students protest abortion, too.

"Being Catholic isn't left or right," said Shawn Storer, one of Baxter's students at Notre Dame, who defines his political affiliation not as Republican, Democrat, or independent but simply as Catholic.

Storer was the valedictorian of his high school in Springfield, Ohio. The son of working-class parents and staunch Democrats, Storer felt a kinship with the Democratic Party, which he associated with his passion for fighting injustice and siding with the poor. But he also opposed abortion—something he had in common with the Republican, not Democratic, Party. He felt conflicted and confused, and by the end of high school he had declared himself an independent.

Pegged by his classmates as the mostly likely to become a politician, Storer landed at Notre Dame, where he found himself outnumbered in some circles by young conservatives. He had never considered himself a liberal—the categories did not seem to apply to his mix of beliefs—but he did not feel at home in conservatism. The relativism of secular leftist campus groups also made him uneasy. So Storer continued to search for a political ideology that could encapsulate his beliefs, one that would not force him to renounce the convictions that he believed were consistent with each other and his Catholic faith.

"I found myself looking for something greater," said Storer. "I was trying to fill this void."

Like McCarthy, Storer encountered Catholic social teaching at Notre Dame, and under the influence of Baxter and books by St. Augustine, Dorothy Day, and the pope, he began to formulate an independent political ideology. He opposes abortion, but he also opposes the death penalty and efforts to put profit before the rights of workers. After struggling to wrest himself from the political categories of right and left that never allowed him to consistently defend the vulnerable, Storer said, he found that "the best way out of it is being Catholic."

"Jesus' message was: 'Turn yourself to God and live your life ordered completely toward loving and serving God,'" Storer said. "In many ways, that's what makes sense to me."

Storer sees prayer and the sacraments as the "glue" that help him stay true to his political convictions.

"The most defiant thing you can do in this world is to go to Mass. You are saying that is the most powerful Lord—the only king."

Of course, many young orthodox Christians do affiliate with political parties. But even those who do so in the highly partisan atmosphere of Capitol Hill say their loyalty to Jesus supersedes their political identity.

"If your allegiance is with the Democratic or Republican Parties, it's not with God. That's wrong. That's idolatry," said Max

Finberg, who works on Capitol Hill and attends the Third Street Church of God, a small service-oriented congregation in Washington's predominantly African American Shaw neighborhood. "Jesus is much more important than Republican or Democrat, or black or white, or male or female, or American or not American, or Protestant or Catholic."

Though Finberg said his first commitment is to Christ, he opted to join the staff of U.S. Representative Tony Hall, a prolife evangelical Democrat from Ohio, because he admired Hall's work on humanitarian issues and hunger relief.

"He loved Jesus and cared about the poor," Finberg said, explaining what attracted him to Hall's political approach.

Finberg said he knows many Christians shun the Democratic Party because it defends abortion and gay rights. But he sees those issues as only a piece of the larger Christian framework and "not defining for a life with God." Despite his differences with more conservative Christians, Finberg said their common bond of faith helps them work together across partisan lines.

"Once you focus on relationships, it's amazing," Finberg said. "This feeling of being a family in Christ is for real."

Tough as it is to ascribe party affiliation to Christianity, a majority of the young believers interviewed for this book are social conservatives, many of whom vote Republican. Many are concerned with the substance of the culture wars—abortion, gay rights, sex education, pornography—though they may balk at affiliation with the Religious Right or at the prospect of declaring war on a culture they would rather evangelize.

Anti-establishment and Anti-abortion

Recent studies have shown a shift toward political conservatism among young Americans. When the National Opinion Research Center compared the views of young adults ages eighteen to twenty-four in the early 1970s with the views of young adults in the late 1990s, it detected significant shifts to the right on some social issues. More young respondents in the 1990s agreed that extramartial sex was always wrong, that the military merits confidence, and that the death penalty should be used for murder. Fewer young adults said that divorce should be easier to obtain and that marijuana should be legalized. Other opinions—on the rights of homosexuals to teach in schools, on women working outside of the home, and on interracial marriages—were more liberal among young adults in the 1990s than among those in the 1970s.[1]

According to another study, UCLA's annual survey of college freshmen, support for legal abortion has declined steadily every year but one since 1990. Then, 64.9 percent of incoming freshmen said abortion should be legal. In 1999, 52.7 percent thought so.[2] A Gallup poll taken in October 2000 found that 40 percent of eighteen to twenty-nine year olds think abortion rights should be more restricted. That proportion of anti-abortion sentiment among the under-thirty crowd was higher than in any other age group.[3]

Indeed, abortion opponents are buoyed by the overwhelmingly young face of today's pro-life movement. They point to the sea of teenage and young adult anti-abortion demonstrators who march on Washington each January and to the rallying cry of Rock for Life, a youth ministry that uses music to spread the anti-abortion message. Meanwhile, abortion rights supporters worry about the lack of support for their cause among the young. Articles noting the aging membership of Planned Parenthood and the difficulty abortion rights groups have in attracting young members quote the new anti-establishmentarians: young adults who use the rhetoric of radicals to explain their opposition to "the abortion industry."[4]

"Being pro-life is being countercultural," said Brother Patrick Reilly, a Catholic whose convictions and passion for politics led him to work for the Boston-based Massachusetts Citizens for Life. "It's almost a rebellion."

Thirty-five days after the *Roe* v. *Wade* verdict, Reilly was "born an Irish Catholic Democrat." As he grew up, he gradually drifted away from the faith and adopted the pro-choice, Democratic party line on abortion. But Reilly began to reconsider the abortion question in college.

As a college student in Florida, Reilly was held up at gunpoint—twice. One holdup occurred while he was working late at a fast-food restaurant, and it sparked a conversion back to the Catholicism of his childhood. The second happened eleven months later, on the campus of Florida State University as he was returning home after a date. Both holdups, when combined with his conversion and the mentoring relationship he developed with a boy from inner-city Tampa, made Reilly reflect on the inherent value of every human life. Abortion no longer seemed morally defensible to him.

"I definitely realized how blessed I was," said Reilly, who recently joined the Brotherhood of Hope, a Boston-based religious community of brothers and sisters. "And I saw how fragile life was."

Unlike Reilly, Steve Sanborn, who was born into a large Catholic family just two years before the *Roe* v. *Wade* decision, always believed that abortion was wrong. He also believed that pro-life politicians on the national level were too compromising on abortion. So, like other young Christians dissatisfied with the political system but concerned about political issues, Sanborn immersed himself in grassroots activism and sought a more direct way to get the pro-life message out onto the highways and byways of America.

Sanborn's idea crystallized while he was working in Alaska during the summer of 1993. Every night on television, he saw news coverage of Americans helping those affected by the devastating floods in the Midwest by sandbagging and donating to displaced families. The coverage got him thinking about how Americans enjoy helping their neighbors, protecting the innocent, and hearing feel-good stories. If he could somehow tap into those sentiments in the context of the abortion debate, Sanborn thought, he could change hearts and minds—and get some positive media coverage for the pro-life cause.

In 1995, Sanborn and a handful of his friends from Franciscan University of Steubenville, a Catholic college in Ohio, decided to start a nationwide anti-abortion pilgrimage across America led by young Christians. The group—which consisted of fewer than a dozen walkers its first summer—started its hike on the beach in San Francisco. The students spent twelve weeks walking more than three thousand miles to Washington, D.C., where they staged a rally at the U.S. Capitol. Along the way, they picked up half a dozen other walkers, talked to more than a hundred thousand people about abortion, prayed and protested outside some twenty abortion clinics, and spoke to dozens of churches, youth groups, and media outlets. Since that first year, Crossroads—the name the group gave to the annual three-month trek—has attracted more than two hundred walkers and has added a second, southern route that leaves from Los Angeles. The walkers rely on donations given along the way, or beforehand, to pay for the RV that accompanies them on the road. They attend Mass as often as possible and say the rosary as a group.

"We are peaceful. We're not nuts or anything," said Sanborn, who has noticed how surprised older adults are when they encounter a crowd of prayerful young adults sacrificing their summer to protest abortion. "It's strange for people to see young people who care about God, who are attempting to be orthodox, good people."

Sanborn recalled one woman he met in Denver who looked to be in her late sixties. She approached him with tears in her eyes and said, "I never expected this. I thought this was going to die with us."

Sanborn said he smiled and told her: "We're not going anywhere. We'll be doing this the rest of our lives."

The way Sanborn sees it, opposition to abortion among the young makes perfect sense. After all, most of the Crossroads walkers were born after 1973. Had their parents made a different—and legal—choice, they might never have been born.

"Our motto has really always been that it could have been us," said Sanborn, who said that argument frequently disarms older abortion rights supporters. "When it comes from younger people, I think people are more willing to listen and they're less able to dispute. I do consider it to be more our fight than anybody else's."

Indeed, much of the political rhetoric of young abortion opponents has a distinctly defiant tone. Protesters at the March for Life in Washington wear black T-shirts with stark, white lettering that says, "You will not silence my message. You will not mock my God. You will stop killing my generation." The Rock for Life Web site features a running tally of deaths by surgical abortion since 1973 and sounds the alarm for young activists by using such flashing slogans as "You can watch them die quietly, or you can Rock for Life" and "Who will cry for the children? Who will be their voice?" Young activists compare legal abortion to slavery and genocide and use the rhetoric of 1960s-era civil rights activists to galvanize support for what they see as the nation's most pressing human rights issue.

"It's the holocaust of our age," said Lauren Noyes, a legislative director for Republican congressman Joseph Pitts of Pennsylvania. Noyes said her evangelical faith, and the anti-abortion cause, led her to Capitol Hill: "I would never, ever have an interest in politics if it weren't for my faith. My passion is really for the pro-life and pro-family issues. That's what drives me here."

Faith Meets Politics

Noyes is a twentysomething Christian who spends much of her time working with the Values Action Team, a coalition of socially conservative congressmen and outside groups that work on legislation dealing with abortion, marriage, and education, among other issues. As warriors on the front lines of the culture wars, Noyes and her colleagues struggle to stand up for their convictions without alienating those who disagree with them.

"Sometimes we give God a bad name," said Noyes. She knows that many liberals consider conservative Republicans—and conservative Christians—"mean and hateful people," and it worries her when nonbelievers associate Christianity with conservative politicians they don't like. "We need to repaint the face of what we do sometimes."

Nina Krig, a twenty-two-year-old evangelical who works with Noyes in Pitts's office, said the label of social conservative sometimes prevents others on Capitol Hill from giving her "the opportunity to love."

"Sometimes I wish people didn't know," said Krig. "Because I'm fighting for all of these things, the door shuts. The temptation is to shut it back."

Krig said she tries to remain humble and admit her mistakes. Like Noyes, Krig's faith is what led her to Capitol Hill in the first place. As an economics major in college, she studied the effects of communism and came to the conclusion that big government destroys the personal responsibility of individuals. She began to reflect on American government and culture and the ways that America's economic system encourages personal responsibility among its citizens. Through it all, she felt her faith leading her to insights about what sort of government allows citizens to be as free as God intended them to be. Her faith-based reflection led her to embrace conservative politics and inspired her to work on Capitol Hill.

"My political perspective definitely came out of my faith and not the other way around," she said.

Now, as a legislative correspondent for Pitts, Krig watches for opportunities throughout the workday—a conversation, for instance, or a quick prayer for a colleague—to live out her faith.

"I have to feel like what I do during the day matters," said Krig. "I couldn't give so many hours of my day just trying to make more money. It has to matter. It has to be impacting lives for the Lord."

Washington—and the political realm at large—naturally attracts devout young believers who are born leaders with a passion for transforming culture. Several Christian organizations have attempted to tap into and contribute to that reservoir of talent and zeal by organizing programs and fellowships that help young adults integrate faith and politics. The Family Research Council, a conservative organization based in Washington, sponsors the Witherspoon Fellowship program for Christian college students. Participants in the program spend a semester in Washington learning—through internships, classes, field trips, and retreats—how to consider cultural and policy questions from a Christian perspective. Focus on the Family, a conservative Christian organization based in Colorado Springs, runs a similar program for college students interested in leadership. And the Council for Christian Colleges and Universities, an evangelical organization that includes about a hundred religious schools, sponsors an American Studies program that brings college students to Washington for a semester to examine public policy and their professional callings as Christians. These initiatives, known as worldview programs, are designed to help young Christians make the connection between their orthodox faith and its implications for politics and society. Most programs are conservative and are concerned with preserving traditional morality in a culture they see as desperately in need of principled Christian leaders. Their emphasis on integration is designed to help young Christians take their convictions from the religious community to the public square, where they can help transform culture from positions of political influence.

Those young Christians who follow their dreams to Washington can find support on Capitol Hill in the form of fellowships and prayer groups designed specifically to meet their needs. Faith and Law, a study group for congressional staffers, gathers several dozen Christians on the Hill several times a year to hear speeches from well-known authors, academics, and cultural figures. The speakers—such as evangelical law professor Phillip Johnson, Catholic theologian Fr. Richard Neuhaus, and Jewish political scientist Hadley Arkes—address questions about public life and public policy from a biblical and, generally, conservative perspective. The audience of Faith and Law tends to be mostly conservative, as well, composed largely of evangelicals and some Catholics. Its organizers also invite non-Christians who may be interested in the topics discussed. Smaller groups also have sprouted from the Faith and Law model, including a subset of discussion groups that formed on the Hill after Chuck Colson and Nancy Pearcey released their 1999 book, *How Now Shall We Live?* which challenged Christians to integrate faith into every aspect of life.

Bill Wichterman, who works as chief of staff for Pitts and helps run Faith and Law, said the gatherings contribute to the formation of a new generation of Christian leaders. Many young politicos will leave Capitol Hill after only a few years, he said. But they will apply what they learned there to careers in media, law, business, and academia.

"Most people on the Hill will end up as leaders in the culture," said thirty-seven-year-old Wichterman, who compares Capitol Hill to a "large Ivy League university" brimming with young overachievers. "So while they're here, we really want to make sure we're encouraging people to discipleship."

The discussion groups and working alliances also encourage ecumenism, by bringing orthodox Christians together across denominational lines to defend traditional morality and fight common enemies. Wichterman said he has seen evangelicals and Catholics working more closely in recent years and coming to better understand one another.

"A lot of us have just realized that there's this whole other side of the church," said Wichterman, who grew up Presbyterian, attends an evangelical church, and considers himself "a 'mere Christian' open to Catholicism." "The areas where we agree are so vast compared to the areas of disagreement. Our differences seem small compared to the assault of the humanist worldview."

An Eternal Perspective

Another group active on Capitol Hill is a private foundation known simply as the Fellowship. Led by Doug Coe, an organizer of the prestigious National Prayer Breakfast in Washington, the Fellowship eschews publicity. Its members work behind the scenes in Washington, across the country, and even internationally to evangelize political leaders. Many young evangelicals on Capitol Hill are involved with the Fellowship and use its evangelization style in their interactions with non-Christians. That style relies heavily on personal witness, one-on-one relationships, and a studious avoidance of religious jargon—including the word *Christian*—that could repel potential converts. Instead, evangelicals active in the Fellowship initiate conversations with non-Christians by talking about the servant leadership qualities of Jesus and the universal lessons that can be drawn from his life.

Personal witness plays a big role in the lives of young orthodox Christians on Capitol Hill. In a cutthroat political atmosphere that rewards pride, ambition, and vengeance, these young adults struggle to practice the opposite virtues: humility, surrender to God's will, forgiveness. They want to lead others to Christ by being a constant example of charity and gospel values. That's a tall order in any profession but especially amid the rancor and frenetic pace of politics.

"The rumor mill is so D.C.—that's one of my biggest struggles," said Sheila Moloney, of the Republican Study Committee. "And praying for your enemies is so hard."

Even when the political stakes are high, serious Christians cannot justify "playing dirty," Moloney said. The eternal stakes are higher.

"We don't see politics and this world as the end."

That eternal mind-set—the idea that a glorious afterlife awaits believers who serve God in this life—helps Christians put political battles in perspective. According to Karin Finkler, a Hill staffer who works on human rights issues, that mind-set also emboldens them to defend the vulnerable. In her international travels,

Finkler has met Christians who are tortured for the same faith that she practices freely in America. Her Christian conviction that worldly power is fleeting and that all power ultimately rests in God helps her pursue her work with passion and courage. And the gospel teaching that those who suffer for Jesus will be rewarded in heaven helps her deal with discouragement.

"I guess what gives me the guts to get in the faces of leaders of other countries is I know that in God's kingdom, those people [who are persecuted] will have incredible crowns," Finkler said, adding that the power of the leaders who torture them now "will be nothing. There's a bigger perspective here that we're working with."

When she encounters the horrific effects of persecution, Finkler consults Psalms 70 and 71 for strength. In them, the psalmist begs God for help and reiterates his trust that God will ultimately bring justice to the oppressed.

"I will hope continually," says the writer, in Psalm 71:14, "and will praise thee yet more and more."

"That is one that I have to repeat to myself," Finkler said.

Hoping and trusting God also extends to career decisions on Capitol Hill. Young aspiring politicians say careerism and selfish ambition run rampant there. Going against that grain can be tough for young Christians who believe that their political success will serve God.

For Max Finberg, political ambition has been a crucial part of his faith journey, which began when he converted to Christianity as a teenager.

"One of my idols has been to run for office," said Finberg. "Most kids think, 'I want to be president someday.' I actually held on to that."

To make it happen, Finberg developed a ten-year plan that involved working on a national campaign, going to law school, and eventually returning to his home state of New York to get elected. That began to change when he attended the National Prayer Breakfast in 1990. Finberg came as "a very partisan Democrat" but found himself inspired by listening to Hall, his future boss, and Doug Coe, the evangelical organizer behind the breakfast. He realized "love your enemies" applied even to his conservative adversaries. Eventually, he also recognized that his ironclad career plan was "Christ inspired but not Christ centered."

"I was only letting God work in different facets of my life—in compartments," said Finberg, a graduate of Tufts University. "I realized I needed to give that up."

Shedding his career blueprint did not force Finberg to renounce his dreams. In fact, he wound up working for Hall—his dream job—first as an intern, then at Hall's Congressional Hunger Center, and finally in Hall's Capitol Hill office. Along the way, Finberg earned a master's degree in social ethics from Howard University's School of Divinity and gained expertise on issues of race and poverty, which he now handles for Hall's office.

"I love my job. It's ideal," said Finberg while sitting in Hall's plush office. "I have far more responsibility earlier on than I would have if I had come the natural route instead of the supernatural route."

Finberg said he still hopes to run for office someday, but his career plan is no longer "set in stone."

"Is this preparation for me sitting in [a congressperson's] seat one day?" asked Finberg, his back to a breathtaking view of the Capitol dome at sunset. "Don't know. If it is, it's great. If not, there's something else out there."

8

THE CALL

He told them, "The harvest is plentiful, but the workers are few. Ask the Lord of the harvest, therefore, to send out workers into his harvest field."

LUKE 10:2

Beads were flying and beer was flowing at the raucous Mardi Gras bash on the outskirts of downtown St. Louis. On this drizzly Saturday in February 2001, thousands of drunken revelers had arisen early to converge in the streets for the nation's third-largest pre-Lenten party.[1]

Just five miles away, a group of more than forty young adults gathered together for camaraderie of a different sort. Most were singles in their twenties and thirties—the perfect demographic for tossing beads and swilling Budweiser. But instead, these young Catholics had gathered at a St. Louis retreat center to learn how they could better integrate their Christian faith into their secular jobs.

Conceived and organized by a handful of young Jesuit scholastics and lay Catholics, the daylong retreat included an address by a philosophy professor from nearby St. Louis University, a Mass, and a panel presentation. Professional diversity abounded: an investment banker chatted with a medical resident, a television reporter with a chemist, a philosopher with a businessman. The atmosphere was cerebral and the energy palpable as young believers who spend their workdays in secular environments gasped the fresh air of fellowship.

During one small-group discussion, eight young adults huddled at a table in the far corner of a crowded conference room. Ignoring the loud buzz rising from the rest of the room, they traded war stories from the world of work.

"Christ has called me to go to law school," said Jim Saunders, a former engineer whose story of a drastic Christ-inspired career move elicited knowing nods from the others.

The thirty-year-old Saunders told the cluster of his fellow Catholics about the perils of defending traditional morality in the legal world. Most of his classmates at Washington University School of Law disagree with his conservative stand on moral questions like abortion, Saunders said. And the same argumentative tendencies that will make him a good attorney also make evangelization a struggle.

"It takes a lot of tact, compassion, and humility," said Saunders, his pursed lips breaking into a smile. "And those are things I've never been good at."

One by one, the professionals swapped tips on spreading the gospel on the job and navigating a worldly workplace. A biologist told of teaching her lab coworker how to pray the rosary. An academic spoke of trying to pay attention to the wallflower students no one else notices. Another said she talks about God at work parties. The group roared its approval as she recounted stories of sharing the gospel with drunken atheist colleagues who interrogated her about her Christian faith after-hours.

The conversation rolled back to Saunders, the budding lawyer, who almost gave up on his secular vocation after his first year of law school. After he learned of the American Bar Association's staunch support of abortion rights and detected the secular sensibilities of law students, he started to wonder if his dream of being an influential lawyer for Christ was naive. Then Saunders thought of Supreme Court justice Antonin Scalia, a conservative Catholic known for his opposition to abortion.

"He's not afraid to carry the cross," Saunders said. "I thought, *You know, if this guy can do it, maybe I can do it.*"

Twenty-four-year-old biologist Karen Pitlyk told Saunders to consider the model for Christian lawyers: St. Thomas More. More gave his life because he refused to support the divorce and remarriage of King Henry VIII of England, she told him. By speaking out for Christ in their secular professions, Pitlyk said, Christians can glorify God just as the martyrs have through the ages.

"When we stand up for our faith," she said, "we pay tribute to them."

Faith at Work

Young Christians intent on spiritual integration choose their careers carefully and pay particular attention to the way their faith informs their work. They are not alone. The connection between spirituality and work is of increasing concern to Americans, as evinced by the explosion of books, conferences, and organizations devoted to the topic. According to a *Business Week* article, the number of workplace spirituality titles hitting the shelves each year quadrupled since 1990, to 79 in 1998. Newspapers from Chicago to Seattle have run feature stories on the proliferation of Bible-study and prayer groups in the American workplace, which—according to the Fellowship of Companies for Christ International—number more than ten thousand.[2] The ranks of corporate chaplains have multiplied. Agencies that offer consultation on workplace spirituality also have mushroomed, from about 24 in 1990 to about 850 in 2000.[3]

Despite the sacred-secular split usually associated with the workplace, Americans are increasingly unwilling to check their faith at the office door. One 1999 Gallup poll found that 48 percent of American workers had discussed their religious faith at work within the past twenty-four hours. Another survey, conducted by the Yankelovich Partners, found that 70 percent of workers polled conversed about faith in the workplace, and half said those conversations happened at least once a month. The survey, which was

conducted for the Lutheran Brotherhood, also found that 55 percent had prayed for guidance in their careers.[4]

Experts credit growing interest in spirituality, coupled with
longer workdays, for the trend. According to a 1999 Gallup poll,
78 percent of Americans felt a need for spiritual growth—nearly
four times as many as articulated that need in 1994.[5] At the same
time that Americans report growing concern about their spiritual
selves, they also lament the creeping influence of careerism and
extended office hours. A Families and Work Institute survey, cited
in a January 2000 *Fortune* article, found that the average American
workweek had grown by 3.5 hours between 1977 and 1997, to 47.1
hours. In the survey, 60 percent of respondents in 1997 said they
"never seem to have enough time to get everything done," as
compared with 40 percent who felt that way in 1977.[6]

A 1999 International Labour Organization report found Americans clocking the longest hours of any workers in industrialized
nations. In 1997, the most recent year studied, Americans worked
an average of 1,966 hours—23 hours more than in 1990.[7]

Many of the books, conferences, and consultants promoting
workplace spirituality adopt a deliberately vague stance toward
organized religion in an effort to attract workers of all religions as
well as those who consider themselves "spiritual but not religious." But some manifestations of the faith-at-work trend are
surprisingly specific in their religious affiliation. Among the
trend's Christian expressions are a host of groups—some new,
some well established—that bring believers together to contemplate the connection between Christ and career. These alliances
serve Christians in nearly every profession, from physicians in the
Christian Medical and Dental Associations, to journalists in
Gegrapha, to lawyers in the St. Thomas More Society.

Young adults often are at the vanguard of movements that reconcile Christian convictions and secular careers. Indeed, many
young believers see a profound connection between their conversion experiences and their choice of careers. They speak of God
calling them to a particular profession for a particular purpose.

Those specific callings tend to involve engaging the broader culture, often in an area that particularly concerned them before their full or adult conversion and sometimes with the explicit goal of evangelization. So an argumentative intellectual may experience a conversion and decide to use his talents as a lawyer defending Christian values. An actress struggling to live out her convictions may experience more serenity when she decides to dedicate her entertainment career to God and seek his glory instead of her own. And a group of doctors in training may gather weekly to peruse Scripture for clues about the way they should treat their patients, professors, and peers.

For these young believers and so many others, a job is never just a job. It is an extension of their faith journey, a way for them to spread the gospel, reverence God, and promote Christian values, which often clash with those of the workplace. To prepare for careers that impact culture and glorify God, these young Christians are forming innovative and action-oriented support networks that allow them to consider the integration question together.

Randy Parks is an associate pastor in New York City and a former InterVarsity minister at Columbia University and New York University. Parks said he sees a movement toward the integration of secular work and Christian faith among young upwardly mobile professionals. To the young adults he has worked with, being a good Christian at work means more than just treating colleagues well. Their fellowship groups tackle the specifics of what it means to be, for example, a Christian mathematician, artist, or business leader—and how their approach to those professions must be different because they are committed Christians.

Parks said most of these believers think seriously about the integration of faith and work. Their thoughtfulness bodes well for Christianity, since these young adults are poised to be the leaders of the future.

"These students are going to have a fairly large, wide range of influence in their business and academic endeavors," Parks said, of the young Christians at Columbia and New York University. "So if they have a strong commitment to Christ, that mission would carry into the workplace."

The mission of transforming culture through Christ-centered work is not limited to Christians with Ivy League degrees or high-status careers. Young believers are striving to serve God through countless different jobs. Their faith is inspiring their sacrificial service to the poor in homeless shelters, their unseen diligence at repetitive tasks as office assistants, and their intimate conversations with non-Christian coworkers while enduring draining physical labor. Though service-sector and blue-collar jobs get second billing in society, these young Christians know that Jesus himself was a carpenter who did a humble job in a small town—and changed the world.

That said, this chapter focuses on young Christians who are pursuing professions that give them the most leverage to impact culture writ large. They are budding doctors, lawyers, investment bankers, computer programmers, journalists, actors, and artists. Many have chosen their careers with the goal of cultural transformation firmly in mind, and they see their high-profile professions as the best way for them to use their gifts in God's service. As noted in chapter 1, the movement toward orthodoxy—and toward an intentional choice of careers that will impact the world for Christ—is not limited to young adults from the best schools or those with the most marketable talents. But it is particularly strong among those young adults, whose professional standing suggests that the movement toward orthodoxy may make up in talent, zeal, and personal influence what it lacks in raw numbers and popular support.

Business, finance, and technology

Mary Naber once worried that God and business could not mix. Torn by her conflicting desires for both, she marched into the office of her Presbyterian pastor in Salinas, California, and presented her career dilemma. She was sixteen.

"I love God," she recalls telling him. "And I love business. So I'll probably just go work in a church or be a missionary, right?"

Wrong, said her pastor.

"He said, and I still remember this," Naber said, "'Mary, Christians are needed in the corporate world, too.'"

That truth—that she could use her talents for God in the secular sphere—set her free. Naber followed her business instincts and wound up tackling a joint major of economics and religion at Harvard. Though her business professors touted her off the unprecedented pairing, Naber persevered, eager to prove that the two disciplines could overlap.

"I [wanted] to find that integration because it made the economics interesting to me," Naber said. "I was so blessed, because when I'm told I can't do something—it just gets me so revved up. It got me totally pumped up about where I could find the integration."

Naber spent her Harvard years combining courses from both disciplines and collecting ideas for a senior thesis upon which her dual degree depended. In the spring of her junior year, she hit pay dirt. She took a class that introduced her to the concept of social investing—using one's money to address ethical concerns, such as supporting organizations that care for the poor and the environment or boycotting pornography and medical companies that perform abortions. Naber, an evangelical Christian, began to delve into a study of Catholic teaching and the way some Catholics consulted their faith to make investment decisions. She dedicated her senior thesis to measuring the performance of portfolios constructed with ethical concerns in mind. Using a regression analysis to judge how each ethical variable impacted returns, Naber found that social investing did not significantly hurt financial returns.

In the spring of 1998, Naber graduated with honors and her two majors. She fell in love with social investing. And she saw her thesis accepted for publication in an investing journal.

"Praise the Lord for that one," Naber said. "I'm totally jived because I get to talk about the Catholic faith in a major secular journal."

Since graduation, Naber has served as a columnist, freelance writer, and conference speaker who introduces Christians—especially evangelicals—to the principles of social investing. She sees her work as an outgrowth of her faith, a way to help believers think about "where they are putting God's money."

"It's a stewardship issue of eternal significance," Naber said. "We talk about tithing 10 percent, and we forget about the other 90."

Naber sees plenty of biblical support for her work in social investing. Case in point: the gospel parable of the three servants who were called by their master to account for how they invested the talents, or money, he gave them.

"A lot of us are going to say, 'I don't even know where these talents are. They're in a fund over here. By the way, your money, Lord, was used to pay for some abortions.' Ugh! Such an important topic and we've totally overlooked it."

Perhaps the most rewarding aspect of Naber's efforts is that they give her opportunities to talk with non-Christians about ethics. Investors acting out of compassion, justice, and love are often open to a discussion about Christian morality, she said.

"Where do these values find their foundation?" Naber asked. "Ultimately, you can only trace it back to Christ, to a loving God. I'm excited about allowing those conversations to take place. This work, which I originally saw as so counter to Christ—what an incredible place to share Christ with others. I can actually bring people into the kingdom. And that's exciting. That's really exciting."

John Chao, a thirtysomething technology consultant for Fortune 500 and Global 1000 companies, spent nearly a decade working on Wall Street while also attending Redeemer Presbyterian Church in Manhattan. In his quest to integrate his Christian faith and secular career, Chao has learned to spot opportunities to witness to Christ in subtle yet substantial ways. Whether treating

employees with dignity and respect, sharing credit with coworkers for a job well done, or steering clear of immoral situations and
foul language when on business trips, Chao—like so many young
orthodox Christians in secular workplaces—constantly brings his
faith to bear on his work. Though opportunities to talk explicitly
about Jesus are sometimes scarce in the business world, he said,
chances to imitate Christ's behavior abound.

"I'm not there to proselytize my coworkers," Chao said. "But
I'm there to live out the gospel."

Chao and Naber share a desire for integration that is common
in the world of business and finance. Christian publications such
as *Life@Work*—an evangelical journal dedicated to "blending biblical wisdom and marketplace excellence"—appeal to an audience
of Christian business executives who seek to witness in their
workplace. Both *Fortune* and *Business Week* have devoted cover
stories in recent years to the influence of spirituality on the marketplace and the ways believers of all faiths are seeking to bring
their whole selves into their work.

The desire for integration sometimes emerges during an early
midlife crisis. Both the *New York Times* and the *Wall Street Journal*
have published features on the advent of an "early midlife crisis"
among Generation-X professionals. Many of these young adults
are changing course early in their careers, opting to shift their priorities away from career success and toward more free time, a sim-
pler lifestyle, or more meaningful work.

Experts blame the crises and disillusionment of young adults
partly on the instability of the job market, which leaves young
professionals cynical about corporate loyalty and careerism.
According to labor statistics cited by the *New York Times,* the
median length of time today's twentysomething workers stay in
one job is just 1.1 years—half as long as their counterparts lasted
in 1983.[8] Others note that those suffering from early angst are the
ones who experienced early, astounding, and in many cases, fleeting success in the dot-com explosion or those who grew up with

enough material advantages or opportunities that they could dismiss materialism earlier than did their parents and grandparents. Even for some who have not yet basked in wealth or career success, the prospect of an endless climb on an increasingly insecure corporate ladder leaves them cold. But the idea of laying down one's life and career for a cause greater than self and a joy more lasting than riches—that's radical enough to capture the imaginations of many world-weary young adults today.

Simon Baker, a thirty-one-year-old private banker and former stockbroker in San Francisco, has seen some young adults in Silicon Valley seek God after losing their dot-com fortune. But others convert in the midst of secular success, as he did. Baker discovered Christianity in his late twenties, when he had a beautiful girlfriend, plenty of party friends, and lots of money.

"The outside looked great," Baker said. "It was just miserable inside. I was just very restless, and I got sick of trying to fulfill it with girls, money, and drink."

When his restlessness led him to accept Jesus Christ three years ago, Baker's life began to change. His relationships grew deeper, and he started incorporating spirituality into his work and social life. Now he prays daily with his business partner at his banking firm. Both are Christians who find prayer helpful in an environment where anxiety intensifies with each market fluctuation.

"It's incredible to have that as a tool when you're dealing with people," Baker said.

His conversion also led Baker to put his skills and contacts to use for God. He started hosting cocktail parties for his peers that featured discussions led by such evangelical standouts as author Os Guinness and journalist David Aikman.

"The first time, I was pretty nervous," Baker said, of his informal evangelization efforts. "I had a lot of secular friends."

The liberal, secular consensus that prevails in San Francisco and Silicon Valley sometimes makes Christianity a tough sell. So Baker was surprised to find some of his friends enthusiastically discussing and debating Christian principles with his guest speakers. Baker believes that enthusiasm for Christianity will grow as the success of the dot-com industry wanes. Now that half of his friends are out of work, Baker said, they are more disposed to think about life beyond the material world.

Before, Baker said, "no one needed Christ in San Francisco. But it's a lot different now. People are really excited to get engaged in that environment. There's a real thirst."

In 1999, Baker formalized the connection between his financial and spiritual interests. He joined Abigail Ochs, a twenty-five-year-old Christian graduate of Princeton, to form a nonprofit organization that promotes philanthropy among young adults in San Francisco and Silicon Valley. The organization, involveX, uses hip marketing strategies and a casual, relational approach to appeal to its Generation-X constituency. Though involveX reaches out to young adults regardless of their religious persuasion, both Baker and Ochs see their philanthropic work as an outgrowth of their Christian faith.

Said Ochs: "If people ever ask me what my motivation is, that's definitely what I talk about. InvolveX is an easy vehicle to do some witnessing."

Ochs grew up in Newport Beach, California, and learned philanthropy from her parents, who started their own charitable foundation in the 1970s. As a child, she reserved a percentage of her allowance for charity. In high school, she organized her friends to volunteer at soup kitchens. In college, she continued to volunteer, but she became more interested in politics. Her passion for philanthropy was rekindled when she moved to San Francisco.

"I started seeing a bunch of my friends get involved in the whole dot-com business and really start making a lot of money," said Ochs.

She noticed that young professionals rarely thought to give their money to charities unless they were asked, and nonprofits rarely thought to ask. While Baker was considering creating a foundation for young investors like him who had disposable income to give to a good cause, Ochs was mulling over ways to introduce her peers to philanthropy. So the two united to form involveX.

With Baker's support, Ochs and another employee now plan parties and volunteer outings that introduce young professionals to organizations that need their help. Ochs plans to eventually return to school for her M.B.A. and to use her training to replicate the involveX model in other cities.

"People want to give back, but I think there's a bit of skepticism," said Ochs, who notices that young adults are more willing to donate to smaller organizations where they can play an active role than to larger philanthropies that simply take their checks. "They get motivated by having ownership in something and seeing the tangible effect."

The desire among some Christians in Silicon Valley to transform their communities was chronicled by *Christianity Today* in 2001.[9] The magazine featured an article that described the fall of the dot-com industry's fortunes and the rise of a "growing network of faith-focused business leaders [that] is determined to save Silicon Valley's soul." The determination of these high-tech executives has supported the success of the Silicon Valley Fellowship, a parachurch ministry that bills itself as "a forum for young Bay Area business professionals of all Christian denominations to explore issues of faith in the workplace, build God-centered relationships, and find encouragement in personal growth."[10] The fellowship offers young believers a chance to mingle with and learn from Christian business leaders. Members take trips to serve the homeless in San Francisco and meet for lunch during their workweeks to talk about their struggles.

For young Christians who work in technology, faith struggles often take an abstract form. The nature of their work poses inherent challenges to an incarnational orthodox faith. In a profession where mental activity is valued over physical activity, it's easy to become overly dependent on computers and to disregard the importance of humanity.

Matt Dorn, a former Calvinist who became an atheist in adolescence, converted to Catholicism while working as a self-taught computer programmer. Dorn said one of the reasons Catholicism attracted him was that it refused the "gnostic split between the mind and the body" that computer technology seemed to foster.

"The Catholic faith is one of the few ideologies that has a defense against that," he said.

While working in a field where virtual reality and technical advances supersede human interaction and connection to physical reality, Dorn appreciates the sensual side of Catholic worship. With the taste of the communion wafer, the smell of the incense, and the acts of kneeling and standing, for example, Catholic worship engages his senses and connects him to God's creation, Dorn said. And Christianity emphasizes the incarnation of Christ—the doctrine that God took on a human body, and therefore the human body merits respect.

His conversion to Catholicism has led Dorn to think, study, and write about the Gnosticism that he sees creeping into postmodern culture via technology and about the ways that a Christian outlook can counteract it. Someday, Dorn said, he hopes to share his insights with a wider audience that is grappling with the spiritual side effects of technological advances.

Law

On a Friday night in February 2001, Harvard Law student George Fibbe was putting his faith to work—literally. The twenty-six-year-old Catholic was toiling all night—and all weekend—on pro bono legal work for the Massachusetts Citizens for Life. The organization was challenging a new Massachusetts law that restricted abortion protesters, and Fibbe wanted to help.

Several other Harvard Law students also were working on the case, as part of their involvement with the Society for Law, Life and Religion, a campus coalition of religious law students who oppose abortion. Of all of the society's activities, Fibbe said, pro bono legal work is among its most popular.

"It's a way to use the legal skills they're getting to do some good in the real world based on their religious convictions," Fibbe said while taking a break from his research.

Though the real world is not always amenable to their convictions, many young Christian lawyers—like young Christians in other professions—seem increasingly willing to go public with their faith commitments. James Kovacs, a recent Harvard Law graduate who works at a Chicago firm, said he has seen several applicants to his firm list their membership in Christian campus fellowships on their résumé. Kovacs, a Catholic who was active in an evangelical fellowship at Harvard, did the same thing. He believes that openness is a reflection of the "evangelical nature" of many young Christians today.

On the legal fast track, Christian law students and lawyers face a host of hurdles to the practice of a devout life. Many complain that the legal world is steeped in relativism, thanks to law professors, lawyers, and judges who dismiss objective truth. Christian law students sometimes lament that they went into the profession to fight injustice but found that many of their professors dismiss that notion as hopelessly subjective and elusive.

That's not the case at the Ave Maria School of Law. The Catholic law school, founded in 1999 as a conservative, pro-life alternative for aspiring Christian lawyers, boldly proclaims its affirmation of the connection between law and biblical morality. The school's Web site promises that Ave Maria students will "consider how the unchanging moral imperatives of the natural law should affect a lawyer's approach to the practice of law. The students discuss not only what the law permits, but whether, in light of the moral law, the law should be amended or reconsidered." It's a novel approach for legal training today, and a growing number of law students seem to be embracing it: in its first year of existence, the school welcomed seventy-seven students—twice the number school officials had planned to enroll.[11]

On the school's Web site, Nathan Manni, a twenty-two-year-old student from Oak Harbor, Washington, explained why he chose to kick off his secular law career at Ave Maria.

"It's easy to get caught up in abstract theories of law and justice that are not grounded in any sense of morality," Manni said. He and his fellow students "chose a place that cultivates the link between our humanity and God's divinity."[12]

Young orthodox Christians in the legal field also face the temptations of what Bob Bordone calls the "corporate trap." Bordone, a lecturer at Harvard Law School and deputy director of the Harvard Negotiation Research Project, said his Christian students talk with him all the time about avoiding the trap. It runs something like this: A young attorney leaves school hoping to contribute to the world in an altruistic way or to work more humane hours than a fast-track corporate lawyer. But he decides to work in a high-powered, high-paying corporate firm for the first few years of his career so he can pay off his hefty law-school debt. (For the 2001-02 school year at Harvard Law, tuition alone hovered around $27,500 per year, or $82,500 for the three years it takes to earn a law degree.) The attorney's plan works for a while, until he grows accustomed to living on a six-figure income and begins to replace his old school debts with the new bills of a luxury lifestyle. Soon money has become an end in itself, new bills have mounted, more work must be done to pay them, and the prospect of giving it all up to live on less becomes unthinkable. "The trap is somewhat alluring," Bordone said.

To deal with the spiritual challenges posed by their profession, members of the Harvard Law School Christian Fellowship hold group Bible studies, where they also discuss such books as Joseph G. Allegretti's *The Lawyer's Calling: Christian Faith and Legal Practice*. Some seek advice on career decisions from professors and lecturers, like Bordone, whom they know to be serious Christians. Bordone said students assume that because he is a school lecturer and not a corporate attorney, he has successfully escaped the magnetism of money.

In fact, Bordone said, he worries about it, too. As a young Catholic who graduated from Harvard Law School in 1997, he hopes to marry and start a family someday soon. And he wants to have enough money to do that.

"I made an initial decision early on, and I felt like it was a good one. But it does get to be tempting."

Many law students and practicing Christian lawyers seek peer support in professional associations to ward off the temptations that accompany a demanding law career. One such organization is the Christian Legal Society, a nondenominational national grassroots network of attorneys, judges, law professors, and law students who work together, as the group's Web site says, "to follow Jesus' command 'to do justice with the love of God' (Luke 11:42; Matthew 23:23)." The society gives its younger members opportunities to meet and learn from established Christian attorneys, and the organization—which was founded in 1961 by four lawyers who met to pray together at an American Bar Association convention a few years earlier—promotes the pro-life cause, pro bono legal work for the poor, and "biblical conflict reconciliation" services for legal disputes. The group's Christian principles and practical support clearly appeal to young adults. Students at more than 160 law schools are involved with the society's campus arm, Law Student Ministries. And student membership has more than tripled since 1997, from 240 student members then to 853 today.[13]

Medicine

Few professional fields tempt their practitioners to careerism and teem with secularism as much as medicine. The challenges to an integrated faith life are copious and daunting in this field, where workaholics are congratulated and Christian medical ethics are routinely challenged. Seeking to live a balanced life, to discover the relevance of faith amid medical work, and to find peace in frenzied secular work environments, young believers in this profession struggle daily with what it means to have a scientific mind illumined by Christian faith.

One weekend in March 2001, 170 medical and dental students gathered in a St. Louis hotel to learn about the integration of faith and science. The standing-room-only crowd heard from Dr. Dale Matthews, a Washington internist and author of the 1998 book *The Faith Factor: Proof of the Healing Power of Prayer.* Armed with a dizzying mass of statistics and studies, Matthews set out to persuade this audience of skeptics, who are accustomed to evaluating arguments by scanning the numbers that substantiate them. His claim: Not only is faith compatible with medicine, it also makes a practical difference in patient care.

Many in Matthews's audience were earning academic credit for their attendance at this conference, and only a slice of them were active in Christian fellowships on their campuses. Some squirmed during his presentation, exchanging skeptical glances during portions of a statistical volley designed to show the curative effects of prayer. But his more general point—that doctors should be open to ministering to their patients' spiritual as well as temporal needs—seemed to find a receptive audience. And when Matthews conducted an impromptu poll, 80 percent of the twentysomething audience members raised their hands to testify that religion was "very important" to them, and about 60 percent indicated that they had attended religious services that week.

The reaction seemed to surprise Matthews, a middle-aged Christian who had cited several studies in his lecture that portrayed health-care professionals as less religious than their patients.[14] In the back of the room, Allan Harmer, the Midwest regional director of the Christian Medical and Dental Associations (CMDA), took the revelation in stride. Harmer said he sees many young health professionals rejecting the religious skepticism of his baby boomer peers.

"The present generation is willing to accept the fact that there are mysteries that we cannot resolve," said Harmer, who oversees CMDA initiatives at about three dozen medical schools. "It's a measure of good medicine to be open to that possibility."

Indeed, the entire health profession seems to be catching on to America's spirituality craze. According to a 2000 survey cited in *American Family Physician,* at least 65 of 126 medical schools and an increasing number of residencies now offer courses on the intertwining elements of religion, spirituality, and medicine.[15] Alternative medicine, holistic health care, and faith healing are hot topics on talk shows and in magazines these days, as are debates about the religious implications of bioethics controversies. Though much of the discussion about spirituality and medicine has taken a vaguely New Age hue, orthodox Christian groups—such as the Catholic Medical Association and the Christian Medical and Dental Associations, both of which are more than seventy years old—continue to thrive.

The CMDA, a fourteen-thousand-member network for Christians in health care, sponsored Matthews's lecture and conference. The group also organizes Christian fellowships on the campuses of medical and dental schools, including St. Louis University and Washington University in St. Louis, whose students packed this conference.

After it ended, seven of the students involved in fellowships at those schools clustered in the back of the conference room to talk about how their faith fit into their medical careers. Though they liked Matthews's idea of praying with religious patients, many saw their faith playing a much broader role in their medical practice—as the reason they went into medicine, the reason they care for patients, and the reason excellence in this profession matters to them.

"I was just totally called into medicine out of the blue," said Samuel Michael "Mike" Davis, a second-year medical student at St. Louis University.

Davis was in the army when he discerned a message from God during prayer beckoning him to become a doctor.

"There's no way I'd go into it otherwise," said Davis, a twenty-nine-year-old married father who earned spotty grades in his undergraduate discipline of anthropology. "So I talked to my wife, and it was . . . interesting."

His wife ultimately agreed that Davis should follow the call. So he returned to school to make up classes he needed for medical school admission. Now he is working on his M.D. and helping coordinate meetings of the CMDA on campus.

Seun Orebiyi, another second-year medical student at St. Louis University and organizer of CMDA campus fellowship meetings, is the daughter of a Nigerian Christian doctor.

She always wanted to practice medicine for the sake of Christ, Orebiyi said. "I knew I needed to use it to serve him."

Orebiyi believes the connection between Christianity and medicine is innate, since both physicians and followers of Christ are called to serve others.

"Being a doctor, that's part of our job," Orebiyi said. A Christian physician sees each patient as "one more person to share Christ with. Being Christians gives us more love for patients."

Many around this circle of doctors-to-be said their study of medicine—despite the reputation of medical schools as havens for secularists—actually has fortified their faith.

"Every day you're learning how amazing the body is," said Elizabeth Fialkowski, a second-year medical student and leader in the CMDA group at Washington University. Seeing the human body in all of its complexity reaffirms her belief that only God could design it. Medical school, she said, "has totally strengthened my faith."

Medicine has also challenged the faith of these students. Kerith Lucco, a medical student and CMDA leader at Washington University, said the secularism and relativism of fellow medical students and doctors makes it tough to integrate faith and work.

Lucco said that Christians who refer publicly to their beliefs are sent a clear message: "That's fine for you, but don't expect me to believe it, too."

Orthodox believers on medical campuses and in hospitals often seek fellowship from other Christians, who help them to consider their medical experiences in the context of their faith. One month after the St. Louis conference and twelve hundred miles away, five students gathered in a cozy dorm room at Harvard Medical School for a dose of that fellowship. The students—four aspiring doctors and one dentist-to-be—formed one of three cell groups run by the Harvard CMDA. The small groups meet individually for Bible study and faith sharing, then come together once a week for a larger fellowship meeting at the medical school.

On this Tuesday night, a young Asian man led his peers in a reading of the twelfth chapter of Luke, which included these lines: "When much has been given a man, much will be required of him. More will be asked of a man to whom more has been entrusted." Tracing his fingers over a Bible littered with yellow sticky notes and wrapped with a book cover made from a Banana Republic shopping bag, the man looked around the room.

"There's so much that we've been given," he said after a long silence. "We've been entrusted with the gospel."

His fellow students were sitting cross-legged on the floor, their shoes heaped in a pile near the door. One student—a tall, soft-spoken young woman who was hosting the gathering—nodded. She told the group how she had heard secular classmates talking recently about the need to share their blessings with the less fortunate and how her secular teacher was emphasizing the attitude of service that doctors should have toward their patients.

"I just thought, wow—they didn't say that because they're Christian, but [that idea] *is* Christian," she said. "It's all about service. That's so true."

A man with a booming voice spoke up. He quoted a Christian speaker he had recently heard on campus who urged young believers not to grow complacent in their witness to the faith. Then he shook his head.

"I believe all of those things," he said. "But on some level it hasn't totally shaken out and infused every part of my body."

The conversation drifted toward evangelization and the ways this small group of believers could share their Christian convictions in the medical field. When it swung around to the ways Christianity helps them survive the high-pressure world of medicine, the young woman smiled, her voice dropping low.

"I just feel so free from the things that are pressures here," she said, referring to the heavy workload and long hours that seem to overwhelm so many in her medical school class. The key, she said, is to "focus on the cross" of Jesus.

With that, they bowed their heads and huddled for twenty minutes of prayer. They prayed for themselves, their families, their friends, their classmates, their medical school. When they had finished, they laced up their shoes and headed to the grocery store. They were hosting a lecture by a medical missionary at the school the next night, and they needed to pool their paltry funds to buy some food for the event.

As she wheeled a grocery cart around the store a half an hour later, Colleen Hanna—the young woman who hosted that evening's meeting—talked about her volunteer work at a nearby crisis pregnancy center that helps needy women cope with unwanted pregnancies and avoid abortion. Seeing women who have come into the clinic after as many as a dozen abortions has convinced Hanna that there is a critical need for Christian doctors with pro-life convictions. She is interested in maternal and fetal medicine, as well as social medicine—a discipline that applies the social sciences and humanities to the fields of health and medicine. Hanna, who was raised in a conservative fundamentalist church and now attends an evangelical church in Boston, said she sees a growing interest among her peers in the spiritual side of medical care.

"People are so interested when they find out you're a Christian," she said. "There's a real sense of the importance of spirituality, the whole feeling that what we're doing now can't be everything."

Mass media and publishing

The ideas were flying at this conclave of North American journalists, who had hastily pulled their chairs into a lopsided, oversized circle in a Potomac, Maryland, conference room. The journalists fired questions at one another as only reporters could: who, what, when, where, how? And the usual favorite: What do *you* think should be done?

What made this gathering unusual—aside from the relatively peaceful coexistence of television and print journalists, who often antagonize one another—was the topic of their discussion. They were not debating politics, swapping story ideas, or jostling for job leads. They were talking about Jesus.

Jesus in the newsroom, to be precise. This collection of some fifty journalists was trading tips on starting Bible studies at work, herding Christian journalists for regional fellowship meetings, and praying for one another's careers. One young woman, who looked to be in her midtwenties, told the group about a Bible study she had started with a handful of coworkers at her California newspaper. Her ensemble, a mix of believers and curious colleagues, gathers regularly at a coffee shop before work for Bible reading and reflection. Her story sparked a series of interrogations by would-be imitators at the conference, all journalists hoping to start similar groups at their own news outlets or in cooperation with journalists at other news outlets in their cities.

A pair of young women, both television journalists at national networks, shared the story of their fellowship in New York City. The group meets on the first Saturday of each month and attracts about twenty Christian journalists from secular outlets around the city, who come to share their struggles and pray for one another's work. Its organizer, a television reporter who said she is often too busy to publicize the gatherings, marveled that the group still manages to attract at least one new person to every meeting.

Other young journalists told of praying—but not outright asking around—to discover other Christians in their secular newsrooms. They spoke of "intercessory prayer teams" of Christians in the field who pray for one another during crisis times. Student journalists asked for help in starting cell groups of Christians in their journalism schools. And one young woman suggested the creation of a mentoring program for fledgling journalists, who could benefit from the guidance of Christians established in the news business.

The group was only one of four such clusters that convened that evening in August 2001. The others—grouped by regions as vast as "India, Asia, Australia, and New Zealand" and "Africa"—had gathered in adjacent rooms to discuss the intersection of their Christian faith and secular trade. The organizers of the Second International Conference of Gegrapha, a fellowship for Christian journalists in the secular media, had opted that afternoon to divide its 250 conference participants into smaller groups so they could discuss the most pressing, pertinent issues in their respective regions.

Unlike the radio broadcaster from China who feared for his life or the newspaper reporter from Malaysia who regularly saw her stories spiked because they criticized the prime minister, the American journalists did not talk of monumental struggles for press freedom. They spoke of subtler pressures: staunchly secular newsrooms where orthodox believers are dismissed, disparaged, or assumed to lack objectivity. Television stations, newspapers, magazines, and radio outlets that squash or skew religious angles. Work environments where devout Christians learn to keep their values and beliefs to themselves lest they lose respect among their secular humanist colleagues. Not all tales were sad ones, and not all American journalists complained of bias. But most resonated with the breathless refrain repeated over and over in their circles during the three-day conference: "I can't believe this exists. I thought I was the only one!"

That sense of solidarity is precisely what Gegrapha founder David Aikman was aiming for when he established the international network in 1998. Aikman is a fifty-seven-year-old retired senior correspondent for *Time* and a senior fellow at the Ethics and Public Policy Center, a nonpartisan Judeo-Christian think tank in Washington, D.C. An Episcopalian who identifies with the church's "evangelical/charismatic wing," Aikman assembled Christian journalists in Washington before taking the fellowship global with a 1999 conference in Chichester, England.[16] He named the fellowship after the Greek phrase—found in the Gospel of John—that was uttered by Pontius Pilate when he was defending his choice of "King of the Jews" as the inscription to be placed over the crucified body of Jesus. Pilate said simply, "What I have written, I have written"—or, "Gegrapha, gegrapha."

"In the highly secular culture of American newsrooms, which are far more secular than society at large, what Christians often face is outright bigotry," Aikman told a reporter from *Insight on the News* during the 1999 conference.

"[Non-Christians in secular newsrooms] tend to react against any belief system they regard as establishment," he continued. "For most reporters, Christianity is still establishment. Also, there's the tremendous hostility toward the 'Religious Right wing' and all of the traditionally conservative clichés collectively associated in reporters' minds with Christianity. If you are, say, a Hindu, you are sufficiently rare not to be perceived as a threat."[17]

At the 2001 Gegrapha conference, American journalists often spoke only off the record about their convictions, hoping to avoid a public branding that could bring them trouble in the newsroom. Poll numbers seem to confirm their perception of colleagues as secular and leftist: a 1980 study found that half of the 286 media elites polled by the Center for Media and Public Affairs rejected religious affiliation, and 86 percent rarely or never attended services. A 1985 *New York Times* poll of print journalists showed that 82 percent approved abortion on demand, 89 percent supported the gay rights movement, and 80 percent disapproved of prayer in public schools.[18] A 1995 Roper/Freedom Forum study found that 89 percent of Washington correspondents had voted for Bill Clinton in 1992 and only 7 percent had voted for George Bush Sr. In a 1996 study by the American Society of Newspaper Editors of more than a thousand newspaper journalists, 61 percent said they were Democrats or liberal-leaning, and 15 percent said they were Republicans or conservative-leaning.[19]

Critics of the media say that bias against organized religion often seeps into stories about conservative morality and Christianity. One study, released in 2000 by the Center for Media and Public Affairs, coded 3,144 media discussions of religion and counted only 7 percent that contained any "spiritual dimension." The religion stories that did refer to theology, the study said, were "disproportionately connected to non-Christian religions with a small membership in this country."

Aikman and the organizers of Gegrapha want to encourage more young Christians to enter and stay in secular journalism. Though the nation's religious press is regarded by believers as vibrant and vital, Gegrapha aims to support the many young Christians who want to venture into the mainstream media outlets that reach the largest audiences. Other Christian organizations are also attempting to help. Media Fellowship International serves Christians in all forms of mass media through a ministry based on confidential prayer and Bible-study sessions. The Council for Christian Colleges and Universities hosts a monthlong summer journalism institute in Washington, which helps aspiring print journalists network with established professionals in the national media.

Many Christians in publishing and the secular media work hard—and pray hard—to achieve integration of their faith and work. Writer Pamela Toussaint, a Christian in her midthirties, has written or cowritten five books, on topics ranging from the health of black women to women's stories of interracial friendship and faith. When she sat down to write her first book—a guide for African American women on pregnancy, childbirth, and motherhood—she had a secular cowriter, a secular agent, a secular publisher, and a bad case of the nerves.

"How do I handle this, Lord?" she recalls asking as she sat down to her computer. "Lord, lead me."

Not only did God lead her, Toussaint said, but he also used her conversations with the doctor who was her cowriter to lead him too. After working closely and talking often with Toussaint, the doctor called her one day and told her he had "received Christ."

"I didn't know God was using me," said Toussaint, who was delighted that the book could now—with the enthusiastic endorsement of her cowriter and a surprising amount of leeway from her publisher—include references to the psalms and suggestions that pregnant women pray over their wombs.

Toussaint's later books also have touched on religious themes. Now she is working on a script for a television drama that she hopes will reach even more people in search of God.

"I don't want to preach to the choir," Toussaint said when explaining why she writes for mainstream audiences rather than for strictly religious publications. "I think I'm more excited when unbelievers who read my work tell me how much they get out of it."

Mitchell Muncy, a thirty-two-year-old Catholic and executive vice president of Spence Publishing, thinks editorial work is a "natural fit" for Christians who want to promote their values without preaching. Muncy oversees the work of a conservative Dallas publisher that has made waves in intellectual circles with such nonfiction titles as F. Carolyn Graglia's *Domestic Tranquility: A Brief against Feminism* and Paul C. Vitz's *Faith of the Fatherless: The Psychology of Atheism*. The books are not Christian, but they are sympathetic to Christianity and western tradition, Muncy said.

"In my professional work, how do you make the truths of the faith appealing and understandable to people? That doesn't happen in the secular world by preaching sermons to people."

Instead, Muncy tries to publish writers who offer historical perspective and point to hopeful conclusions. He avoids publishing work that he finds trivial, sensational, or sordid. He also tries to live his faith at work in more mundane ways—by working hard and treating colleagues with Christian charity. Muncy is a member of Opus Dei, an orthodox association of mostly lay Catholics who seek to live their faith more fully in the secular world by viewing all work as God's work. Muncy said the group's priests and prayer routines give him the spiritual formation he needs to more effectively witness to Christ in the secular world.

"You're not doing anything different" as an Opus Dei Catholic who works in the secular realm, Muncy said. "You're doing the same things in the right way and hopefully for the right reasons. You're turning even work that's secular into a prayer.

"I try to do my work very well," Muncy continued, "not because that's going to advance me professionally, but because God wants our professional work to be well done, because that's the way he has chosen for most of us to live our faith."

At the office, Muncy said he tries to "offer up the daily tasks and trials" to God, and his faith helps him temper his naturally tough management style. He said his spirituality prompts him to consider the needs of employees as well as of the company when making decisions.

"This doesn't preclude having a professional outlook," said Muncy, who added that the best thing for some people is to leave a job they cannot do well. "It's just having that deeper concern for the whole person."

That concern extends to the editors and writers Muncy meets on the job. When networking at a conference, for instance, he tries to work with colleagues from other companies for the common good and to pay attention to their personal, as well as professional, concerns. Muncy asks a "workaholic" magazine editor if he is getting enough rest, for instance, and he discusses life's big questions with a group of nonbelieving professional men in Dallas over regular lunchtime get-togethers. The conversations are not necessarily religious. But they are part of Muncy's spirituality.

"In Opus Dei, it's typically called the apostolate of personal friendship. It's not 'One more soul on your belt.' That's not the point, either. It's having that genuine interest in a person."

Arts and entertainment

As they nestled into an overstuffed couch with an unobstructed view of the empty stage, the two women surveyed the packed room with a mix of expectancy and cool confidence. Both were actors who looked to be in their early thirties. Both had the arched eyebrows, sleek coiffures, and lanky figures of runway models. One was white; one was black. They were college chums and Christians who had made the show business pilgrimage together, first to New York City, then to Hollywood. On this night in April 2001, they joined nearly a hundred other actors, writers, and "newbies" to seek advice about show business in, of all places, a church.

Of course, First Presbyterian of Hollywood is not your typical church. An evangelical congregation dedicated to serving Christian artists and entertainers in Los Angeles, First Presbyterian stands in the shadow of the Hollywood sign, just off Sunset Boulevard. Its sprawling complex includes a sanctuary, a theater, and about half a dozen other buildings that allow it to host fellowship meetings like this monthly gathering for Christian entertainers known as Third Thursday.

At this assembly, Christian entertainers and aspirants congregated for more than mere fellowship. They gathered to network, swap cards and contacts, and hear from a keynote speaker with a reputation as a "dream maker." Their goal: to launch entertainment careers that glorify God.

But tonight, the two women who came looking for acting advice were out of luck. The evening's star was an agent for writers, not actors. A few minutes after the women arrived, the handsome literary agent ambled onto a stage decorated with a television set and several votive candles. He opened his speech with an Our Father, bowing his head as he prayed in front of his audience. Then he proceeded to tell his own conversion story before dishing out concrete advice to the mostly thirtysomething audience on what it takes to be a screenwriter for prime-time television. His counsel: Write ceaselessly. Intern at studios and learn the process. Work in teams. And work hard.

The congregation of would-be standouts hung on his every word. His was the wisdom of a Christian who did the impossible: made it in Hollywood and survived with his faith intact.

Like orthodox believers in every profession, young Christian artists and entertainers often commence their careers with grand visions of transforming culture for Christ. But many soon find themselves fighting for their spiritual lives, barely able to cling to their values in private, much less convert others. Surrounded by colleagues who overwhelmingly reject conventional morality and organized religion, young Christian entertainers and artists struggle to defend the faith when necessary without needlessly isolating themselves or injuring their careers.

Many fail at that balancing act. Yet young Christians say the risks are worth taking, because the stakes are so high. Consider the perks of working in a place like Hollywood: believers can use their creativity for God, reach audiences that might never set foot in a church, and produce movies, music, and other artistic projects that subtly but powerfully illustrate Christian principles. Their efforts stand to make a huge impact on America's future: a 1999 Kaiser Family Foundation study found that the typical American child spends an average of more than thirty-eight hours a week—nearly five and half hours a day—watching television, listening to music, and consuming various other media.[20] If young Christians could shape the content of that media flood, they could change the way Americans think about religion, morality, and life in general. Along the way, they might also change the minds of artists and entertainers who deprecate Christianity, creating a ripple effect that could transform American popular culture.

"Hollywood is a mission field," said David Schall, director of entertainment ministries for First Presbyterian and founder of Inter-Mission, a four-thousand-member network of fellowships for Christian entertainers. "Our purpose is to change Hollywood from the inside out."

Inter-Mission, which was founded in 1987, has outposts in Los Angeles, New York, and Minneapolis. It supports such "sister ministries" as Act One, a monthlong seminar that attracts aspiring Christian screenwriters, and Actors Co-op, a theater company run by Christians that operates on the grounds of First Presbyterian. Also working with Inter-Mission is Associates in Media, an umbrella organization affiliated with Campus Crusade for Christ that includes such fellowship groups as Mastermedia International, for entertainment executives, and Premise, for writers and others who affect film and television content.

Opportunities abound in other arts-and-entertainment centers too: Christian actors in Manhattan flock to The Haven, a popular weekly Bible study, or attend acting workshops at The King's College, an evangelical school in New York's Empire State Building. Other fellowships include Open Call, Entertainment Fellowship, the Arts and Entertainment Ministry, Media Fellowship International, Catholics in Media Associates, and the Nashville Christian Musician's Fellowship, organized by Artists in Christian Testimony.

Mike Chapman, of Associates in Media, said he sees a "whole new level of communication and cooperation between ministries in Los Angeles." Chapman traces that unity to the growing recognition—particularly among young evangelicals—that secular art and entertainment can be used for good as well as evil.

"It's only really now in the past five years that the church is starting to catch a vision for Hollywood in the mission field," said Chapman, who has lived in L.A. since 1987. "Before, there were maybe fifteen hundred believers out there. Now, there are maybe eight thousand. I think it's God. I think God is burdening Christians to come to Hollywood."

Many young evangelicals in Hollywood tell stories of once feeling stuck in the "Christian ghetto." Still reeling from a pietistic upbringing that sheltered them from secular society, they see Hollywood, and the arts in general, as the final frontier to be conquered for Jesus. Their heroes are Christians like the late Bob Briner, whose best-selling 1993 book, *Roaring Lambs,* challenged believers to stop hiding their talents under the bushel basket of an evangelical subculture and start bringing them to bear on secular society. Their models are artists like the Christian members of Sixpence None the Richer, a platinum-selling folk-rock band whose songs for mainstream audiences are uplifting but not overtly religious. Weary of the culture wars that shaped the 1980s and 1990s, these young believers want to win souls for Christ through persuasion and artistic excellence—not picketing or preaching. Many find that they need the support of fellow believers in the business, as well as churches friendly to the arts, to achieve their vision.

Jeff Charlton, a Los Angeles actor in his midthirties, was raised in a conservative Baptist church in LaGrande, Oregon. He clung to his childhood faith through his college years. But as he began to pursue an acting career at the end of college and into graduate school, Charlton was plagued by persistent doubts about the compatibility of Christianity and artistic freedom. The theology he had learned as a child made him suspicious of the arts, yet he felt called to acting—a profession that lacks institutional support in many Christian churches.

Charlton became increasingly frustrated by his inability to find a Christian approach to the arts that offered a theological context for his work. When he went to church, he heard sermons full of platitudes that had no bearing on his struggles as a Christian actor seeking to glorify God while taking his craft seriously. So he stopped going—for four years.

"I believed Christianity was absolutely true and the best way to live, and that my church experience was irrelevant," Charlton said.

After attending graduate school in Indiana, Charlton moved to Chicago and prayed for a new church, one that would help him integrate his faith and his craft. He found an Evangelical Free church where the pastor gave practical sermons, supported the arts, and affirmed Charlton's work.

Eventually, he found churches that ministered specifically to entertainers, like First Presbyterian of Hollywood.

Now Charlton belongs to First Presbyterian and its Actors Co-op, a church-sponsored theater company that opens its meetings with prayer and requires members to sign a statement of faith to join. Though it performs secular shows that have won positive reviews from such secular strongholds as the *Los Angeles Times,* the Co-op's atmosphere is decidedly different from anything Charlton experienced before. Instead of making raw sexual jokes backstage, he and his fellow cast members take prayer requests from one another. And the church that supports them reaches out to struggling Christian actors with rent money, food donations, and worship services that incorporate the arts.

"I've never seen a church do this," said Charlton, who also works at the Co-op's box office. "In my experience, the church has been, in a lot of ways, hostile to the arts."

Efforts to engage culture through art have gained momentum particularly among young evangelicals who were previously segregated from secular culture, theologically and otherwise. A similar trend has emerged among devout young Catholic actors, artists, and screenwriters. Many young Catholics never experienced the same degree of isolation within a Christian subculture that evangelicals did. But their exposure to secular liberalism—which seeped into many Catholic schools and parishes after Vatican II—has given them a similar desire to transform culture. Often inspired by adult conversions to orthodoxy and spurred on by Pope John Paul II's denunciations of America's "culture of death," these young Catholics want to use their creativity to restore a "culture of life."

"I used to equate living a zealous Catholic life with ministry," said Patrick Coffin, an aspiring Hollywood screenwriter who graduated from the first Act One screenwriting class in 1999. "I certainly don't think that anymore."

Coffin is a self-proclaimed "raised, rebelled, and returned Catholic" in his thirties. He fell in love with theater in college but pursued theology and teaching in the wake of his adult conversion back to Catholicism. Eventually, he opted to combine his loves by writing screenplays that convey truth without preaching.

"Souls are not saved by movies," said Coffin, who works as a headhunter to support his budding writing career. A Christian in Hollywood who attempts overt evangelization with his movies "will become Pat Boone. But if you're trying to be too much of a stealth bomber, you become one of them."

The ideal movie is not a mix of the two extremes, Coffin said, but an honest film that conveys "the truth of the human condition."

Unlike Coffin and other Catholics, who come from a faith tradition loaded with sacraments and symbolism, many Protestants grew up in churches that eschewed visual imagery and spiritualized Christianity. Those churches often regarded art and symbolism as too "worldly" and passed their views on to budding Protestant artists. As a result, Protestants—and particularly, evangelicals—have historically attempted to use the arts and entertainment more for overt evangelization than subtle symbolism. Though many young Protestants today are making a conscious effort to avoid didactic projects and tap into the power of symbolism, the religious background of these artists, and of their counterparts from more liturgical churches, still tends to shape their work.

Barbara Nicolosi, a Catholic and director of the Act One program for Christian screenwriters, explained the difference between her Catholic and Protestant writers. The Catholics make better use of allegory in their writing, Nicolosi said: "They believe in the power of symbols because they are surrounded by them."

Protestants, and especially evangelicals, "really believe in the power of truth and in the power of change and redemption. Catholics are very cynical about that."

Today, many young Protestants and Catholics are working to mend the fissure between Christianity and the arts that developed during the Reformation and to heal the division between their faith traditions. Their desire to do so is reflected in the trend toward symbolism and liturgy in worship that has surfaced among young Christians across the denominational spectrum, as well as in concrete initiatives that unite Christian artists with one another.

Young believers who want to blend faith and art belong to such organizations as Christians in the Visual Arts and the International Arts Movement, or I AM. They attend conferences on "Art as Prayer: Prayer as Art" in New York City and "Art and Soul" at

Baylor University in Waco, Texas. They read *Image: A Journal of the Arts and Religion*; listen to *Mars Hill Audio,* an audio magazine that explores connections between Christianity and the visual and literary arts; and circulate Pope John Paul II's "Letter to Artists," which argues that beauty is essential to the church.

Thinking about the power of beauty is what led Tashya Leaman to study landscape architecture. A twenty-eight-year-old Mennonite from Pennsylvania, Leaman always appreciated her faith tradition's emphasis on simplicity, pacifism, and links to the land. But when she traveled with missionaries from her church to Peru, she felt limited by their singular focus on planting new churches there. She saw many other needs among the people—for political, economic, and educational help—and she decided to look for a career that would allow her to "bridge the gap" between her secular interests and her Christian faith.

"I was looking for more of a holistic approach," said Leaman, a graduate of Messiah College, an Anabaptist school in Pennsylvania.

Leaman spent her first few years after college working in international development for several Washington-based think tanks and visiting war-torn areas around the world. The more she thought about world peace, the more she began to reflect on her Mennonite heritage and the connections between beauty, the land, and human harmony. In December 2000, she quit her office job and began working in a floral shop in Georgetown as a sort of "sociological study." She was fascinated by the way urbanites in the sterile city flocked to the shop seeking beauty.

Inspired by what she observed at the flower shop and guided by a landscape architect who had grown up in war-torn Lebanon, Leaman enrolled in a three-year graduate program in landscape architecture at Cornell University. She plans to spend her life designing spaces of beauty and artistry in the midst of war-torn countries and violent neighborhoods.

"Beauty impacts people's ability to live in peace," said Leaman, who believes that the process of a community's landscape

revitalization, as well as its aesthetic outcome, can help enemies reconcile with one another. "God created everything. He's created the
natural environment and each person. I want to bring life back to
God's landscape, to help mend relationships with one another. I hope
that that will eventually impact society at large and the world."

Many orthodox Christians believe their faith—and, by extension, their belief in objective standards of truth and beauty—
makes them ideally suited to creative careers. Taking as their
motto Philippians 4:8—in which Paul exhorts believers to focus
on "the true, the good, and the beautiful"—young Christian
artists try to use their talents to impart some truth or inspire some
wonder that leads patrons to God.

There is no shortage of patrons seeking explicitly Christian art
and entertainment. The popularity of Christian music, books, and
movies among the young—a reflection of the broader popularity
of evangelicalism among that group—has been analyzed in secular publications from *Entertainment Weekly* to the *New York Times,*
as writers and entertainment executives struggle to understand
why such explicitly religious materials appeal to the young. The
cover of the July 16, 2001, issue of *Newsweek* featured the faces of
nineteen teenagers in a mosh pit at a Christian rock festival. Red
and black letters shouted the prevailing sentiment at the summer
gathering, which attracted fifty thousand Christian music fans:
"Jesus Rocks!" Inside, pictures of praying and playing youths were
mixed with the sort of raw data that makes industry executives
drool: the Left Behind series, a collection of apocalyptic Christian
novels, has sold some 28.8 million copies. The Christian *VeggieTales*
cartoons have sold 22 million videos. And record sales of contemporary Christian artists reached $747 million in 2000.[21]

Despite the obvious market for explicitly Christian art and
entertainment and the freedom Christian artists have to express
their faith in the religious genre, many direct their energies into
the secular realm, where they try to shape projects that are not
overtly religious.

Bridget Finney, a Catholic in her twenties, has spent three years pursuing a screenwriting career in Hollywood. While doing so, she has taken work at a film production company in Beverly Hills—a job that allows her to review mounds of potential movie scripts.

"It's an adventure every day," said Finney. "At my job now, I'm like a soldier trying to defeat evil, trying to stop evil scripts from getting made."

When Finney sees a particularly debauched or godless script, she gives it a negative evaluation. If that does not stop the company from pursuing it, she said, she starts "praying like a maniac" that it will not turn into a movie. Finney uses e-mail to enlist the prayers of her network of Christian friends in Hollywood. Sometimes, she said, the prayer chain works and the script gets rejected.

Still, Finney has learned to pick her battles. Though she thought she would never work for a company that produced horror films, for instance, she now sends out letters promoting those films as part of her job.

"I've learned to have more compassion, because here I am," Finney said in a spring 2001 interview near her office. "In spite of my best efforts, I'm not perfect. Why do I expect everyone else to be?"

The struggle for Christians in the entertainment industry—and in all fields, for that matter—is to find the middle ground between stringency and capitulation. Failures are inevitable, particularly in a place like Hollywood. Work is scarce, and there is always someone waiting to take the place of an actor or writer with "religious hang-ups" or moral qualms. Young Christians hoping to get to the top and someday use their influence for Jesus have been known to take shortcuts that derail their orthodox faith.

"We've seen too many good people come into the industry and lose their souls in the process," said Nicolosi, of Act One. "In making the compromises, you lose the ability to be an effective apostle."

Nicolosi, like many Christians in Hollywood, can tell tales of believers who started with godly intentions and wound up "selling

out" by writing scripts or acting in films that contradicted their Christian convictions. Believers in the entertainment industry need to spend time with other Christians who support them and hold them accountable, she said.

Many young Christians interviewed for this book listed the support of other believers among their key sources of career guidance. But many also said that such support has its limits, since fellow believers are often just as confused as they are about where to draw the line as a Christian artist or entertainer. Can a Christian produce an R-rated movie? Should a Christian actor do a nude scene? Are swear words acceptable in a script? And what projects are simply off-limits to orthodox believers?

Christians will come to different conclusions, said Ryan Finnelly, a twentysomething evangelical who works in Hollywood, "because how to make a film isn't in the Bible."

Ryan Finnelly and his wife, Emily Finnelly, recently attended a conference that addressed questions of Christianity and filmmaking. The conference featured Scott Derrickson, a young writer and director who made waves in Christian circles for cowriting *Hellraiser V: Inferno,* a horror film released in 2000 that featured a Los Angeles detective trapped in hell and attacked by demons. Derrickson is a Christian who attends the First Presbyterian Church of Hollywood.

At the conference, Derrickson explained his motives for making the film. He wanted to show that the detective's sins of drug use and infidelity had horrific consequences and to use fear and gore to make viewers think about life after death.

"It's a genre where you can preach," Derrickson said, in an April 2001 interview. When fellow believers ask him why he is not portraying "the true, the good, and the beautiful" in his films, Derrickson reminds them that sin and damnation are Christian truths.

"The truth is, many people do not get redemption," he said. "Many things that are true are not beautiful. I have the instinct and the capacity to look at the harder truths, and I think as artists, we have to do that."

For her part, Emily Finnelly said, she respects Derrickson's careful deliberation about *Hellraiser*. But she still worries that films that exclude the hope of resurrection overlook the most important truth of Christianity and could lead viewers to despair. If Christians in Hollywood must feature graphic sex, drug use, and despair in their films to be accepted and successful, she said, "then I don't have a job here."

The Finnellys are both graduates of the Los Angeles Film Studies Center, a Christian institution that sits in a particularly strategic position for cultural engagement. The center is less than two miles away from Universal Studios and less than a mile from Warner Brothers Studios. Though its location alone could probably attract a healthy crop of college students, the center—which is sponsored by the Council for Christian Colleges and Universities—offers aspiring filmmakers much more than proximity to celebrities. Its students get an inside peek at Hollywood and a leg up on other neophytes, thanks to the center's classes and internship arrangements. To enter the program, students must assent to a statement of faith that precludes "sexual immorality, homosexual practice, adultery, theft, and dishonesty"; forbids alcohol, tobacco, and illegal drugs; and requires them to "make the Lordship of Jesus Christ central to all I do."

Though the center is rooted in a conservative theological tradition, its Faith, Film, and Culture class is anything but traditional. The instructor, a Christian screenwriter with a broad smile and a gift for energizing his students, spent his last class of the spring 2001 semester castigating the Religious Right for its rigorous moral standards. His slide presentation featured clippings of controversial speeches by Jerry Falwell and snapshots of anti-gay protestors at the funeral of slain gay student Matthew Sheppard.

In the midst of the presentation, the instructor moved toward a white board at the front of the class and plotted a chart that listed "Heroes, Villains, Audience, Message" on the top and "Old Testament History, Prophets, Gospels, Paul" on the side. Prodding his students for answers, he took them through his

interpretation of the Bible. In his equation, the hero of the gospel was Jesus, its villains were the self-righteous, its audience was everyone, and its message was "love and grace, except for the self-righteous." Other parts of the Bible are "in-house documents" meant only for believers, he said, and their condemnations of sin—such as the Pauline exhortations against sexual license and homosexuality and Old Testament warnings about the consequences of transgressing God's laws—should not be broadcast to the general public.

"We have become the moral thought police, telling everyone else to shape up," he said. It's no wonder, he added, that nonbelievers in Hollywood and elsewhere "think we're hateful, think we're judgmental."

The instructor took some flak from the aspiring filmmakers and screenwriters in his midst. A few wondered aloud at the implications of this vision of Christian tolerance. Does this mean they should not tell others they are Christian? Does it mean they should not confront a Christian friend who is sinning and remind him about what the Bible says about his behavior? Or does being tolerant require them to emphasize only what Jesus said about forgiveness, without mentioning the strict moral standards he championed?

One young man with a furrowed brow raised his hand.

"Where do you draw the line on the church, then?" he asked. "It seems so gray, because I *want* people to keep me accountable. How do you address anything like that in any kind of Christian media?"

The screenwriter grinned.

"The day that our church is dispensing too much grace, then we can worry about it," he said. "Are we ever going to err by being too libertine? Ain't gonna happen folks. And your reaction just told me that."

After the class ended, the screenwriter was deluged by students. Many gushed about how profoundly he had changed the way they thought about their roles as Christians in Hollywood. When asked if he saw any danger in encouraging young Christians to keep their views on sin and morality to themselves, he smiled again and shook his head.

"I think the danger is that we'll just continue to beat up the culture rather than to embrace the culture," said the instructor, who asked that his name not be used, lest some of his unbelieving colleagues in Hollywood learn that he is Christian and associate him with the Religious Right.

While the problem of alienating unbelievers is a real one among Christian artists and entertainers, the opposite danger is also prevalent—that of embracing the culture too much, to the point of capitulation. Young believers who enter arts and entertainment hoping to share their Christian convictions with others often find that their desire for acceptance from secular colleagues leads them to keep those convictions quiet. In a culture where individual autonomy reigns supreme, many young believers seem destined to slip into the very relativism that their orthodoxy would refute. The most susceptible to such relativism often are those raised in strict fundamentalist churches. Eager to enter and transform the secular world they were sheltered from as children, many young Christians swing to the opposite extreme. They naively accept even the most heterodox projects and principles in the name of "engaging the culture."

Alan Wolfe saw a strain of that trend among college professors and students at evangelical schools. In his 2000 *Atlantic Monthly* article "The Opening of the Evangelical Mind," Wolfe noted the growth in both the quality and quantity of evangelical scholarship in recent years, and his take was overwhelmingly positive. But he also said that today's evangelicals "are democratic to a fault," and their eagerness to find value in every idea and person can impede their ability to make good judgment calls. Wrote Wolfe: "Evangelicals have created institutions as sensitive and caring as any in America. The downside of all this is that evangelicals sometimes find themselves with no adequate way of distinguishing between ideas that are pathbreaking and those that are gibberish."[22]

Ken Myers, a former National Public Radio editor and the creator of *Mars Hill Audio,* has long argued that his fellow

Christians need to resign their suspicion of the physical world and secular culture and become more culturally engaged. His audio magazine helps its more than ten thousand subscribers do just that, by providing interviews with authors, poets, musicians, and scientists. Despite his obvious concern for connecting with culture, though, Myers recognizes the dangers of capitulation that confront American Christians, especially evangelicals.

"We can be fully engaged and we can be fully assimilated," said Myers, when speaking in August 2001 to a crowd composed mostly of evangelicals. The group had assembled at a resort outside Washington, D.C., to discuss how they could impact popular culture.

Moving from a "mindless" rejection of the arts and culture to a "mindless" embrace of worldly values is not progress, Myers said. The better path is to engage culture where appropriate, but with discernment and the knowledge that some media are simply not conducive to the Christian message.

As an example, Myers played a jarring, discordant excerpt from what sounded like a satanic rock song. The lyrics were written by a Christian and adapted from *Precious Remedies against Satan's Devices,* a Puritan classic written by Thomas Brooks in 1652. Despite its creator's good intentions, Myers said, the song's harsh, agitating media undercut its message. When Christians become so concerned with blending in that they copy and promote even the negative aspects of popular culture, he said, "we're too engaged. We have become truly worldly."

Life in the Balance

Few places more clearly illustrate the problem of cultural capitulation than Hollywood, but young believers across the nation, and in every profession, face similar struggles. As orthodox Christians grapple with ethical decisions on the job, they sometimes make concessions against their principles in the short term, hoping they can use those compromises to reach a position of power later.

Once in power, they tell themselves, they will be safe enough to stand up for their convictions and influential enough to do more good than if they took a stand now.

It's the classic ends–justify–the–means argument, applied to the realm of evangelization and cultural influence. And though Christians in Hollywood, in the boardroom, or in the hospital might balk at that characterization of some of their own decisions, most admit that accommodation to secular culture and its values is a clear and present danger to their faith.

Andy Crouch, a former campus minister at Harvard University and the editor in chief of *re:generation quarterly,* cowrote an article on this topic with *RQ* editor Nate Barksdale in the winter 2000–01 issue of the magazine. The piece's title—"Roaring Lambs or Bleating Lions?"—echoed the title of Bob Briner's book *Roaring Lambs,* which has inspired so many young Christians to engage secular culture. Though the article acknowledged the "deep" resonance between *RQ*'s vision for its young readers and Briner's, it highlighted the problems inherent in such a quest for secular power—even if that quest is driven by a desire to spread the gospel.

"What is unfortunately missing from *Roaring Lambs*' vision of cultural transformation is awareness that being in power more often than not transforms one into a bleating lion," wrote Crouch and Barksdale.

> *The pop universe (whether that's pop music, pop writing, or pop politics) allots power on its own terms, for its own purposes. This means, among other things, that those "real Christians" who are given the most power and popularity are not likely to be those who directly challenge the society's dominant values—and in more or less subtle ways (ranging from doctrinal creativity to lifestyle choices) they are likely to reinforce those values, even while imparting a pleasant, positive, religious—but above all tolerant—glow to the proceedings.*

The solution, they argued, was for Christians who aspire to change culture to go back to the gospel for guidance.

"The teachings of Jesus suggest that true power can be accessed via a very unlikely source: from being aligned with the truly powerless, from serving those who cannot serve you back."[23]

In an interview after the article appeared, Crouch talked about the seduction of power and popularity that he witnessed among cultural elites at Harvard University, where he worked as an evangelical campus minister for nine years. Christians zealous to use their time at a prestigious university for God, or to funnel their talents into a successful career for God, sometimes rely too much on their own "strategic thinking," Crouch said. They make elaborate plans to gain the most influence and reach the most people, rather than relying on God to gently guide them toward what he wants them to do. Surrounded by other elites in their schools and professions, they can fall into the trap of living for the approval of others and chasing after the "idols" of money, power, and fame.

"I pick up a lot of this," said Crouch. "It's like this 'wanting to be invited to the party' sort of thing: 'God's put me here and I'm gonna just work my tail off.' But the people who are actually the most effective for God are the ones who are most relaxed."

A center of power like Harvard—or Hollywood—can tempt Christians to chase after the approval of others, Crouch said. But it can also lead them to recognize and root out their own craving for human approval and replace it with greater zeal to do God's will.

"I've just had to let God burn that out of me, that need for affirmation," Crouch said. "The more that I put to death those fleshly things, the more I get to be in those settings and preach the gospel."

When he gets access to power as the editor of a magazine and a former Harvard campus minister, Crouch said, he takes it. But he also accepts less prestigious speaking engagements.

"I will go anywhere I'm invited," said Crouch, who takes his culture-transforming cues from the gospel. "Jesus didn't spend much time saying, 'I wonder how I can get access to Herod.' Jesus goes wherever he's invited."

9

THE FUTURE

For I know well the plans I have in mind for you, says the LORD, plans for your welfare, not for woe! plans to give you a future full of hope.

JEREMIAH 29:11

With conservative churches attracting committed Christians, liberal churches hemorrhaging members, and young believers working overtime to spread their faith, the future of orthodoxy in America looks bright. Moral relativism and the specter of an increasingly hostile popular culture cast long shadows over this crop of religious young adults. So do the twin threats of cultural isolation and cultural assimilation. But these believers know the dangers that lurk in their path, and many are taking thoughtful approaches to defend against them. To succeed in transforming their church and culture, they will need to continue building on two crucial characteristics of their orthodox movement: ecumenism and balance.

The Perils of Orthodoxy

Ecumenism, as understood by the young orthodox Christians interviewed for this book, is not an excuse for overlooking deep theological divisions. Nor is it another word for syncretism, the fusion of all beliefs and practices into one formless faith. Many young believers were raised in churches that prized tolerance and acceptance above the search for truth. Still scarred by the theological confusion that approach engendered, they are deeply suspicious of a relativistic ecumenism that dismisses differences rather than acknowledging them, hashing them out, and working together in spite of them.

That suspicion could make them terrible ecumenists—or terrific ones. The most committed members of a denomination frequently are the least likely to work with outsiders and understand views that contradict their own. Strains of that insularity are plainly apparent in this crop of orthodox believers, especially among conservative Catholics, evangelicals who inherited heavy doses of anti-Catholicism, and members of some Orthodox churches.

Yet many committed young believers excel at ecumenism, precisely because they can clearly articulate the distinctiveness of their faith traditions and they believe that universal truth is knowable. If these young believers continue to embrace opportunities to work together across denominational and even interfaith lines without airbrushing significant theological differences, they have the potential to transform American religion and culture. If they refuse to do so, recoiling instead into their various subcultures to avoid the ideologically impure, their effects on American culture will be diluted and their obedience to Christ's gospel imperative of unity will be incomplete. That insularity also will damage the credibility of their movement, relegate it to the fringes of society, and perhaps even repel their own children, who are apt to rebel against the subculture as did some of these believers and many of their parents.

The subculture, of course, is not entirely unhealthy for orthodox believers. As noted in chapters 2 and 4, supportive faith communities are crucial to the survival of a confessional faith in a pluralistic society. So too are strong families and vibrant churches that hand down the faith with clarity and confidence. The failure of so many families and mainline churches to do this is precisely what has attracted many young believers to orthodoxy, where they finally found the clear answers they never heard at home or in Sunday school.

The struggle of today's culturally engaged orthodox Christians boils down to a search for balance. As the old maxim goes, Christians should be *in* the world but not *of* the world. But what is the right balance between fidelity to a confessional faith and interaction with a pluralistic secular culture? On the one hand, these believers feel compelled to huddle together and protect their Christian convictions from contamination. On the other, they feel driven to reach out and share those convictions with others. In the gospel, Jesus tells them they must do both—and indicates that the stakes are high for those who ignore that directive:

> *You are the salt of the earth; but if salt has lost its taste, how shall its saltness be restored? It is no longer good for anything except to be thrown out and trodden under foot by men.*
>
> *You are the light of the world. A city set on a hill cannot be hid. Nor do men light a lamp and put it under a bushel, but on a stand, and it gives light to all in the house. Let your light so shine before men, that they may see your good works and give glory to your Father who is in heaven. (Matthew 5:13–16)*

For those who heed the call to practice a vibrant faith that bears witness to the world, the question evolves into a more practical one: How, exactly, does that command apply to their lives? An evangelical in Hollywood might believe it requires him to write secular screenplays that send subtle messages about grace and redemption. A nun might decide that it requires her to spend her days and nights in fervent, contemplative prayer for the believers on the front lines of the culture wars. Still other Christians might shine their light in medical missions, around office watercoolers, in the pages of secular newspapers, or behind the sound booth at Christian rock concerts. Some veer dangerously close to assimilation into a culture that repudiates their faith. Others teeter toward an isolated smugness that masquerades as piety or privatizes a faith they are too ashamed to share. And most stumble down a middle path, dodging worldliness this moment, ducking self-righteousness the next, trying to keep their eyes focused on the God who makes their struggle worthwhile.

When navigating the narrow road of orthodoxy, believers are often drawn to the extreme that most closely aligns with their denomination. Conservative Catholics, besieged by fellow Catholics and the culture at large, tend toward defensiveness and isolation. Condemnations of them as judgmental and self-righteous sometimes reveal the critic's own prejudices against orthodoxy. But often those criticisms are deserved, as many young Catholics who adhere to papal authority or revere liturgical tradition regard liberal Catholics or non-Catholics with a mixture of condescension and contempt. Some seem doomed to repeat the mistakes of a pre–Vatican II church that gave too little credence to the laity and of cultural Catholics who confuse accidentals of the faith with its essentials. Many young orthodox Catholics are sensitive to this problem, but many others spend so much time with like-minded friends that they fail to realize how others perceive them. If they do not guard against that tendency toward rigidity, they could render their orthodox revolution irrelevant.

For most young evangelicals, the hazard is exactly the opposite. Terrified of being branded as the intolerant Religious Right, many have swung to the other end of the spectrum, tripping over themselves to prove how relevant, culturally engaged, and non-judgmental they are. These Christians understandably want to avoid the pitfalls of a fundamentalist attitude that turns off potential converts and sympathizers. But the relational emphasis of evangelical theology cannot justify capitulation to the culture.

Difficult as it is for orthodox believers to achieve balance, it can be done. Those who do it best cite prayer, Scripture study, and the sacraments—not human strategies—as the keys to their success. Rather than believing that the church needs to be more like the world, these young adults long ago decided that the world needs to be more like the church—at its best. And most of them have seen enough of the secular world to be wary of its seductions.

Most also are more focused on transforming culture for Christ than finding a safe niche where they can hide. These young believers want to work across denominational lines toward their common goals, and many have already invested themselves in friendships, alliances, and institutions that foster ecumenism. For evangelicals in search of the sacraments, that ecumenism may lead them to liturgical churches. For many others, including Catholics, it may help them appreciate parts of the Body of Christ they never knew.

Ultimately, the common enemies of secularism and relativism may lead orthodox Christians beyond mutual admiration and back into unity. In the meantime, these young believers are building ecumenical alliances—in the realms of home and school, politics and public life, media and culture, and the church—that have the potential to institutionalize their movement, renew their church, and transform their culture.

Guarding the Family against the World— and a Backlash

If any realm of life can indicate the direction these young believers are taking and the direct impact they will have on American culture, it is the sphere where they have the most influence: their own homes and families. Pope John Paul II, a hero to many young believers, has said that the "new evangelization" of today's society cannot succeed without Christian families. "To the extent in which the Christian family accepts the Gospel and matures in faith, it becomes an evangelizing community," the pope wrote in his 1981 exhortation *The Role of the Christian Family in the Modern World.*[1]

Predictions are risky, but the combination outlined in chapter 5—of fierce determination to avoid divorce, strong faith communities that support marriage vows, and ardent belief in marriage as a divinely blessed bond—portends well for the marriages of these young believers. And just as strong marriages bode well for the future of orthodox families, so strong orthodox families bode well for the strength and stability of American culture.

Countervailing trends do exist. Many Christian newlyweds are children of divorce, and studies show that spouses whose own parents divorced are about one and a half times more likely to divorce than those whose parents stayed married.[2] Studies of fundamentalist and evangelical churches have found that their members divorce at the same or higher rates than the general population. And in many parts of the Protestant Bible Belt, the divorce rate is roughly 50 percent higher than the national average.[3] A study by the Princeton University Center for Research on Child Wellbeing found that Southern Baptist couples are more likely to divorce than the general population.[4] Catholics tend to fare slightly better: the divorce rate for couples married in the Catholic Church is 15 to 20 percent lower than that of the general population.[5]

Experts offer varying explanations for the link between evangelicalism and divorce. Some say Bible Belt couples tend to marry younger and suffer from the strain of lower incomes. Others point to the idealized vision of marriage that evangelicals have and the lack of marriage preparation offered in their churches. As for the relative success of Catholic marriages, experts cite the extensive marriage-preparation classes mandated by the Catholic Church for engaged couples and the church's practice of forbidding remarried people from receiving communion if their first marriage has not been annulled by the church. Catholics themselves often credit the grace that accompanies sacramental marriage in the Catholic Church.

Another explanation for the lackluster success rates of Christian marriages is the crucial and oft ignored distinction between those who claim membership in a church and those who are regular churchgoers. The young believers described in this book fall solidly into the latter category, and they are intent on adhering to admonitions against divorce. Their sense that their commitments are countercultural, and that secular society could conspire to undermine them, only strengthens their resolve to stay together. Just as patriotism flares when a war is raging, so the convictions of orthodox Christians solidify in the face of secular opposition. That defense mechanism may protect these couples from many of the moral quagmires they will face as they navigate secular culture together.

Young believers can also look to a host of faith-based movements for marriage and family support. The initiatives range from Christian men's groups run by the Promise Keepers movement, which aims to produce better husbands and fathers, to the institution of covenant marriage laws in Louisiana and Arizona and the rise in premarital counseling for young evangelicals. The courtship movement—embraced by some evangelicals and conservative Catholics—is gaining steam among parents who want to take an active role in guiding the love lives of their teenage children. Its goals dovetail neatly with those of many orthodox Christians who want to spare their children the anguish they experienced while dating in a sex-saturated society. Here, too, young believers who would propagate the faith must walk a fine line between protecting their children and segregating them. If they rein their children in too tightly, they could witness a backlash not unlike the one that led their baby boomer parents to reject traditional religion and morality and instigate the sexual revolution.

Among orthodox Catholics, the statistical possibility for lasting marriages may correlate with their adherence to a widely contested church teaching, the ban on artificial birth control. Couples who use the church-approved method of natural family planning (NFP) instead of contraception post miniscule divorce rates: only 2 to 5 percent divorce, as compared to roughly 50 percent of the general population.[6] Those who eschew artificial birth control for religious reasons are often more likely than most Catholics to heed church prohibitions on divorce. But they credit NFP directly for the difference in divorce rates, since the method forces them to have frequent discussions about intimate issues that couples using artificial birth control can avoid.

While it is true that many American Catholics ignore church teaching on contraception and other issues of sexual morality, most young Catholics interviewed for this book agree with the church's teaching against contraception—some even cited it among the reasons for their conversion to Catholicism. A small but growing number of Protestants also has warmed to the concept of avoiding artificial contraception.

Whether using birth control or not, many young believers of all denominations say they want large families or, at least, families larger than the ones they were raised in. They look forward to thwarting the status quo by regarding their many children as blessings, not burdens. Young orthodox Catholic parents in particular hope that the sheer number of children raised in homes like theirs will affect the attitudes of the next generation about such contentious issues as contraception, abortion, and, more generally, the moral authority of the Catholic Church. Many of these young conservatives are, essentially, hoping to outnumber the opposition. Indeed, the influx of orthodox children—if they remain orthodox into adulthood and carry on the tradition of having large families—could significantly shift the direction of the American Catholic Church in years to come. If these children adopt their parents' morally conservative voting patterns and entertainment tastes, they could also have an exponentially increasing impact on American culture.

Another promising trend for the propagation of an orthodox faith is the homeschooling movement. Children of conservative Catholics and Protestants who are educated at home and in networks of like-minded peers typically resist much of the secularization that affects their peers and exhibit more attachment to their faith and families. With the support of the courtship movement and orthodox Catholic and evangelical colleges geared specifically to students who attended high school at home, homeschoolers may avoid intimate interaction with unbelievers, and even Christians of other denominations, for most of their youth.

That's a victory for orthodox parents who want to protect their children from religious pluralism and moral relativism. But few Americans will escape those realities forever, and young believers who want their children to change the world will need to carefully consider how to prepare those children for the clash of cultures that surely awaits them. Again, balance is key: children deserve enough protection to maintain their innocence and enough freedom to acquire the tolerance and charity demanded by a pluralistic culture. If orthodox parents fail to strike that balance, the faith of their children could be swallowed up by secular culture when those children encounter pluralism head-on. If they succeed, their families could be the most lasting legacy of their orthodox movement.

Selling Out or Opting Out

As if the preservation of an orthodox faith in a pluralistic culture was not daunting enough, today's young believers are also intent on merging religion and public life. So far, their attempts to effectively engage in politics without selling out religious principles have been promising. But power corrupts, and the choices these cultural leaders make in the political realm could make or break their orthodox revival.

For orthodox believers in a liberal democratic society, the classic conflict is this: how do they live as tolerant citizens of pluralistic America while still adhering to the moral and religious absolutes of orthodoxy? The testimonies in this book clearly demonstrate that a glut of religious and ideological choices fuels the search for certainty. But just as orthodoxy thrives in pluralism, the two also can clash—sometimes violently.

As Americans struggle to make sense of the terrorist attacks by Islamic extremists in 2001, the question of religion's role in the public square has become newly relevant. As true believers and citizens of pluralistic America, these young Christians are uniquely positioned to defend the proper role of religion in a secular state and to defend traditional morality as the basis for civil law. They also stand poised to rescue the church from enmeshing itself in unholy political alliances or isolating itself into political impotence. First, though, they must wrestle with the twin political temptations of selling out and opting out. For orthodox Christians who hope to transform culture for Christ, both are deadly.

Selling out, by means of careless capitulation or unwise alliances, is a perennial danger for Christians who engage in politics. Political expediency often makes it tempting to compromise on key moral points for the sake of broadening a coalition or to conflate religious ideals with allegiance to a particular political party or leader. Young orthodox believers will be tempted by the left to dilute their defense of moral standards and by the right to overlook the needs of the poor and powerless. Neither concession squares with orthodox Christianity.

Faced with the difficulties of navigating a theologically permissible third way, some young orthodox Christians will be tempted to opt out of politics altogether. Unwittingly, they may cooperate with secularists who want them to "keep their beliefs to themselves," by staying home on election days, refusing to associate with people outside their sectarian circles, and sequestering their children from a pluralistic culture that seems increasingly threatening. These believers may come to see theocracy as the only true answer to what ails government—not unlike Muslim extremists who believe the world could be rid of its evils if only Islamic law were enforced everywhere.

Of course, this view defies a key tenet of orthodox Christianity: namely, the idea that all of creation is fallen and only God, through his Son, can redeem it. So no government will ever be perfect until Jesus returns to restore all things, and even an airtight Christian subculture will suffer from sin so long as its inhabitants are human. Contempt for liberal democracy also disregards the fact that the religious freedom orthodox believers enjoy is a direct result of America's tolerance for all religions—including ones that fly in the face of orthodox Christianity. Political disengagement by orthodox Christians would impoverish the culture, marginalize the church, and squander a valuable opportunity to make American society more conducive to Christian virtue.

The preservation of their orthodox faith, and their vibrant Christian witness to the world, depends on the ability of these young believers to cling to the "Jesus first" principle so many of them have adopted to decide political questions. They must avoid the dual extremes of capitulation and isolation and forge ecumenical and interfaith alliances that amplify their political influence without diluting their values. It's a tall order for a group of young believers still settling into adulthood, but some precedents do exist for such political alliances among orthodox believers. One example is Evangelicals and Catholics Together, the 1994 declaration that grew out of a coalition led by evangelical Chuck Colson and Catholic Fr. Richard John Neuhaus. Signers of the statement rejected such things as abortion, pornography, and euthanasia and lauded family-friendly public policies that do not make the poor "virtual wards of the government." "We strongly affirm the separation of church and state," the statement said, "and just as strongly protest the distortion of that principle to mean the separation of religion from public life." The Christian unity fostered by ecumenical political alliances such as this one has the potential to bleed beyond the public realm into the life of the church, where ecumenical understanding among orthodox believers is so desperately needed.

In matters of traditional morality and the family, orthodox Christians also have begun to forge alliances across the interfaith spectrum and with secular conservatives. To attract a broader constituency, orthodox Christians must do battle with the pervasive moral relativism and secular humanism that rebuffs their moral absolutes. Their best hope is to start in their own churches and neighborhoods, mobilizing the "mushy middle" of Americans who consistently tell pollsters that the moral decline of society is their chief concern. Religion is most powerful when addressing those concrete concerns about family, meaning, and morality, as many converts to orthodoxy can attest.

As young orthodox believers move into the political realm, they are taking their Christian convictions with them. If they strike the right notes of balance and ecumenism, they have the potential to reinvigorate America's civil discourse and reshape American culture.

Importing Campus Conversions into the Real World

In the realm of education, tomorrow's young orthodox Christians may find the road already paved for them by today's young believers. Young orthodox Christians are uniting across denominational lines to engage the secular academy and challenge their liberal co-religionists. Their confidence in absolute truth is energizing relativistic classrooms and their insistence on openly articulating religious and moral principles is testing the tolerance creed of their secular colleagues. If these students continue to blend faith and reason without being co-opted by campus relativism, the church and the American academy will be richer for their contributions. Perhaps even more important for their movement will be the ability of orthodox believers to import campus ecumenism and enthusiasm into the real world of local churches and national alliances.

In the classrooms of Catholic schools, many orthodox believers are cheering a new development: the church requirement, adopted by U.S. bishops in 1999, that Catholic theologians ask their bishop for permission to teach theology, Scripture, or church history. The hotly contested move was a response to *Ex Corde Ecclesia,* Pope John Paul II's document on Catholic higher education that called for a revival of the thousand-year-old European tradition. The bishops also were responding to widespread concern among American Catholics that Catholic colleges were shedding their Catholic identity and that dissenting theologians were teaching ignorant students only critiques of Catholic doctrine, or no doctrine at all. Many Catholic theologians worry that the requirement will stifle academic freedom in Catholic schools, while many orthodox Catholics are relieved that a crackdown on dissenters may ensue. But the concrete results of the requirement have yet to be measured, and since universities are autonomous, bishops likely will have a tough time enforcing it.

Another interesting trend for orthodox Catholics on campus is the advent of Catholic studies programs, which have started to sprout at secular and Catholic schools around the nation. Those programs could pave the way for a recovery of the Catholic intellectual tradition in the secular academy and the conversion of a new subset of students. They may also pose a formative challenge to the postmodern academy's dismissal of tradition and absolute truth.

Evangelicals also are enjoying an intellectual awakening, as more head to secular schools and into secular academic careers. The ranks of evangelical intellectuals are being fortified by world-view programs, run by such organizations as Focus on the Family and the Family Research Council, which teach Christian college students how to integrate their faith into their academic endeavors and future careers.

Campus evangelical fellowships continue to gather students by the dozens, even hundreds, each week to praise Jesus at secular schools, and their popularity shows no signs of abating. These fellowships tap into the energy of the young while spreading the orthodoxy of old. They attract Christians from every denominational stripe and give them a template for the ecumenical alliances they may form later in life.

Young orthodox Catholics also are launching popular "renegade" fellowship groups at Catholic and secular universities, in a reaction against more liberal campus ministry programs that have failed to clearly articulate the faith or spark student interest. Catholic campuses across the country are seeing revivals of rosary recitations and eucharistic adoration—traditional devotions that some older campus ministers have tried unsuccessfully to discourage.

Popular as they are, these parachurch groups have their limits. Students who immerse themselves in a vibrant campus fellowship often become disillusioned when they graduate and cannot replicate their experience at the local church. Campus leaders frequently fail to prepare students for the more solitary faith journey that often follows graduation or, in the case of conservative young Catholics, for the challenges of dealing effectively and charitably with liberal parish leaders. They may also fail to connect college students with local churches where they can learn from believers of other ages and worship in larger, less homogeneous faith communities.

For Catholics, the best solution to the inevitable bursting of the college bubble is to steep students in the sacraments, which can keep them moored to their faith when fellowship fades. Many Catholic graduates who revere the sacraments still feel the awkwardness of the transition into a parish where singles are scarce and singles programs are banal. Church leaders clearly need to pay more attention to this postcollege cohort. But young orthodox Catholics who are anchored by the sacraments often are the ones who start new parish ministries that mimic the best of what they experienced in college.

Single evangelicals have more fellowship options than Catholics, but they do not have the sacraments or the institutional loyalty to moor them to a particular church. They often bounce from church to church after college, seeking to recapture an idealized parachurch experience that did not prepare them for life after graduation. Many evangelical and Catholic campus ministers are working to address these problems, get students involved in local churches, and—for Catholic students—get them rooted in the sacraments that will nourish them when fellowship wanes. But the difficulties of sustaining faith after college remain daunting for young believers and pose serious challenges to the longevity of an orthodox movement among the young.

Courage and Charity: Keys to Church Renewal

Like leaven in the church, young orthodox Christians are the best hope American Christianity has for renewal. Their enthusiasm, creativity, and commitment to seeking truth make these young believers ideal reformers of mainline and evangelical faith communities that have wandered into worldliness, complacency, or insularity.

Many of these young believers will contribute to the divisions in their churches. They may become co-opted by conservative factions, judge their elders too harshly, or huddle together in peer groups that reinforce their own views and do not impact the larger church. They may cling to the prejudices that make it impossible to work across denominational lines toward Christian unity.

Many others will use their convictions to challenge—not simply critique—fellow believers. Their overriding zeal for the gospel and Christian unity will propel them to speak the truth with charity. And their talent for personal witness and distaste for a quarantined faith will lead them to share with the rest of the church the treasures they have found in orthodoxy.

For those who balance truth and love, courage and charity, their impact on the church will be powerful and lasting. The trends set so far by these believers suggest that many of them will fall into this latter category of effective reformers. If church leaders consent to learn from these young orthodox Christians, they could spare the next generation of Christian children much of the confusion and anguish that afflicted these young adults.

A good way to judge the impact young believers are already having on the church is to consider the current trends in religious education. In evangelical churches, classes on engaging the culture are becoming a staple, thanks largely to the desire that young evangelicals have to move beyond their Christian subculture and interact more with secular society. In Catholic parishes, young adults who grew up without a strong faith formation are supporting plans to reform religious education. Many have taken it upon themselves to start adult catechism classes, Bible studies that incorporate Catholic doctrine, or question-and-answer sessions with priests that help parishioners learn the faith. Their efforts echo institutional changes in the Catholic Church: the U.S. bishops recently decided to prepare a "reader-friendly" national catechism suitable for study by young adults that addresses issues of faith as they relate to American culture.

Religious education for children also has been influenced by young orthodox Catholics, who are flooding their parishes and Catholic schools to give the next generation the solid catechesis they did not receive. In some dioceses, these young believers clash with older, more liberal teachers who resent their conservative take on theological and moral issues. The *National Catholic Reporter,* a weekly for progressive Catholics, published an article in 2000 about the critics of Franciscan University of Steubenville graduates. According to the *NCR,* the school runs the largest Catholic undergraduate theology program in the nation and sends out more than seven hundred graduates to work in various aspects of religious education.[7] Church leaders in some dioceses, like Peoria, Illinois, and Sioux Falls, South Dakota, purposely hire the graduates because of their staunch orthodoxy. But others say the students are self-righteous and divisive.

This criticism of young orthodox Catholics is common. Young adults have a natural tendency to see life in black and white, with no room for compromise even on minor matters. And conservative Catholics often are overly alert to the missteps of those they regard as inadequately orthodox. At the same time, the argument of orthodox Catholics—that church leaders who disregard Vatican dictums on personal morality and liturgical tradition are tampering with the substance of the faith—makes sense. Swallowing concerns about abuses in their parishes will not make the problems—or their resentment—disappear. Rather than waging war or hiding behind an icy truce of tolerance, these young believers should pick their battles, focus on the reforms that matter most, and use the tensions of parish life as an opportunity to practice patience and love of one's enemies.

Conservative Catholics can find consolation in the fact that the clergy is growing more sympathetic to their grievances. As the ranks of liberal religious dwindle, young conservative clergy and religious are rising up to take their place. Catholic parishes and schools are already feeling some effects of the trend toward orthodoxy among young priests: more emphasis on tradition and the sacraments, stronger sermons against abortion and contraception, and more attention to moral and spiritual reform than to the political and social reforms favored by baby boomer priests. As one *New York Times* article put it in 2000, research has shown that "the youngest and oldest priests share similar views, while the generation of Vatican II stands isolated between them."[8]

For liberal Catholics at the 2000 national conference of Call to Action in Milwaukee, the future looked grim. The conference spilled over with gray-haired radicals, priests wielding canes, and nuns dressing as defiantly as septuagenarians can. But young adults were scarce. To fill a meeting room reserved for "the next generation," conference organizers defined young adults as anyone between the ages of eighteen to forty-two—a move that provoked snickers among the college-aged students in attendance. High on the list of concerns at the conference were the conservatism of young seminarians and the overwhelming sense that today's young Catholics no longer care to wage the battles for women's ordination, married priests, and democracy in the church, battles that consumed their baby boomer predecessors.

In mainline Protestantism, a similar generational divide has appeared between young evangelical Episcopalian converts and older, more liberal church leaders. Pairing up with elder conservative clergy in their home churches and more conservative Anglican clergy in developing nations, these young evangelicals are fighting the culture wars inside the American Episcopal Church. Two hot-button issues are the ordination of active homosexuals and the blessing of same-sex unions. Young conservative Episcopalians often feel torn about such debates, wondering whether they should stay in the Episcopal Church and fight the progressive national hierarchy or flee to Catholic or Orthodox churches where the official church line remains morally conservative. The future for these individuals and their churches remains uncertain. Some Episcopalians say a church split is inevitable. Others say conservatives can hold the line by attracting still more young conservative evangelicals who crave liturgy to the Episcopalian fold.

In the area of youth ministry, church-based programs and parachurch outreaches are a promising vehicle for spreading orthodoxy to the next generation. Young Life, an evangelical youth ministry founded in 1940, dispatches some two thousand staff members and more than ten thousand volunteers to spread Christianity to teenagers. Life Teen, a Catholic equivalent started in 1985, hosts more than seven hundred programs world-wide, and an estimated seventy-five thousand teenagers attend Life Teen Masses and meetings each week. Rounding out the realm of youth ministry in Protestant and Catholic churches are mission trips—an increasingly popular phenomenon among evangelical teenagers—as well as eucharistic conferences for Catholic teenagers and young adults.

In addition to supporting existing youth ministry programs, church leaders would do well to listen to young orthodox believ-ers about what new initiatives are needed. If they do, they will hear that churches need to be bolder in proclaiming Christian doctrine—particularly the reality of sin and the need for salva-tion—which is absent from so many mainline churches but attracts converts by the thousands to so many evangelical ones. They might also hear that conforming their churches to the world repels the young, but challenging the young to conform to Christ inspires and attracts. Just ask the leaders of conservative evangeli-cal fellowships that attract students by the throngs on secular cam-puses. Or ask Pope John Paul II, a man who convenes young adults by the millions for World Youth Day festivals that celebrate sacrifice and sanctity.

Catholic leaders in particular should reassess the power and promise of orthodoxy for youth ministry. In an age when worldly values have largely overwhelmed Catholic identity among the young, orthodoxy accentuates that which is most distinctive about Catholicism—its rituals, tough teachings, and traditions. This grassroots orthodox movement has arisen spontaneously among young Catholics battling to save their faith from secularization. Older church leaders should resist the urge to view the movement through the liberal-conservative lens that dominated their day. They should foster its growth with solid catechesis. And they should be sensitive to the creative, communal instincts of orthodox Catholics, who are eager to establish such events as praise-and-worship eucharistic adoration sessions and small-group catechism studies in their parishes.

The creativity of young orthodox believers, and their penchant for ecumenism, already has taken root in communities across America. An ecumenical band of Christians in Chicago seeks out male hustlers in the Boys Town neighborhood, offering them food, prayers, and prodding to get off the streets.[9] A Catholic woman in the diocese of Fort Wayne–South Bend organized an ecumenical celebration for the signing of a statement in which Catholics and some Lutherans announced their agreement on the doctrine of justification. In East Palo Alto, California, two evangelical women spent so much time ministering to children in a drug-infested neighborhood that they finally moved into an abandoned crack house so they could live closer to "their kids." And at the subway stop beneath Grand Central Station in Manhattan, a crowd of born-again Christians of every race and hue gathers on Sundays to sing evangelical praise songs for passersby. "It's God's calling in my life," said a young woman with a soft Caribbean accent while performing in January 2001. "He gave me a voice. He wants me to use it for him."

In the Catholic Church, international lay movements are getting a boost from young Americans who want to live their faith in a more intentional way. Regnum Christi and Opus Dei in particular attract young orthodox Catholics seeking solid spiritual direction and the support of like-minded believers. Critics say these groups are secretive, controlling, and rigid, while members defend them as supportive enclaves in a hostile world. Indeed, members of Regnum Christi and Opus Dei tend to be leaders in the church and world who are confident in their orthodoxy and strategic in their evangelization. The religious orders associated with these groups are vibrant, and the lay members of these groups are among the most energetic and committed Catholics in the church. But their insularity can sometimes blind members to the faults of the group and make them too suspicious of outsiders to effectively engage—and learn from—the world.

In the realm of worship, the trends are conflicting. Some young believers crave tradition. Others want contemporary worship. A large majority seek more meaning in their worship, and many are finding that meaning in the Eucharist—the cause of deep, profound conversions for a great many Catholics and Orthodox Christians. For most Protestants, the Bible is their sole source of authority, and fidelity to God's word remains their litmus test for judging the merits of a preacher or the health of the church. Catholics and Orthodox Christians hope that attention to Scripture will eventually lead Protestants to join their churches, which maintain that they have the apostolic authority to definitively interpret the Bible. And Catholics in particular hope that the teaching authority of the Roman Catholic Church will continue to attract conservative Protestants who worry that their own churches are slipping into the same moral relativism that they see engulfing the culture. For their part, many evangelicals wish Catholics and other liturgical Christians could unite with evangelicals under the banner of *mere Christianity,* a term used by C. S. Lewis to describe orthodox Christians of all denominational stripes.

The tide could turn either way, but interviews of the young believers in this book seem to indicate that this generation craves mystery and a connection to the traditions that the modern world has stripped away. Those yearnings bode well for the historical churches in general, and the accompanying desire for moral guidance from a trusted authority figure portends a positive future for the Catholic Church in particular.

Sharing the Gospel with Flexibility and Fidelity

Most young adults who have committed to orthodoxy are equally committed to evangelism. Their efforts to spread the faith range from innovative media and cultural initiatives to small-scale conversations and community building. Protestants often miss opportunities to connect their movements to local churches because of their suspicion of institutions. Catholics sometimes lack the clarity and cultural savvy of their evangelical cousins. The most successful endeavors blend evangelical flexibility with Catholic instincts for institutionalization and focus unapologetically on Jesus, his church, and the life-altering demands of orthodoxy.

As connoisseurs of popular culture, most young orthodox Christians attach great importance to the mass media and secular communication tools. Examples of electronic evangelization and media support for the faithful abound, from the reams of e-mail prayer requests that these young Christians trade daily to the scores of fans that pack Christian rock festivals.

In order to evangelize effectively, these young orthodox Christians must have resources and support. For Catholics and those who want to learn more about Catholicism, there is the Eternal Word Television Network (EWTN), a worldwide satellite feed founded by septuagenarian nun Mother Angelica. EWTN features extensive programming for teenagers and young adults, including radio and Internet resources for those who want to listen to a commentary about the canonization of saints, check out the day's Mass readings online, or e-mail the host of such youth-geared shows as *Life on the Rock*. Catholic Answers, an apologetics and evangelization outreach, supports youth ministries, magazines, and a call-in radio show for listeners who want help in sorting through Catholic doctrine. Those more prone to print can choose from a healthy number of orthodox publications, ranging from the hip and sassy *Envoy* magazine— which promises "100 % unadulterated orthodox Catholicism" to its audience of budding apologists—to the more scholarly *Crisis*.

While Catholics plunge deeper into the traditions that make them distinct, young evangelicals are moving from their strong and vibrant subculture into mainstream culture and, in some cases, toward ecumenism. Those wanting to consider culture from a Christian perspective embrace outlets like *Mars Hill Audio,* an audio magazine; *Books and Culture*, a cultural review; and *re:generation quarterly,* a magazine run by young orthodox ecumenists. *RQ*'s founders also host the Regeneration Forum, a network of readers' groups in twenty-five cities, and the Vine, a periodic conference that brings several hundred young believers together to discuss faith and culture.

Jennifer Jukanovich, who founded the Vine in 1999, first began thinking about staging ecumenical gatherings for her peers while in Washington, D.C., where she was spending a semester of her junior year of college as an intern with the American Studies Program, a worldview program run by the Council for Christian Colleges and Universities. In Washington, Jukanovich caught an ugly glimpse of the divisions between Christians in the political arena. Liberal Christians and conservative Christians worked separately, she said, and often harbored deep suspicions about one another.

"It just made me wonder, *What's going on? What could we do as a generation?*" said Jukanovich, who is in her late twenties.

Jukanovich returned to school—Gordon College, a Christian school near Boston—and ran for student body president during her senior year, pledging to unite students across denominational lines. She organized an ecumenical conference that featured a Catholic speaker—a bold move on a largely evangelical campus that does not employ Catholic professors. Later, she helped plan similar conferences for political leaders in Washington. After pairing up with the leaders of the Regeneration Forum, Jukanovich launched the Vine in 1999 by asking about a hundred young Christians of various denominations to invite their Christian friends who were in positions of cultural influence to attend. The result: conferences like the 2000 gathering, which brought together aspiring priests, ex-Catholic evangelicals, inner-city schoolteachers, and financial analysts, among others.

Jukanovich can tick off concrete results of the relationships formed at Vine gatherings, ranging from the funding of a youth center in New Orleans to the rebuilding of earthquake-damaged homes in El Salvador. She also believes the relationships will bear fruit in the years to come, as emerging leaders in the church and culture break down barriers and learn more about their fellow believers.

"One conversation could change a life," Jukanovich said.

Relationships that unify and strengthen the church are the ultimate goal of initiatives like the Vine and the Regeneration Forum. Other grassroots groups formed by young believers also follow that relational model of evangelism, which appeals to a generation that treasures authentic community, informal alliances, and personal stories. Such gatherings often are bereft of a hierarchy or sermons and instead center on young believers hearing each other's testimonies.

On the West Coast, an informal network of about two hundred young Christians and their seeker friends gathers annually at a resort in Lake Tahoe, California. The retreat, known simply as Tahoe, is a loosely structured event with an emphasis on fellowship and fun. Believers of all denominations are welcome, but its invitation has a distinctly evangelical flavor, as evinced by the assurance that Tahoe will be "no more or less religious than Jesus himself. Jesus was about relationships that cross many borders and boundaries, not about religion; he just wanted people to come to know and experience him." Many of the same young Christians who attend Tahoe also belong to affiliated evangelical fellowships in Los Angeles, Portland, and Seattle known as The Thing or, in San Francisco, The Rock—grassroots initiatives organized by young adults seeking to share the gospel in an informal setting. The events often eschew traditional elements of a worship service in order to make seekers feel more comfortable and to appeal to a younger audience.

Creativity is a hallmark of evangelical initiatives. Young believers use the Internet to advertise Bay Area Christian coffeehouses with such stealth names as Catacombs and Fish Bowl. In the Minneapolis area, teenagers and young adults gather in movie theaters and coffee joints for their "house-church" meetings.[10] Still others gather by the thousands for such Christian extravaganzas as the One Festival, a four-day youth gathering that was held in Memphis, Tennessee, in June 2001 and featured more than ninety Christian bands, fifty speakers, and eleven thousand attendees.[11] The festival offered guided spiritual retreats and Christian rock bands with names like Soul Junk. Its brochure invited young Christians "to mosh in dance, contemplate in prayer. To live dangerously, and give extravagantly."

The unconventionality of evangelical worship, and the reluctance of some evangelicals to use religious words like *Christian* and *church* for fear of turning off nonbelievers, has some drawbacks. When Christians pit "loving Jesus" against "organized religion," they appeal to a relativistic culture eager to dispense with the traditional morality and spiritual disciplines that organized religion usually entails. And they go against the grain of the gospel story itself. In fact, Jesus *was* religious: he was an observant Jew who went to synagogue, observed Passover, and described his ministry as a fulfillment—not an abolition—of the Jewish religious tradition.

Evangelicals rightly emphasize the joy that a relationship with Jesus brings—and often do a far better job at that than their counterparts in Catholic, Orthodox, and mainline Protestant churches. But without an accompanying emphasis on the sacrifices that a follower of Jesus must make—of praying when things seem hopeless, forgoing pleasures in which nonbelievers indulge, going to church when they do not feel like it—the seed of conversion will fall on rocky ground. And without the nourishment of a structured faith community, where young adults can learn from mature Christians who have been living the faith for decades, the conversion will wither and die. Budding young evangelists should keep that in mind as they reach out to make disciples who will not only love Jesus but also do his will.

In their quest to spread the gospel and transform culture, a small but growing number of evangelicals are reconsidering the riches of tradition. At a conference for Christian professionals on the eastern shore of Maryland, a few dozen artists, journalists, intellectuals, and congressional staffers gathered over Labor Day weekend in 2001 to talk Christ and cultural renewal. Most were evangelicals and many were in their twenties and thirties. Over the course of four days, they heard from such leading evangelical thinkers as commentator Ken Myers and bioethicist Nigel Cameron about what it might take to transform American culture. The retreat was sponsored by Faith and Law, a Christian fellowship on Capitol Hill, and the Wilberforce Forum, a wing of Chuck Colson's Prison Fellowship Ministries.

As usual, though, opinions varied about how Christians should shape society. Many in this gathering argued for meetings with Christian friends in Hollywood and on Capitol Hill, who could create more family-friendly entertainment and use their cultural influence to promote projects and products with a biblical worldview.

But others argued that rather than encouraging more consumerism and aggrandizing the role of popular entertainment, Christians should take new paths—by encouraging their children to read the classics, for instance, or using their churches as incubators for more modest dress—that defy the hegemony of popular culture. And some, including Myers, suggested that they look to tradition for guidance in transforming culture.

As young evangelicals are probing the riches of tradition, young Catholics are discovering the thrill of evangelization. Their efforts often lack the marketing savvy and mass appeal of evangelical endeavors, and Catholics who blend orthodoxy and charismatic elements generally attract larger crowds than strict traditionalists. But a growing number of orthodox Catholics are realizing that they have much to learn from their Protestant cousins—and the great saints of their own Catholic tradition—about the art of evangelization. Spurred on by the exhortations of Pope John Paul II and by their own postconversion zeal, many are using the Internet, mass media, and face-to-face encounters to extol the treasures of their faith.

One example of that blend of evangelical fervor and Catholic tradition is NET Ministries, or National Evangelization Teams Ministries. The nonprofit organization supervised by the Archdiocese of Saint Paul and Minneapolis uses a hundred young Catholic volunteers to spread the gospel around the nation. The volunteers travel by van to Catholic dioceses across America to give retreats and, as their literature says, "invite all they meet to give their lives to the only one who can satisfy their hungry hearts—Jesus Christ." The volunteers interact with about seventy thousand young people in the course of their service year. When it ends, an estimated 90 percent continue to serve actively in the Catholic Church, and 10 percent enter the priesthood or religious life. Also based in Minnesota is Saint Paul's Outreach, a ministry designed to give Catholic young adults an experience of Christian community life and a deeper understanding of their faith. Since the outreach began in the mid-1980s, hundreds of young Catholics have passed through its programs, including several dozen who have entered religious communities or taken religious vows after their experience at Saint Paul's.

Budding Catholic evangelists in St. Louis can join the REAP team, or Retreat, Evangelization and Prayer team, an archdiocesan-sponsored youth ministry that farms out groups of teenagers and young adults to area schools and parishes to give talks on Jesus, the Catholic faith, and chastity. A national band of Catholic missionaries affiliated with Regnum Christi, Youth for the Third Millennium, is composed of evangelists who range in age from about fifteen to nearly thirty. In cities where a large Catholic event is taking place, they sometimes go door-to-door to spread the word—and the faith. Young Catholic apologists can hone their evangelization skills at summer conferences sponsored by the

Franciscan University of Steubenville in Ohio, which offers workshops on such topics as "Born-Again Catholic" and "The Seven Deadly Sins of Catholic Apologetics." The university also sponsors a popular series of traveling summer conferences for teenagers from Atlanta to Denver, which combine exuberant praise music with the preaching of Franciscan friars in floor-length habits. In the past two decades, more than 100,900 teenagers have participated in Steubenville's summer conferences.[12] Also available to zealous young Catholics are manifold Web sites that give them information on everything from the latest papal address to the latest attack on Catholicism in mainstream media.

Like their evangelical cousins, many young Catholics use the mass media to promote the gospel. But young Catholics focus more on the institutional church than evangelicals do—an inclination that can tend toward insularity if they do not maintain their focus on outreach and evangelism. Where they do maintain that focus, their efforts have a better chance of taking root than initiatives that do not connect young believers to a larger church body.

Consider the case of Steubenville's rock-and-roll conferences. There, as in any orthodox Catholic setting, priests, nuns, and other ecclesiastical authority figures are present in abundance, and the sacraments, traditions, and hierarchy of the Catholic Church are celebrated, not disparaged. The result is often an odd juxtaposition of tradition and innovation, nuns and drums, kneelers and mosh pits. The same questions that arise in evangelical circles about the suitability of the media to the message also arise in Catholic settings. And just as pious hysteria tends to fade after evangelical revivals, so it also tends to fade after Catholic youth rallies. Yet the deference given to the institutional church and its leaders at such distinctly Catholic events largely protects against the possibility that seekers who convert there will fall in love with Jesus but reject the church that Catholics believe he founded.

As young orthodox believers move into the new millennium, they face a host of challenges to their evangelism efforts. To overcome them, they will need to learn from one another's strengths, work together to spread gospel essentials, and balance their flexibility with fidelity to the larger faith communities that sustain them.

A New Day

The cramped kitchen was littered with party snacks, soda bottles, and glasses of wine. In the dining room, a spread of chopped vegetables and tortilla chips mingled with abandoned beer cans and candles. Some thirty young adults filled the modest apartment on this Saturday night, perched on sofas, leaning against walls, sitting and kneeling on the floor. Their lively conversation muted, their laughter fading, the crowd began to contemplate together the week's horrific events.

Four days earlier, terrorists had hijacked four American planes, striking the World Trade Center towers in New York, the Pentagon in Washington, D.C., and an abandoned coal mine in Pennsylvania. It was too soon to know how or why the attacks happened, who orchestrated them, or how many thousands of bodies would turn up in the rubble. America was shrouded in an eerie silence that week in September 2001, its flags lowered to half-mast, its houses of worship packed, its rescue workers toiling around the clock in New York and Washington to recover victims of an unknown aggressor.

Against that backdrop, this band of twenty- and thirtysomething Catholics flocked to a friend's apartment in St. Louis. For much of the night, they engaged in the usual banter: chatting about politics, giggling at photos from a recent wedding, finding out who was getting engaged, getting married, getting pregnant. But the heart of this gathering was not small talk or stress relief. At this party, like so many others attended by this circle of friends, the focal point was prayer.

At ten o'clock, the glasses had stopped clinking and conversation had ceased. Alone and as couples, the young adults had taken their seats and hit their knees to pray for their nation. On the Feast of Our Lady of Sorrows—the day Catholics set aside each year to contemplate the pain that Mary endured while watching her Son suffer and die—the group prayed a solemn rosary. Men and women took turns offering their own thoughts and petitions before leading the group in another round of prayers.

"Forgive us our trespasses as we forgive those who trespass against us," they murmured, reciting the Lord's Prayer that opened each of the rosary's five decades. "Lead us not into temptation, but deliver us from evil."

They prayed in quiet unison, their voices achieving a reassuring rhythm that seemed to gain momentum as the moments passed. Former atheists and repentant partiers mixed with lifelong Catholics and future priests. Elementary school teachers and youth ministers prayed next to doctors, lawyers, and philosophers. A slim young man in jeans and a T-shirt paused at the end of the rosary to read a statement from Pope John Paul II, who had inspired his own vocation to become a Jesuit priest, as well as the Christian conversions of many in the room. Attention was fixed on the young man as he read from a computer printout of the pope's address.

"The human heart has depths from which schemes of unheard-of ferocity sometimes emerge, capable of destroying in a moment the normal daily life of a people," the pope had said the day after the attacks. "But faith comes to our aid at these times when words seem to fail. Christ's word is the only one that can give a response to the questions which trouble our spirit. Even if the forces of darkness appear to prevail, those who believe in God know that evil and death do not have the final say. Christian hope is based on this truth; at this time our prayerful trust draws strength from it."

In the silence that lingered, eyes opened, heads lifted, and all made the sign of the cross. Slowly, the crowd began to mingle again, talking softly of the way they saw God bringing good out of even this catastrophe. Friends exchanged hugs. Some dabbed their eyes. Others spoke of the need to balance justice and forgiveness in the inevitable military response. Still others spread word of interfaith groups assembling to promote reconciliation, hatched ideas for op-ed articles to make sense of the tragedy, and compared breathless anecdotes about the rise in public displays of faith in the days since the attacks.

Just outside the second-floor apartment, a crane hoisted an oversized American flag above the treetops, one so large that even motorists from miles away could see its stars and stripes. As the clock ticked toward midnight, away slipped an extraordinary week marked by public prayer services and communal grief, a week when "God bless America" fell from the lips of even the most hard-bitten television reporters. And ushering in the new day was a small band of Christians gathered in an upper room, intent on using their faith to transform a nation.

NOTES

Chapter One: The Faithful

1. Sally MacDonald, "City Experiences Priestly Revival While Nation Lacks Men of Cloth," *Seattle Times,* Sunday, 31 January 1999, sec. B1.

2. Lauren Winner, "Gen X Revisited," *The Christian Century* 117, no. 31 (8 November 2000): 1146.

3. George H. Gallup Jr., *The Spiritual Life of Young Americans* (Princeton, N.J.: The George H. Gallup International Institute, 1999), 24, 40–41, 44.

4. H. J. Cummins, "Young Faith: Most Teens Consider Religion Important— and That May Translate into Healthier Lives," *Newsday,* 27 May 2000, sec. B1.

5. Tim Padgett, "And to the Latin Mass," *Time,* 7 June 1999, 65.

6. William Dinges, Dean R. Hoge, Mary Johnson, and Juan L. Gonzales Jr., "A Faith Loosely Held: The Institutional Allegiance of Young Catholics," *Commonweal* 125, no. 13 (17 July 1998): 13.

7. Diana Jean Schemo, "Priests of the 60's Fear Loss of Their Legacy," *New York Times,* 10 September 2000, sec. 1.

8. "The Faithful Are Casual at This Sunday Service," *New York Times,* 16 March 1997, sec. 1.

9. David C. Newman, "Lift High the Cross: A Scrutiny," *Fifteen Minutes,* 13 April 2000.

10. *Promise Keepers Online,* Promise Keepers, 9 October 2001, <http://www.promisekeepers.org/faqs/core/faqscore28.htm>.

11. Marcella Bombardieri, "Taking Root: As Youths Explore Judaism, Some Parents Rebel," *Boston Globe,* 15 March 2000, sec. B1.

12. Peter Beinart, "The Rise of Jewish Schools," *The Atlantic Monthly* 284, no. 4 (1 October 1999): 21.

13. Mary Therese Biebel, "For Some, Chastity Is the Real Turn-On," Associated Press, 28 March 1999.

14. Richard Nadler, "Glum and Glummer: Social Conservatives Must Learn to Accentuate the Positive," *National Review* 50, no. 18 (28 September 1998).

15. Chris Branam and Michael Rowett, "No Sex before Nuptials," *Arkansas Democrat-Gazette,* 20 July 2001, sec. B1.

16. Ruth Padawer, "Casual Sex Loses Its Appeal for Youth, 'Neo-Traditionalism' Replacing 'Free Love,'" *Bergen County (New Jersey) Record,* 8 December 1999, sec. A1.

17. Mieke H. Bomann, "Volunteering Grows Dramatically but Nature of Work Changes," *South Bend Tribune,* 7 March 2000, sec. A2.

18. Trinity Hartman, "Youths More Likely to Volunteer Than Vote," *Fort Worth Star-Telegram,* 19 March 1999, sec. 1.

19. Julia Duin, "Conservative Values Take Hold on College Campuses," *Washington Times,* 28 January 1999, sec. A2.

20. G. K. Chesterton, *Orthodoxy* (San Francisco: Ignatius Press, 1995), 17.

Chapter Two: The Search

1. Elizabeth Clarke, "Ten Trends in Religion," *Palm Beach Post,* 9 February 2001, sec. 1E.

2. David Briggs, "Gen X-ers' Quest for Faith Takes a Personal Route," *Arizona Republic,* Sunday, 21 January 2001, sec. J3.

3. "Teenagers' Beliefs Moving Farther from Biblical Perspectives," *Barna Research Online,* George Barna and Barna Research Group, Ltd., 23 October 2000, <http://www.barna.org/cgi-bin/PagePressRelease.asp?Press ReleaseID=74&Reference=B>.

4. David Briggs, "Young Catholics Are Staying Put," *Dallas Morning News,* 14 November 1998, sec 1G.

5. Kelly Ettenborough, "Where Has God Gone?" *Arizona Republic,* Sunday, 25 February 2001, sec. J1.

6. William Dinges, Dean R. Hoge, Mary Johnson, and Juan L. Gonzales Jr., "A Faith Loosely Held: The Institutional Allegiance of Young Catholics," *Commonweal* 125, no. 13 (17 July 1998): 13.

7. James Langton, "Magazine Cashes In on Opulence by Spurning the Humble Millionaire," *London Sunday Telegraph,* Sunday, 15 October 2000, 33.

8. Diana Jean Schemo, "Priests of the 60's Fear Loss of Their Legacy," *New York Times,* Sunday, 10 September 2000, sec. 1.

Chapter Three: The Church and Worship

1. George Gallup and Alec Gallup, "More Than Half of Teens Are Religious," *Asheville (North Carolina) Citizen-Times,* 28 October 2000, sec. B2.

2. Juan Williams, "Spirituality and Religion in America in the New Millennium," *Talk of the Nation,* National Public Radio, 21 December 2000.

3. Richard John Neuhaus, "A Candid Word about an Untold Story," *First Things,* April 2001, 63.

4. Dean R. Hoge, "Amazing Growth: The RCIA Story: Survey of Persons Who Were Received through the RCIA," *United States Conference of Catholic Bishops,* January 2000, <http://www.usccb.org/evangelization/data.htm>.

5. John Burnett, Linda Wertheimer, and Robert Siegel, "Eastern Orthodox," *All Things Considered,* National Public Radio, 28 January 1997.

6. Jeff Jensen, "American Pious: Don't Tell Yahoo!" *Entertainment Weekly,* spring 2000, 10th anniversary issue, 77.

7. "Faith Communities Today," The Hartford Institute for Religion Research, 6 December 2001, <http://fact.hartsem.edu/>.

8. Willard F. Jabusch, "Young and Conservative: Young Catholics," *America* 177, no. 10 (11 October 1997): 5.

Chapter Four: Faith Communities and Fellowship

1. Gary O'Bannon, "Managing Our Future: The Generation X Factor," *Public Personnel Management* 30 (22 March 2001): 95.

2. Arthur Paul Boers, "Learning the Ancient Rhythms of Prayer," *Christianity Today,* 8 January 2001, 38.

3. William C. Graham, "Shallow Book Lacks Fresh Truth," *National Catholic Reporter,* 9 March 2001.

4. Bishop Richard C. Hanifen, "The Study of the Impact of Fewer Priests on the Pastoral Ministry," *United States Conference of Catholic Bishops,* June 2000, <http://www.usccb.org/plm/update.htm>.

5. Uwe Siemon-Netto, "Orthodoxy Lures Young Men to Priesthood," United Press International, 10 January 2001.

6. Brian W. Clowes, *Call to Action or Call to Apostasy?* (Front Royal, Va.: Human Life International, 1997).

7. Diana Jean Schemo, "Priests of the 60's Fear Loss of Their Legacy," *New York Times,* Sunday, 10 September 2000, sec. 1.

8. Colleen Carroll, "Chaplains of Schools That Belong to the Council for Christian Colleges and Universities," (survey), February 2001.

9. Wendy Murray Zoba, "Youth Has Special Powers," *Christianity Today,* 5 February 2001.

10. Kristina Stefanova, "Development Falls Short: Anacostia Housing Doesn't Lure Businesses," *Washington Times,* Sunday, 6 May 2001, sec. A1.

11. Diane Granat, "Virginia vs. Maryland," *Washingtonian,* April 2001, 80.

12. Teresa Mask, "25 Years and Growing," *Chicago Daily Herald,* 1 October 2000.

13. "Promise Keepers Plans 18 Events in 2001, None in Colorado," Associated Press, State & Local Wire, 27 December 2000.

Chapter Five: Sexuality and Family

1. Karen S. Peterson, "Unhappily Ever After: Children of Divorce Grow into Bleak Legacy," *USA Today,* 5 September 2000, sec. 1D.

2. Anne Jarrell, "The Face of Teenage Sex Grows Younger," *New York Times,* Sunday, 2 April 2000, sec. 9.

3. Sharline Chiang, "College Students Shun Politics," *Daily News of Los Angeles,* 26 January 1999.

4. William Mattox, "The Next Hip Trend: Saving Sex for Marriage," *Washington Times,* 22 February 1999.

5. Ivy McClure, "Springtime for Virginity," *The Women's Quarterly* (summer 1999).

6. Linda J. Waite and Maggie Gallagher, *The Case for Marriage* (New York: Doubleday, 2000), 183 n. 27.

7. John Meroney, "Loving True Love," *re:generation quarterly* 4, no. 1 (spring 1998).

8. Alex Witchel, "Counterintelligence: 'Rules' Books Sell Millions, but Mr. Right Takes a Hike," *New York Times,* 6 May 2001.

9. Mark Galli, "An Interview with Joshua Harris: The Man Who Ignited the Dating Debate," *Christianity Today,* 11 June 2001.

10. George Gurly, "Wendy Shalit's *Modesty* Proposal Infuriates Feminists, Says Loose Sex Conduct Takes Power from Women," *New York Observer*, 22 February 1999.

11. Jeffery L. Sheler, "The Mormon Moment," *U.S. News & World Report*, 13 November 2000.

12. Alisa Blackwood, "Unmarried Partners Living Together on the Rise," Associated Press, 23 June 2001.

13. Tamala M. Edwards, "Single by Choice: Flying Solo" *Time*, 28 August 2000.

14. "Types of Families," *Public Agenda Online*, 23 June 2001, <http://www. publicagenda.com/issues/factfiles_detail.cfm?issue_type=family&list=1>, citing "Statistical Abstract of the United States—1999" (U.S. Census Bureau, 2000).

15. Rick Marin, "Is This the Face of a Midlife Crisis?" *New York Times*, 24 June 2001.

16. Stanley Rothman and Amy E. Black, "Media and Business Elites: Still in Conflict," *Public Interest* (spring 2001): 72–86.

17. Mary Rourke, "Faith, Hope, Chastity," *Los Angeles Times*, 29 April 1994, sec. E1.

18. Mary Beth Bonacci, "You Scratch God's Back, He'll Scratch Yours?" *Real Love Productions*, 10 May 2001, <http://www.reallove.net/ articleshowphtml?ID=92>.

19. Pope John Paul II, *The Role of the Christian Family in the Modern World (Familiaris Consortio)* (Boston: St. Paul Editions, 1981).

20. Alan Wolfe, "Liberalism and Catholicism," *The American Prospect*, 31 January 2000.

21. Diane Urbani de la Paz, "They Don't Have Rhythm: But Some Couples in the East Bay Do Use Natural Birth Control," *San Francisco Chronicle*, 7 April 2000.

22. Kristin Vaughan, "More Are Embracing Idea of Natural Family Planning," *Boston Globe*, 2 August 1999, sec. B1.

23. Sam and Bethany Torode, "Make Love *and* Babies," *Christianity Today*, 12 November 2001.

24. T. Keung Hui, "More Teachers Answer to 'Mom,' 'Dad,'" *Raleigh (N.C.) News and Observer,* 28 July 2001, sec. A1.

25. Allan Carlson, "Domestic Partners," *World,* 20 May 2000.

Chapter Six: The Campus

1. Kelly Monroe, ed. *Finding God at Harvard* (Grand Rapids, Mich.: Zondervan Publishing House, 1996), 348.

2. Michael Paulson, "Evangelicals Find Place at Mainstream Colleges," *Boston Globe,* 20 February 2000.

3. Michael Rust, "Christian Colleges Stay the Course," *Insight on the News,* 30 August 1999, 14.

4. Alan Wolfe, "The Opening of the Evangelical Mind," *The Atlantic Monthly* 286, no. 4 (October 2000): 55.

5. Kelly Kurt, "Faith-Based Schools Grow as Students Seek Academics and Spirit," *Chattanooga Times Free Press,* 14 October 2000, sec. F4.

6. Pope John Paul II, *Faith and Reason (Fides et Ratio)* (Boston: Pauline Books and Media, 1998), 129.

7. Gene Yasuda, "'Noles Top the Polls: FSU No. 1 in Fun and Football," *Orlando Sentinel,* 26 October 1993.

8. David Cho, "Campus Christianity Draws Asian American Students," Knight Ridder News Service, 18 April 1999.

9. Terry Mattingly, "Catholic Colleges Urged to Respect Values," Scripps Howard News Service, 16 October 1999.

10. Margaret Talbot, "A Mighty Fortress," *New York Times,* 27 February 2000.

11. Greg Barrett, "Just Like Home: College Caters to the Home-School Team," *Tulsa World,* 8 June 2001.

12. Philip Walzer, "Robertson Reflects on His Brainchild, Regent U., at 25," *Virginian-Pilot,* 30 May 2001.

13. Lauren Winner, "Policy Wonks for Christ," *Christianity Today,* 13 November 2000.

Chapter Seven: Politics

1. Karlyn Bowman, "Opinion Pulse: The Generation Gap," *The American Enterprise* 12, no. 2 (1 March 2001): 60.

2. John Leo, "The Joy of Sexual Values," *U.S. News & World Report,* 1 March 1999, 13.

3. Alicia Montgomery, "Has Choice Lost Support?" *Salon.com,* 29 January 2001, <http://www.salon.com/politics/feature/2001/01/29/choice/index.html>.

4. Jennifer Baumgardner, "The Pro-choice PR Problem," *The Nation,* 5 March 2001; Alicia Montgomery, "Has Choice Lost Support?" *Salon.com,* 29 January 2001, <http://www.salon.com/politics/feature/2001/01/29/choice/index.html>.

Chapter Eight: The Call

1. Diane Toroian, "Soulard Mardi Gras Is a Swell Party but Can't Be Ranked As World's Third Largest," *St. Louis Post-Dispatch,* 7 March 2000.

2. Michelle Conlin, "Religion in the Workplace," *Business Week,* 1 November 1999, 150.

3. Alex Tizon, "Spirit at Work: More Are Integrating Their Religious and Professional Lives," *Seattle Times,* 13 September 2000.

4. Religion News Service, "Faith Often a Topic at Work, Study Finds," *Los Angeles Times,* 22 August 1998, sec. B4.

5. Marc Gunther, "God and Business," *Fortune,* 9 July 2001.

6. Jerry Useem, "Welcome to the New Company Town," *Fortune,* 10 January 2000.

7. Laura Pappano, "Running Out of Time: Are You Working More and Playing Less Than You Used To? Or Does It Just Feel That Way?" *Boston Globe,* 25 June 2000.

8. Rick Marin, "Is This the Face of a Midlife Crisis?" *New York Times,* 24 June 2001.

9. Tony Carnes, "The Silicon Valley Saints," *Christianity Today,* 6 August 2001.

10. *Silicon Valley Fellowship,* Silicon Valley Fellowship, <http://www.svfellowship.org>.

11. "Religion, Ethics, and the Law—An Integration,"*The Ave Maria School of Law Web Site,* Ave Maria School of Law, <http://www.avemarialaw.edu/curriculum/religion.html>; "Ave Maria School of Law Opens to First Class," <http://www.avemarialaw.edu/news/news082200.html>.

12. *The Ave Maria School of Law Web Site,* Ave Maria School of Law, <http://www.avemarialaw.edu>.

13. *Christian Legal Society,* Christian Legal Society, <http://www.clsnet.org>.

14. Dale A. Matthews, *The Faith Factor: Proof of the Healing Power of Prayer* (New York: Viking, 1998), quoting Todd A. Maugans and William C. Wadland, "Religion and Family Medicine: A Survey of Physicians and Patients," *Journal of Family Practice* 32, no. 2 (1991): 210–13.

15. Walter L. Larimore, M.D., *American Family Physician* 64, no. 3 (1 August 2001): 373, quoting Harold G. Koenig, Michael E. McCullogh, and David B. Larson, *Handbook of Religion and Health* (New York: Oxford University Press, 2001).

16. James Harder, "Aikman Raises a Global Spiritual Perspective," *Insight on the News,* 18 September 2000.

17. Aimee Howd, "Keeping the Faith in the Newsroom," *Insight on the News,* 27 September 1999.

18. Don Feder, "Reporters Don't Get Religion," *The Weekly Standard,* June 2000.

19. John Wicklein, "That 'Liberal Media' to Blame," *The Quill,* October 1997; Eleanor Randolph, "GOP Finds That Media-Bashing Is the Right Path," *Los Angeles Times,* 22 July 1996; and Robert L. Bartley, "The Press Pack: News by Stereotype," *Wall Street Journal,* 11 September 2000.

20. "Kids and Media at the New Millennium," *The Henry J. Kaiser Family Foundation,* November 1999, <http://www.kff.org/content/1999/1535/ChartPack.pdf>.

21. Lorraine Ali, "The Glorious Rise of Christian Pop," *Newsweek,* 16 July 2001.

22. Alan Wolfe, "The Opening of the Evangelical Mind," *The Atlantic Monthly* 286, no. 4 (1 October 2000): 55.

23. Andy Crouch and Nate Barksdale, "Roaring Lambs or Bleating Lions?" *re:generation quarterly* 6, no. 4 (winter 2000–01).

Chapter Nine: The Future

1. Pope John Paul II, *The Role of the Christian Family in the Modern World (Familiaris Consortio)* (Boston: St. Paul Editions, 1981).

2. "U. Professor Says Divorce Doesn't Affect Kids Like It Used To," Associated Press, 12 August 1999.

3. Blaine Harden, "Bible Belt Couples 'Put Asunder' More, despite New Efforts," *New York Times,* 21 May 2001.

4. Larry Witham, "Southern Baptists Seek to Cut Divorces," *Washington Times,* 14 June 2001.

5. Kelly McBride, "Churches Help Prepare Couples for Marriage," *Spokane (Washington) Spokesman-Review,* 18 October 2000; John R. Donahue, "Marriages Are Made in Heaven," *America,* 30 September 2000.

6. Carmen Staicer, "My Journey to Natural Family Planning," *Midwifery Today and Childbirth Education,* 30 September 1999, quoting Mercedes Arzu Wilson, *Love and Family* (San Francisco: Ignatius Press, 1996), 261.

7. John L. Allen Jr., "What Kind of Model Is Steubenville?" *National Catholic Reporter,* 11 February 2000.

8. Diana Jean Schemo, "Priests of the 60's Fear Loss of Their Legacy," *New York Times,* 10 September 2000, sec. 1.

9. Jonathan Nelson, "Hustlers on the Road to Emmaus," *re:generation quarterly* 4, no. 4 (winter 1998).

10. Martha Sawyer Allen, "House of the Lord," *Minneapolis Star Tribune,* 2 December 2000, sec. 5B.

11. Jody Callahan, "One Festival's Fees to Shelby County to Total $102,700," *Memphis Commercial Appeal,* 23 June 2001, sec. B2.

12. John L. Allen Jr., "What Kind of Model Is Steubenville?" *National Catholic Reporter,* 11 February 2000.

INDEX OF NAMES

INDEX OF SUBJECTS